The Last
of the Duchess

Also by Caroline Blackwood

CAROLINE BLACKWOOD

The Last
of the Duchess

A COMMON READER EDITION
The Akadine Press

The Last of the Duchess

This COMMON READER EDITION published 2000 by The Akadine Press Inc., by arrangement with the Estate of Caroline Blackwood.

Grateful acknowledgement is made to the following for permission to reprint previously published material: Cleveland Amory: Excerpt from *Who Killed Society?* by Cleveland Amory. Reprinted by permission of Cleveland Amory. The Famous Music Publishing Corporation: Excerpt from "I Want to Be a Bee in Your Boudoir" by Richard Whiting and George Marion. Copyright © 1930 (renewed 1959) by Famous Music Corporation. Reprinted by permission of Famous Music Publishing Corporation. David McKay Co.: Excerpts from *The Heart Has Its Reasons* by the Duchess of Windsor. Copyright © 1956 by the Duchess of Windsor. Reprinted by permission of David McKay Co., a division of Random House, Inc. Enoch Pratt Free Library: Excerpt from *The American Mercury*, June 1944. Reprinted courtesy of the Enoch Pratt Free Library, in accordance with the terms of the will of H. L. Mencken. Hugo Vickers: Excerpt from *Laughter from a Cloud* by Laura, Duchess of Marlborough. Reprinted by permission of Hugo Vickers, literary executor to the Late Laura, Duchess of Marlborough.

A COMMON READER EDITION and fountain colophon are trademarks of The Akadine Press, Inc.

ISBN 1-58579-001-X

10 9 8 7 6 5 4 3 2 1

For Evgenia, Ivana, Sheridan and Hugo Vickers

$\mathcal{T}$his examination of the bizarre fate that befell the Duchess of Windsor first interested me as a story about the rich and famous, so many of whom at the end find themselves at the mercy of those in their employ. This account was written in 1980. For obvious reasons, its publication was delayed until the death of the Duchess's necrophiliac lawyer Maître Blum. When I was first sent by the British *Sunday Times* to interview Maître Blum (who at that point claimed, although this has been disputed, to hold the Duchess's power of attorney and had seized the right to act as her spokesperson), I had no idea that I was going to be given so many contradictory statements as to the Duchess's current condition. The Duchess was old. I took for granted that like that of countless aged people, her physical state of being was unlikely to be perfect. It was only when her lawyer started to tell me blatant, joyful lies about the life of the Duchess, both past and present, that I became interested in trying to discover the reasons why these seemingly pointless lies were being fed to the world press. As her lawyer had cast a total *cordon sanitaire* of silence around the true situation of her distinguished protegée, I entered into arenas of speculation. For me this story became a real study in the fatal effects of myth. A dark fairy tale, it seems a lesson for those who are vulnerable to being overprotected. That is not to say the Duchess's friends and those looking after her were not doing their best to see that she was properly cared for. Maybe only time will elucidate the pure and total truth.

The Last
of the Duchess

I first became aware of Mrs. Simpson, the future Duchess of Windsor, when I was a child living in Ulster. I was then too young to understand the furor she was creating, but the violent emotion that she aroused made me curious about her. To an embattled Protestant community whose very identity depended on their loyalty to the British crown, Mrs. Simpson was a figure who was regarded with horror. She was a threat to the church and the monarchy. She symbolized sex and evil. Eyes were rolled and voices dropped to grim whispers whenever her name was mentioned. I heard her described as "that dreadful American divorcée." Mrs. Simpson then started to intrigue me because the last two words of this menacing epithet were made to sound so very much worse than the "dreadful."

It was quite a long time before I could make out what she had done. When the future King of England first declared his desire to renounce the throne in order to marry her, it was seen as a tragedy and something so obscene and shocking it had to be hidden from the children.

Yet because her crime was kept secret from me and I picked up only ripples of the loathing she inspired, Mrs. Simpson started to become a figure of mystery and glamor to me. She had done something that the adult world seemed to consider unspeakable.

I first associated Mrs. Simpson with mysterious, attractive sin and later with loss, for I lost my coronation cup. A few months after the abdication I bought a mug in a local souvenir shop. Provincial as it has always been, Northern Ireland at that point was ahead of its times for it had produced a souvenir of an event that was never to take place. My chunky, vulgar mug celebrated the coronation of Edward VIII. My cup only became precious to me because I noticed that it had an electric effect on everyone I showed it to. Peculiar expressions came over their faces as they looked at it. As an object it was able to arouse extremely complex feelings of anger, disgust, and betrayal. On one side of the mug there was a gaudy picture of Edward VIII's handsome profile. He looked noble and golden wearing the Crown.

Although it was obvious no one liked my mug, I was told I must keep it forever. It could only become increasingly valuable. Its future value as a collector's item was incalculable.

I treasured my coronation mug for many years and then as time went by, it got lost. Whether it was stolen by some perceptive thief or whether it somehow got used as an ordinary cup and got broken in the sink, I was never to know. For a while I had the nagging sense of guilt about its loss. Once it vanished, it seemed all the more precious, and it joined the horrible ever-accumulating list of valuable things that I had let slip from my possession for want of proper care.

Inevitably, with the passing of the years, my remorse over the loss of this irreplaceable cup faded. Then in 1980 the English *Sunday Times* asked me to write an article on the Duchess of Windsor and my old childhood curiosity about this woman, who had given my mug its rarity value, revived.

Francis Wyndham, the senior editor, told me that Lord Snowdon had an interesting project. He wanted to photograph the Duchess of Windsor. It was suggested that I fly over to Paris in order to write a description of the taking of this unusual photograph.

My first reaction to this proposal was one of bemusement. How could Lord Snowdon want to photograph the Duchess of Windsor? How could he want to photograph her, when the Duchess must surely be dead?

"Do we know that the Duchess is in any condition to be photographed?" I asked.

It was apparently very hard to find out. All that was known was that the Duchess had been bedridden and in seclusion for several years. She was living in France in a huge house on the edge of the Bois de Boulogne. Lord Snowdon had no idea what state the Duchess was in. His whole project was therefore rather delicate.

The Duchess of Windsor was now apparently eighty-four. She was under the sole control of an ancient female lawyer called Maître Blum. This old woman was about the same age as the Duchess and very much feared and respected in Paris. She held the Duchess's power of attorney, and she had become her spokesperson. She was in complete control of the Windsor estate. Anyone who wished for information about the Duchess had to contact Maître Blum. Francis Wyndham would do this and let me know if Lord Snowdon's imaginative enterprise was feasible.

I very much hoped that it would be. I felt that it would

be extremely interesting to meet the Duchess of Windsor and I very much wanted to see her legendary and beautiful French house. It also struck me that it might be interesting for someone to take a photograph of Lord Snowdon caught in the act of photographing the Duchess. One royal divorcée taking a snap of another. Surely this would have a certain historic value and be a record of an event that had an Alice in Wonderland unreality.

I soon learned that Lord Snowdon's project was out of the question. Francis Wyndham had spoken to Diana Mosley, wife of Sir Oswald Mosley, England's Fascist leader. Sir Oswald had been a friend, admirer, and imitator of Hitler. In the thirties he had the dream of becoming Great Britain's führer. He organized a group of young English thugs who became known as the Blackshirts. Mosley's unattractive followers very much resembled the members of Hitler's Youth Movement. They roamed around London in their dark-shirted uniforms searching for Jews and "foreigners" whom they could bait and beat up. Once war was declared between Great Britain and Germany, Sir Oswald and his beautiful, aristocratic wife, Diana, were both put in jail. They were imprisoned for their openly pro-Nazi allegiance and activities.

Diana Mosley was just as fervently "keen" on Hitler as her husband. She gave him a nickname and liked to refer to him as "Darling Hittles." Her sister, Unity Mitford, also a British upper-class beauty, was more seriously involved with him. As his pre-war guest, she fell passionately in love with the führer. On learning of the British declaration of war, she attempted suicide. Her attempt failed and she survived but she remained for many years brain-damaged and incapable of speech.

After the war, Sir Oswald and his wife were released from jail but apparently felt too unpopular to be comfortable living in England. They later moved to France. There they met another notorious couple who were living in France because they were not welcome by the British establishment. The Mosleys became close friends of the Duke and Duchess of Windsor.

In Francis Wyndham's conversation with Lady Mosley, he had learned that she was very worried about the Duchess. She was frightened that she might be in the most terrible condition. Maître Blum had not let Diana Mosley visit her for three years. The Duchess was locked away in her Paris house on the edge of the Bois de Boulogne. If the Duchess's friends were not allowed to see her, it was highly unlikely Maître Blum would dream of permitting her to be photographed.

In the course of trying to ascertain the current health of the Duchess, he had noticed that when anyone made any reference to Maître Blum they spoke of her with an awe that was curiously akin to pure terror. They invariably described her as "formidable" and "belligerent." He felt that it might be interesting to set up an interview with Maître Blum herself. This bellicose old *éminence grise* who was lurking behind the stricken Duchess suddenly seemed to be emerging as rather an intriguing figure. I agreed with him and he said he would see if an interview with the old lawyer could be arranged.

If I was going to interview Maître Blum, I wanted to

learn something about her, so I bought a copy of *The Windsor Story*, the work of two American journalists who ghosted the autobiographies of the Duke and Duchess, and then produced a best-selling book of their own in which they maintain that the Duke's life, once he renounced the throne, was all misery, recriminations, and regrets. I looked up Maître Blum in the index.

Maître Blum had only two references and she was sketched in very roughly, yet something of her commandeering and unforgettable personality still jumped from the page. "Maître Suzanne Blum," Bryan and Murphy wrote, "whose shrewdness had much impressed the Duchess and on whose judgement she had come to rely . . ."[1] This kind of elliptical statement whets the reader's curiosity. When, precisely, did Maître Blum's shrewdness first impress the Duchess? At what point did this notorious American from Baltimore start solely to rely on her old French lawyer's judgement?

Describing Maître Blum, they wrote that she was "a woman of about the Duchess's age." Her reputation as a trial lawyer was "quick, cool, clever, and tough."

Bryan and Murphy went on to say that Maître Blum had gone to New York fleeing the German occupation and she had studied law at Columbia University. In 1958 she'd represented Rita Hayworth in her divorce from Aly Khan and her other Hollywood clients had included Charlie Chaplin, Jack Warner, Darryl Zanuck, Walt Disney, and Merle Oberon. Her first husband had also been a lawyer. He was the Paris correspondent for Allen and Overy, the English law firm whose solicitor Sir Godfrey Morley had always represented the Duke. It was Maître Blum's first husband who, said Bryan and Murphy, "brought her to the Windsors' attention."

They gave an account of the Duchess of Windsor sending for Lord Mountbatten soon after the Duke's funeral. The Duchess was distraught. She was convinced she was bankrupt, she thought that the French government was going to turn her out of the beautiful house in Neuilly that they had given the Windsors free. She saw herself as penniless and about to be forced to sleep on the streets. Apparently, both she and the Duke were always haunted by a neurotic terror of poverty.

Lord Mountbatten reassured her. The Duke had left her everything. The Duke did not leave a penny to any charity or friend or relative or servant. The only exception was Countess Mountbatten, one of Lord Mountbatten's daughters. She had the dubious good fortune to be bequeathed an inscribed royal family tree.

Over the years the Duke had given the Duchess jewels estimated as worth more than six million dollars. He had inherited some of them from Queen Alexandra so he had given the American divorcée some of the British Crown jewels.

Lord Mountbatten begged the Duchess not to panic. He assured her she could not have inherited less than several million pounds. He felt certain that as France had been so generous towards the exiled Duke, it was unlikely that after his death they would change their tactics and expel and penalize his widow.

Lord Mountbatten was quite right. The French government soon informed the Duchess she would not have to pay any death duties on his estate. In this she was uniquely favored. They also told her she could retain her free house in the Bois de Boulogne for her lifetime.

Reassured by Mountbatten that she was in no danger of becoming a pauper, the Duchess asked him what she should eventually do with so much money. She had no close family relations of her own. She felt she would like to do something to perpetuate her late husband's memory. Maybe it would be a good idea if she formed a Duke of Windsor foundation. "Do you think Charles would become involved with it?"

Lord Mountbatten felt certain that Prince Charles would be delighted to become chairman of the foundation. All the Duchess had to do was name the charitable organizations the Duke would have liked to support and the trustees would apply the income to his memory.

"She clapped her hands," according to Bryan and Murphy. Here I started to feel a little skeptical. How did they know that the Duchess, who was then nearly eighty, made this girlish and gleeful gesture? Were these journalists both in the room while she and Mountbatten thrashed out this very private financial transaction?

"It's a *wonderful* idea!" the Duchess said. "I'll get Godfrey Morley to redraw my will at once, then we'll clear it with my French lawyer." Then the bombshell fell. The Duchess's French lawyer was none other than the all-powerful and controversial Suzanne Blum.

Sir Godfrey Morley, who had acted for the Windsors for umpteen years, never received any instructions to form a Duke of Windsor charitable foundation. When he next heard from the Duchess, she informed him that the whole idea of the foundation had been abandoned and she no longer required his services. From now on her sole legal advisor was going to be Maître Blum.

Sir Godfrey Morley never knew what had brought about his abrupt dismissal, or how and why Maître Blum had dissuaded the Duchess from forming the foundation. When Lord Mountbatten heard the news that the Duchess's charitable project had been abandoned, he was apparently maddened. "Damn it," he said, "the money was *his*, not hers!"

Maître Blum only made one more slight appearance in Bryan and Murphy's version of *The Windsor Story*. Yet her brooding presence still dominated the final chapter.

The Duchess by this time in their narrative was in very serious physical condition. She had suffered two severe falls, and in one of them she had fractured her hip. Her mind had become enfeebled and disordered. She failed to recognize old friends. She forgot things. She rambled. She was tactless. She made social gaffes.

The Duchess ate less and less. She drank silver mugs of vodka. She developed a gastric ulcer which perforated and she was rushed to the American Hospital. She remained there for six months. The royal family did not invite her to Princess Anne's wedding. But they did send her some flowers.

The Duchess became increasingly lonely and depressed. She got more and more morbid and seemed to long for death. She asked her friend Lady Monckton to escort her body to Frogmore, the royal burial ground at Windsor, where she hoped she would soon be buried alongside the Duke. She was released from hospital and she returned to her house on the Bois de Boulogne.

Then on the second-to-last page of *The Windsor Story*, there was the most ominous passage. "The gates are locked and Maître Blum is the sole keeper of the keys. Recently the poor invalid Duchess's circle has shrunk to include only her doctors and nurses, two or three servants, and—to be sure—Maître Blum."

CHAPTER TWO

*H*aving found out all that *The Windsor Story* could tell me about the Duchess's keeper, I telephoned Sir Godfrey Morley, the Duke of Windsor's rejected solicitor, and I asked him if he could tell me anything about her. Was it true that Maître Blum had taken total control over all the affairs of the Duchess? "I've lost my memory," he bleated desperately. "I'm a very old man. I'm retired. I can't tell you anything. I can't remember anything anymore. Why don't you speak to Maître Blum directly? I'm sure she'd love to speak to you. But I would never advise you to get on the wrong side of her—you know that in her time she represented five of the major Hollywood film companies. I think that sums her up . . . Anyway, speak to Maître Blum. Don't try and speak to me . . . You will find that Maître Blum is the most imperious and volatile lady . . ."

Sir Godfrey certainly sounded rather antediluvian and croaky. But I wondered if he had really lost his memory or whether the painful moment that the Duchess had suddenly fired him under the instigation of Maître Blum was not a moment he deliberately wished to recall.

Lady Mosley was in London, so having failed to get any valuable information from Sir Godfrey, I decided to try to speak to her. When I reached her on the telephone, she said she had become stone deaf. I then realized that if

I hoped to talk to people who had once surrounded the Duchess, I must expect to encounter the hurdle of various physical disabilities.

I explained that I wanted to visit to learn something about Maître Blum. Because of her deafness, Lady Mosley misunderstood me and appeared to think that I wanted to come round to give her publicity for a book she had just completed on the Duchess of Windsor. I kept shouting that this was not the purpose of my visit, but the misunderstanding persisted and still thinking that I was going to write a plug for her book, Lady Mosley with great sweetness and graciousness asked me if I would like to come for tea.

We had tea in her bedroom. She sat in a chair looking extremely elegant. Her aristocratic and chiseled face was still incredibly beautiful. She was charming and she was also exceedingly modest. "My book on Wallis is really rather rubbish. But please don't print that in the *Sunday Times*. There's nothing very new in it. I've just retold the story of the abdication and all the things all of us know." Her huge ice-blue eyes had a childish, yearning expression. She was so beguiling that she made one forget that she had spent her life yearning for a Europe united by a repressive Fascist leadership.

She apologized for receiving me in such an ugly house. It was not hers, she insisted. It was borrowed. She was only in London for a few days. The house in which we met was indeed rather dingy and gloomy, and Lady Mosley's famous taste and flair for creating beautiful surroundings was certainly not much in evidence.

"I hope you won't be too horrid about my book," she said.

"I'm not reviewing your book," I shouted. "I was hoping that you could tell me something about Maître Blum."

"Maître Blum?" She seemed amused. I discovered that if I sat on her left side and bellowed, it was sometimes possible to make her hear me. "What do you want to know about Maître Blum?"

"I want to know what she is like. I may be going to interview her."

"Maître Blum is quite a remarkable old character. It's hard to describe what she is like. She's not like anything that any of us have ever met. You will really have to meet her. She's a very fiery and vociferous old woman. She doesn't care what she says. She's outrageously outspoken. You ought to hear her denouncing the royal family. She feels that they have always maltreated the Duchess. She launches into the most terrible tirades against them, she curses them to high heaven, and she calls them every kind of name. Her husband tries to stop her. It makes him frightfully nervous . . ."

"Does Maître Blum have a husband?" I was starting to form an imaginary picture of this bellicose old lawyer and it astonished me to hear that at her advanced age she was still married.

Diana Mosley said that Maître Blum was married to some kind of general. He might be French. He might be Prussian, she didn't quite know which. Whatever his nationality, I found the news that Maître Blum was married to any kind of general very unlikely and therefore riveting.

According to Lady Mosley, Maître Blum was about eighty-four—roughly the same age as the Duchess. Her husband, General Spillman, was younger than she was. He was only about eighty but the poor man looked well over a hundred. Possibly his life with the Maître had aged him. Despite his high military rank, he seemed petrified of his wife.

"Is Maître Blum very frightening?" I asked.

"Well, in a way, Maître Blum is very frightening indeed. Between you and me, she gets really quite peculiar and crazy on the subject of the Duchess."

"How do you mean?" I said.

"Well, Maître Blum is wildly loyal to the Duchess. All that's rather good. People have been so horrid about Wallis . . . But Maître Blum certainly carries her loyalty a bit far. I've been extremely nice about the Duchess in my book. But I think Maître Blum is furious with me. I spoke to her last week and she was icy cold." Lady Mosley laughed but she suddenly seemed vulnerable and wounded. "I don't think the silly old thing thought my book was nice enough about the Duchess . . ."

"Did you like the Duchess?" I asked her.

"Oh yes, I really did. Wallis was such fun and she was so kind to us. She was so gay and she entertained so beautifully. Her food was always absolutely delicious. She had such style . . ."

"I believe that you are now rather worried about the Duchess. Is that true?"

Lady Mosley was extremely worried about the Duchess. It was worse than that. She was in despair about her, but she didn't know what she could do. She was sure that Maître Blum meant very well but she really wished that Maître Blum would let her visit her old friend. She wanted to see for herself that the Duchess was being properly cared for. Supposing, for example, that the Duchess didn't like her nurses—who would she complain to? It was so important that old and bedridden people had kind and sympathetic nurses.

"Poor Wallis has been so alone since the Duke died," she said. "She is really most unlucky. She doesn't have one single close relation. Her only family is the royal family and, as you know, they have always hated her. They don't care what Maître Blum is doing to her."

"What is she doing to her?" I asked.

"Well, she is keeping her alive. And I can't believe that's very kind. She keeps operating on the poor little thing. She made her have yet another ghastly major operation just a few months ago. It's too awful to think about . . . All that pain . . . And what's the point of it? Maître Blum keeps saying that 'il faut respecter la vie.' But I'm not so sure about that. The Duchess is eighty-four. Wouldn't it be kinder to let her go?"

"Is Maître Blum a Roman Catholic?" I asked.

"I don't know what she is. She's obviously Jewish but I suppose she may also be Catholic. All I do know is that she takes this firm line. It was just the same thing when she took away the Duchess's vodka. Why did she have to take it away from the poor little creature? Why couldn't Wallis be allowed at least one tiny glass in the evening?

After all, she was already eighty-one at that point and her vodka was really all she had. But Maître Blum couldn't see my point when I put it to her quite gently and politely. It made her furious. She said that the alcohol was bad for the Duchess's blood pressure. It was terrible for her 'tension' and all that. She was outrageous if I'm to be honest. She really screamed at me that *'il faut respecter la vie!'* "

I asked Diana Mosley if the Duchess had been a heavy drinker. She hesitated. Finally she admitted that after the Duke's death, the Duchess drank rather a lot.

"I don't think poor Wallis was very happy in that period. It was a horrible time for her. When she lost the Duke, in a way, she lost everything."

Later I told Francis Wyndham that Maître Blum had taken away the Duchess's vodka. "Don't you think that sounds cruel?"

"It's one of the cruelest things I've ever heard," he said. "No wonder she's become a living vegetable."

While I was talking to Lady Mosley I asked her if the Duchess was still conscious.

"I'm afraid she often may be. That's the ghastly nightmare. One doesn't like to think how much she may be suffering. I've been so desperate about her, I've even toyed with writing to Prince Charles. I thought he might be able to do something for her. They say he has a kind heart."

"Do you think she wonders why you never come and see her?"

"I'm afraid she may well wonder. That's the frightful thing that worries me all the time. The Duchess may not realize that Maître Blum refuses to allow her to be visited.

We all accepted her marvelous hospitality in the old days. It's too dreadful if poor Wallis thinks that now she is old, and ill, and widowed, we have all deserted her."

"When you saw her three years ago," I asked Lady Mosley, "how did the Duchess seem then?"

"Oh, it was too upsetting and awful to see her. The poor little thing was lying there on her side. Her big blue eyes were open and she was staring desperately in front of her. She never said a word. And something had gone horribly wrong with her sad little hands."

I asked Lady Mosley if she thought the Duchess recognized her. She couldn't tell. But presumably the Duchess could still recognize people because Maître Blum claimed that her blood pressure went up whenever she saw any of her old friends. That was the ostensible reason why Maître Blum had forbidden her to be visited. Lady Mosley felt that the Duchess might prefer that her blood pressure rose at the sight of a friend rather than be condemned by Maître Blum to this frightful isolation.

"Who was the last person who managed to get in to visit the Duchess?" I asked Lady Mosley. She said that the last person she knew was a diplomat called Walter Lees. He had been very upset by what he saw. He said that the Duchess was being fed through her nose.

"Through her nose?" I asked, horrified.

"Yes, I'm afraid she was." Lady Mosley shivered. "Maître Blum only let him take a little peep through the door. But he managed to catch a glimpse of a ghastly black pipe which was stuck up her nostril."

"Poor Duchess," I said.

"Exactly," Lady Mosley agreed. "It would have broken the Duke's heart if he'd known what was going to happen to Wallis after he'd gone. He wouldn't have been able to bear it. He loved her so . . ."

"Did the Duke adore her?"

"Oh yes, he certainly did. Until the day he died, he was absolutely besotted by her. It's all rubbish when people try to make out that he regretted not being able to lay cornerstones and take all those silly salutes, wearing a hat with a plume. He loathed all those dreary royal duties. He was always bored stiff by that kind of thing. If one sat next to the Duke at dinner, he was never really listening to what one said to him. His eyes were always staring up the table. He couldn't take his eyes off Wallis . . ."

"Was Maître Blum very close to the Duchess?" I asked. "I don't understand how she got into this position of power."

"Maître Blum never really knew the Duchess. That's the nightmarish part of the whole thing. It's also the big joke. She only got to know Wallis once she started to lose her mind."

"When did the Duchess start to lose her mind?"

"Well, about five years ago the Duchess began to get rather vague."

"And this vagueness was caused by illness, not alcohol?"

"It was caused by illness," Lady Mosley said firmly. "Although I'm afraid Wallis probably did drink a bit more than she should have. You know she had a terrible fall. And then naturally everyone said she only fell because she was drunk. But remember that Wallis always had horrid things said about her. You have no idea how much hate mail she received at the time of the abdication. She was showered with death threats and obscene letters. They came from all over the world. Great bags of them. It made her really miserable . . ."

"I understand the Duchess was quite tough."

"Yes, the Duchess certainly was rather tough. But if it seems as if everyone in the whole globe needs to write and tell you how much they would like you to be dead . . . Who has ever had to deal with that? The Duchess was quite tough. But she wasn't tough enough for that. No one could be . . ."

As I was leaving, I asked Lady Mosley two last direct questions. "Is Maître Blum nice? Do you like Maître Blum?"

She hesitated. She lowered her voice to a whisper as if she were frightened that Maître Blum in her apartment in Paris could hear her across the Channel speaking indiscreetly in London. "Well, not exactly," she said evasively. "But for goodness sake," she added jokingly, "don't print that. I don't want any trouble from her. She might bring an injunction against my book and that would be too ghastly and tiresome."

Lady Mosley seemed terrified of Maître Blum. It was ironic that Diana Mosley, who had so boldly endured her wartime imprisonment as a pro-Nazi, now should appear to feel so intimidated by this ancient Jewish lawyer.

CHAPTER THREE

*A*fter I had left Lady Mosley, I started thinking about the unusual predicament of the Duchess. This frivolous American woman once had so longed to be royal and never quite succeeded. Now in her death, she appeared to be receiving a truly royal, and the most cruel and modern, V.I.P. treatment. From Lady Mosley's account, the Duchess seemed to be enduring a death just as agonizingly prolonged as that of Franco and Tito. There had been political reasons for the barbaric way in which Tito and Franco were kept alive and chopped about by surgeons, endlessly resuscitated. They were martyred because the fear existed that severe political unrest might be created by their demise. But why was the poor old Duchess being kept alive? Surely no one could pretend that any form of unrest could be caused by what the Irish might call her "passing."

After having seen Diana Mosley, I telephoned the biographer David Pryce-Jones, who had written an article on the Windsors for *The New York Times*. "What's Maître Blum like?" I asked him. "I hope to interview her."

"Personally I find her the purest horror and nightmare!" he said. The very mention of her name seemed to make him violently agitated. "Maître Blum tried to sue my article, of course. She made endless trouble for me. She rang every other newspaper and told them she was suing *The New York Times.* She also showered me with hate mail. And even though I knew it was all coming from Maître Blum, she still managed to upset me. It's not very pleasant having all that poison arriving every morning at breakfast."

"Who was the hate mail meant to have come from?" I asked.

"Gardeners, cooks, old retainers of the Windsors. They denounced me as a monster for writing ill of their marvelous ex-employers."

I asked him if Maître Blum had been successful in her suit against him.

"Of course she wasn't." His reply was outraged. "I hadn't written a word that she could sue me for. Being Jewish she didn't like me pointing out how wildly pro-Hitler the Windsors were. But there was nothing she could do about that because it's all documented and on record. Maître Blum likes to pretend the Windsors led lives which were as pure as the driven snow. Her theory doesn't wash very well if you examine the facts. What a ghastly and unscrupulous couple they both were . . ."

Later I read a copy of his article and I could understand that Maître Blum with her apparent worship of the Windsors wouldn't like it very much. He stressed the fact that they accepted the invitation to stay with Hitler in Berchtesgaden in 1937, that two years previously when he was Prince of Wales, the Duke made a speech in which he said that war between England and Germany was unthinkable. This made him a popular figure in Germany and Joachim von Ribbentrop, then ambassador to England, and later

Hitler's foreign minister, was encouraged to get in touch with him.

Maître Blum should have been grateful to Pryce-Jones that he made no mention of the startling telegram that was sent to Hitler's go-between by the Duke when he was on his way to take up his appointment as governor of the Bahamas. In this telegram the Duke offered his services to Hitler if they were ever needed.

Maître Blum should have also been thankful that he never referred to the fact, that after the defeat of Germany, when the German Foreign Office records were seized by the Allies, Winston Churchill arranged that various other documents which revealed the extent to which the Duke of Windsor had carried on his mindless flirtation with Hitler be destroyed. Churchill saw them as too embarrassing for the current British monarchy and British public to be worth preserving.

If, as I'd been led to believe, Maître Blum deified the reputation of the Duchess of Windsor, she should have considered herself fortunate that the article which she'd tried to sue made no allusion to the treatment the Duchess is well known to have received from the German führer when she made her ill-advised trip to visit him in Berchtesgaden so close to the outbreak of the Second World War.

On the arrival of the Windsors the black-mustached Nazi dictator instantly treated the Duke with a fawning and effusive respect. He barely greeted the Duchess. He put his arm around the Duke's shoulder in a chauvinistic and brotherly "leader to leader" embrace, and he started taking him off to his private study. The Duchess tried to follow her husband, but Hitler made a contemptuous gesture of the hand in which he instructed his guards with their swastika armbands to close the door in her face. Wallis Windsor was left outside. She was excluded and humiliated. She never really forgave Hitler for causing her such mortification. She only remembered the rudeness with which he'd treated her. After this incident she never much sympathized with her husband when he continued to nourish very woolly and unrealistic fantasies in which he saw himself as one day becoming the crowned King of Germany. Within the Duke's ridiculous pipe dream, the Duchess would reign beside him as his rightful Queen. In this fanciful, yet evilly mindless scenario, Hitler would act as his most devoted Prime Minister.

Although David Pryce-Jones had refrained from making use of this material, there were other things in his article which I could see that Maître Blum, with her notorious loyalty towards the Duchess, was bound to detest.

He referred to the man who was destined at birth to become King of England and Emperor of India by the Grace of God as "first and foremost a chap in plus fours and checked tweeds of a brassy yellow and blue, a chap for cocktail shakers and golf clubs, a perpetual adolescent schoolboy, a chinless wonder, a twit. Who in the world does he resemble more than P. G. Wodehouse's Bertie Wooster . . ."

As Maître Blum, apparently, regarded the Duchess as a near to sacred being, she clearly would not like the

American public to read that her heroine had been married to a figure who was no more consequential than a Bertie Wooster.

I asked David Pryce-Jones how Maître Blum dealt with matters as delicate as the Windsors' Fascist activities. Apparently she dealt with them in exactly the same way that she dealt with all other aspects of their lives which might be held up to criticism. If any unpalatable facts turned up about the Duke and Duchess, Maître Blum simply denied they were true. If she were to be asked why the Windsors agreed to become the guests of Hitler in 1937, she would have said that the Duke was interested in German housing or some such drivel. Maître Blum made a big point of the Duke's passionate interest in cheap German housing developments and as far as she was concerned, that was sufficient explanation why so close to the outbreak of war the Windsors accepted Hitler's invitation to be his guests.

I asked Pryce-Jones if Maître Blum had become senile; she was after all a woman of eighty-four. He said Maître Blum was not in the least senile. On the contrary, her mind was sharp as a new pin. You would never dream she was an old brute of eighty-four. She had the step of a young girl. No one could be more spry. She was obviously going to outlive all of us.

He said she was one of the rudest and most snobbish women he had ever met in his life. When he interviewed her, she never stopped insulting him. She called him "*ordure.*" She had called him a "dirty jackal" and various other disparaging names. She had a paranoid dislike of journalists and in a sense she had to be commended that she made no concessions toward them.

"Do you think she will agree to see me?" I asked him. He very much doubted it. Maître Blum had been so enraged by his article that he felt that she would never agree to be interviewed again. "Maître Blum really doesn't want a grain of publicity at this point. I don't think she wants the focus of public attention drawn to all the things she is up to."

"What is she up to?" I asked. He seemed to be hinting that her activities were sinister. He didn't want to say. He couldn't bear to have any more trouble from Maître Blum. She'd made his life miserable after he wrote the article on the Windsors and now he was unwilling to run any risk that she might sue him for slander. She had used extremely dirty tactics when she'd tried to bring her libel suit against him. In his article he'd written that Maître Blum was married to a "retired general." As she couldn't prove libel on any other count, she had claimed that her husband had been defamed by this statement.

"But that's insane," I said.

He agreed that it might seem slightly insane but added that if I ever managed to see Maître Blum, I would soon learn that, although many of her actions could seem superficially demented, they almost always had an underlying diabolical cleverness.

It appeared that under French law it was indeed libelous to say that any general was retired. French generals could die, they could fade away, but they must on no account retire. Maître Blum failed in her suit against Pryce-

Jones because it was too hard for her to convince an American jury that her husband had been defamed. But if Pryce-Jones's article had been reprinted in France, he would have been in serious trouble. Everything I heard about this old lawyer made her sound a figure whom it was exceedingly dangerous to offend.

David Pryce-Jones warned me that even if I were to meet Maître Blum, I would learn nothing about the Duchess. It would be the same if I started to question anyone else who had been in her immediate circle. I would meet with a wall of silence. No one would speak to me for they would all be too frightened of reprisals from Maître Blum.

"How does this woman manage to exert such a tyrannical hold?" I asked.

Apparently Maître Blum had drawn up the Duchess's will and as a result she was in a position to "dangle golden carrots." She let it be known that those who were wise enough to bow to her will might later receive substantial rewards.

Pryce-Jones also warned that whatever I wrote about the Duchess, Maître Blum would detest it and most likely try to sue me.

"Could anyone write anything that Maître Blum would consider nice enough about the Duchess?" I asked.

"No one in the world could possibly write anything that the Maître would feel was nice enough about the Duchess."

CHAPTER FOUR

*A*fter talking to Pryce-Jones,
I wrote to Maître Blum asking if she would see me. I first
tried to write to her in French, but with the help of various
dictionaries and bilingual friends the language of my letter
became embarrassingly high-flown so that with its rolling
subjunctives it had a Racinian flavor which I felt she rightly
might find off-putting and inappropriate.

Finally I decided to write her in English which, I assumed, she must speak if she had been to Columbia Law
School. I said that I was writing about the Duchess and
would be grateful if I could interview her.

Waiting for her reply, I tried to find someone who
liked Maître Blum so that I could get a different perspec-
tive on her personality. Lady Dudley, who had accompanied the Duchess to the Duke's funeral, suggested that I
talk to Lady Tomkins, who had been British ambassadress
to France during the period when the Windsors lived in
Paris. Apparently she was a friend of Maître Blum and
might be able to tell me something about her. Lady Dudley
herself preferred not to talk about either the Duchess or
her old lawyer. I assumed that understandably she dreaded
having trouble from Maître Blum. This response was becoming increasingly familiar. I telephoned Lady Tomkins,
who was in the country, and asked her if she'd been a
friend of Maître Blum.

"Well, I know her," she said. "But she's not a friend of mine. Whoever gave you such a strange idea?" She sounded aghast. "Maître Blum is not the sort of woman one could have as a friend."

"What's she like?" I asked.

"Suzanne Blum is rather a splendid old girl."

This was the most favorable thing I'd yet heard anyone say about the Maître.

"She defends the Duchess like a lioness with her cubs. And after the Duke died, believe me, the Duchess was quite lucky to have a lawyer as formidable as Maître Blum. I have to say that the behavior of the royal family was quite tactless at that point. They had snubbed the Duchess for years and then once the Duke was gone, they started making friendly overtures toward her because they wanted her jewels and possessions. The Duchess was much too clever not to see through that. She always hid the royal swords before Mountbatten visited her. And she made sure Maître Blum was present too. Otherwise he'd have pocketed objects from her dining room table."

Later this was corroborated by Mrs. Brinsley Plunkett, who was another close friend of the Duchess. She also remembered Wallis Windsor hiding her swords before Mountbatten came to see her. "He was always trying to get those swords. I suppose it was because he was a soldier."

Lady Tomkins went on to say that whatever one felt about Maître Blum, one had to admit she always had been excellent in defending the Duchess's "French interests."

"French interests?" I could understand that this unusual Duchess from Maryland might have American or even English interests. Conceivably she still might have self-interests although even this in her new unhappy state of ill health was doubtful. But how could she possibly have French ones?

"It's all this business of her will," Lady Tomkins said.

"To whom does the Duchess plan, eventually, to leave her possessions?" I asked.

Lady Tomkins didn't know. Only Maître Blum could tell me that. All Lady Tomkins knew was that the Duchess had told her she wanted to leave everything to France because it was the only country that had been kind to her. "Everything that I own is mine," she had told Lady Tomkins. "I don't care what the royal family thinks. All the jewelry the Duke gave me is mine and I could melt it down if I felt like it."

Lady Tomkins sympathized with Wallis Windsor's rebellious position. The Duchess had always had the most fabulous taste and flair for decorating her houses, which were filled with the most dazzlingly beautiful objects— marvelous Sèvres snuffboxes, fantastically rare and valuable Meissen figurines of her favorite pug dogs, and so on. Altogether she had formed the most amazing collection of furniture and china. Lady Tomkins felt it would be fitting if her possessions were bequeathed to France, the country which had exempted her from any form of taxation. There could be a room in some French museum where her things could be on public display and it could be known as the "Windsor Room."

"Do you think Maître Blum would be in favor of this?" I asked.

Lady Tomkins felt that Maître Blum, being French

herself, might well approve of it. As the Duchess's lawyer, she must know all the slights the Duchess had received from the royal family. It was unlikely that she would therefore have much sympathy for the acquisitive and proprietary attitude with which they now regarded the Duchess's estate.

I asked her if it was true that the Duke had given the Duchess Queen Alexandra's emeralds and rubies. If the Duchess now had Crown jewels in her possession, would that justify the eagerness of the royal family to have them returned?

Lady Tomkins only knew that the Duchess always wore the most beautiful jewelry she had ever seen in her life. Whether some of the jewels were bona fide Crown jewels she found it impossible to say. The Duchess used to have all her antique stones recut because she liked only modern settings. If some of them originally had belonged to Queen Alexandra, you would have to be a jewel expert to know. A lot of the Duchess's jewelry was stolen when she was staying with Laura, Duchess of Marlborough. If the Duchess had owned any Crown jewels, most of them must have been seized at that point by burglars. Obviously the Duke replaced them for her with money obtained from insurance. But the fact remained that it was unlikely that many of the gems the Duchess now owned were originals. And even if one or two could technically be described as Crown jewels, Lady Tomkins failed to see why the royal family should get into a tizzy about them. Surely they already had enough Crown jewels of their own.

Lady Tomkins had such a forthright, commonsensical

approach to this whole subject. Coming from an ex-ambassadress it was both surprising and refreshing.

"Wallis was very maligned," she said. "The royal family always blamed her for making the King abdicate. But it was the Duke who wanted to do it. He was such a stubborn character. No one could have stopped him from doing what he wanted to do. He adored Wallis and if they wouldn't let her be Queen, as far as he was concerned—that was that. And he continued to adore her. Any conversation one ever had with the Duke, he always had to bring Wallis into it. 'Oh, you must tell Wallis this . . . Oh, that will amuse Wallis . . .' "

Lady Tomkins remembered asking the Windsors to dine and the Duke had adored the violet-coated almonds she served him. "Wallis, Wallis, you must taste these delicious almonds!" he shouted excitedly up the table. "Darling, we really must get some of these."

This anecdote had a so-what quality which I found typical of many others that are recounted about the Windsors. But Lady Tomkins felt it had importance in that it proved that if ever the Duke was thrilled by anything, his immediate impulse was to share his pleasure with his wife.

Lady Tomkins had liked the Duchess very much. She found her charming and witty and extremely kind.

"In what way was she kind?" Lady Mosley had also mentioned the Duchess's kindness.

When Lady Tomkins had gone down to stay at the Mill, the house the Windsors owned outside Paris, she found the most lovely cut carnations in a priceless glass bowl beside her bed. The Duchess asked her if she had noticed them and told Lady Tomkins she had put them there herself. I could see this was kind but not quite as immeasurably kind as Lady Tomkins clearly saw it. I hoped the Duchess hadn't cheated in any way, that one of her maids hadn't really put the carnations in the British ambassadress's bedside bowl.

"Wallis did a superb job in horribly difficult circumstances," Lady Tomkins said.

"She was the most perfect hostess for the Duke. No one in the world could have done it better. When she entertained, her dinners were always extremely grand and yet also gay and informal in an American way. A very clever mixture. The Duchess made the Duke a marvelously happy man and everyone should be grateful for that. Admittedly, there was that unfortunate business with Donahue but that soon blew over . . ."

"Donahue?"

"Yes, Jimmy Donahue. He was heir to the Woolworth millions. A very nasty piece of work indeed. I was always extremely fond of the Duchess but I'm afraid she really went too far with Donahue . . ."

I asked if the Duchess had fallen in love with Jimmy Donahue.

Lady Tomkins wouldn't say that falling in love was quite the right way to put it. The man was a raging homosexual. She couldn't believe the liaison was very physical. But there was no doubt the Duchess had become deeply involved with him and the poor Duke had suffered horribly in that period. It had all been quite distressing.

"He was the most ghastly man, Donahue. I don't

know what Wallis saw in him. He was mixed up in the most hideous scandal. It was only hushed up because of the Woolworth millions. If I remember, he may have killed a man, you know. Admittedly only inadvertently. He may have inadvertently killed a waiter . . ."

"Is Jimmy Donahue still alive?" I asked her. Just as the Duchess's ancient, volatile lawyer appeared to be a figure whom it would be very interesting to interview, now the Duchess's criminal lover was also starting to emerge as an equally colorful character whom it would be intriguing to meet.

"Jimmy Donahue committed suicide. He jumped off a roof or something, I'm sure he had good reasons . . ."

I thanked Lady Tomkins for all that she had told me and asked her if perhaps we could meet after I'd seen Maître Blum. She seemed quite eager to do this. An ex-ambassadress, I wondered if she might feel very bored living with a retired, wheezy husband in the rainy English countryside and missed all her old, glamorous, diplomatic, Parisian duties. She appeared to be glad of the opportunity to hark back to the past and talk about the Duchess.

The days went by and I got no answer from Maître Blum. David Pryce-Jones had told me she was a woman who had all "the hauteur" of a reigning monarch and I was worried that the letter I had written her had been too casual, that finding it insufficiently deferential, she would not deign to answer it.

I read various books about the Windsors for if Maître

Blum were ever to consent to see me, obviously she would expect me to be familiar with every detail of their strange saga.

There was still no reply from Maître Blum and finally I decided to put through a call to Paris. I was tired of the suspense and I wanted to know once and for all if she was going to see me.

A French woman answered Maître Blum's telephone. *"Qui parle? Qui parle?"* she shouted angrily. I had an immediate frisson of pure terror. Could it be her? I had no clear image of what "her" would be like. Maître Blum was obscured for me. She seemed like Jove hidden in the black clouds of a mythical thunderstorm. I sensed only her awesome power and I had become infected by the fear she inspired in those who knew her. My moment of panic was needless. I was not speaking to Maître Blum. The gruff woman's voice said that Maître Blum was *"en voiture"* and she would be arriving later. I then waited another twenty-four hours before making another attempt to speak to her. When I got the same curt reply, I began to feel it was hopeless. I didn't believe for a moment that Maître Blum was "en voiture." How could a woman of that age constantly be traveling in such a hectic fashion? Just as she guarded the Duchess from visitors, Maître Blum, obviously, had a ferocious female guardian who protected her from the outside world. I decided I would put through one more call to Paris, and if I was palmed off once again with the same excuse, I must resign myself to the fact I was never going to meet the Duchess of Windsor's lawyer.

Then on the last call that I made, Maître Blum herself

answered. I was appalled. When Stalin in his last years was sealed away, dangerous and brooding in the Kremlin, no stranger could have put through a call and reached him personally. It therefore shocked me that the fierce and despotic Maître Blum, whom I'd begun to see as equally unapproachable, should turn out to be so unbecomingly accessible. I braced myself for one of her volatile outbursts. I waited for a display of her famous rudeness. But she was disquietingly polite. Her voice was modulated and manlike. She apologized for not having answered my letter. She had been in the country and she had just got back to Paris. The only day she could see me would be next Monday. On Tuesday she planned to return to the country. I quickly said that I would fly over to Paris and come to see her on Monday. After having spent so much time trying to get in touch with this unfathomable figure, it was awful to realize that if I were to delay just one day, she would elude me and once again be endlessly "en voiture." Maître Blum said she looked forward to seeing me. Her English was fluent but she had a strong French accent. She sounded alert and energetic. I would never have guessed I was speaking to a very old woman.

After our meeting had been arranged, it occurred to me that my whole preconception of the Duchess's keeper might be totally wrong. The civility and reasonableness with which she had treated me were not the qualities I had been led to expect from her. Maybe Maître Blum was a much more sympathetic figure than her general reputation implied. Lady Tomkins could very well be right. Maybe Maître Blum was a "splendid old girl."

The day before I went to Paris to see Maître Blum, I lunched with my aunt Mrs. Brinsley Plunket. She had seen a lot of the Duchess in the old days, but ever since poor Wallis became "Blumed," she had realized it was hopeless to try to see her. She felt the Duchess had made the greatest mistake of her life when she had fired her loyal private secretary, John Utter.

"Why did she fire him?"

"It was just one of those horrible mistakes people make . . . I have been told it was all that ghastly Blum's fault; the woman came zooming in the moment she heard the Duke was dead and tried to make the Duchess think that all her staff were cheating her. Poor Wallis was in a terrible state just after his death. Her health was getting worse and worse. She didn't know what to do with her life. She became really paranoid and she thought the whole world was against her. Obviously that clever old beast Blum knew exactly how to work on her paranoia. She did a sort of purge and she tried to get rid of everyone who'd ever been fond of the Duchess. She wanted Wallis to herself. And once that old lawyer got her way I'm afraid life has been hell for the Duchess."

I asked if Maître Blum had exerted a great influence on Wallis Windsor before the death of her husband.

Mrs. Brinsley Plunket gave an impatient little shake of the head.

"I don't think she had any influence at all. I suppose she must have been hovering around somewhere like a vulture, in the background, waiting for the Duke to die . . . It's possible she handled a few little dreary legal matters for the Windsors but that would have been the extent of it."

I asked Mrs. Plunket if she'd met Maître Blum. She apparently had never set eyes on her, nor did she want to. She didn't think the woman sounded in the least attractive. When she'd last tried to visit the Duchess she'd been forced to speak to Maître Blum on the telephone.

"The horrible old brute was extremely rude to me . . . She was unbelievably impertinent considering that I'd always been a close friend of Wallis. She sort of growled and barked rather like a furious dog barks . . . She said she certainly couldn't allow me to endanger the life of the Duchess."

Mrs. Plunket, who was a tiny, frail figure, immaculately groomed, approaching eighty, and of the most mild, unthreatening appearance, trembled with anger as she remembered this insult.

"Endanger!" she said. "How dare that awful creature accuse me of trying to endanger the life of poor Wallis! If the Duchess was too ill to want to talk, I only wanted to peek my head through her bedroom door. I wanted to wave to her . . . I wanted to blow her a kiss and maybe put some flowers by her bed . . . I only wanted Wallis to know that I hadn't forgotten her. And then her lawyer had the nerve to pretend that she was frightened I might go rushing into her bedroom and stab her with a kitchen knife or bring in a machine gun and riddle her with bullets! It was unbelievable!"

Mrs. Brinsley Plunket said that she'd had reports from various friends that Maître Blum now liked to claim that for years she'd been on intimate social terms with the Windsors, that she'd attended all their lavish parties, and been their constant and favorite guest.

"I really saw a lot of the Duchess before the Duke died," Mrs. Plunket said. "I was often in Paris in those days . . . I certainly never once saw Maître Blum at any of the dinners which the Duchess gave."

Mrs. Brinsley Plunket also thought it suspicious that the Duchess had never once told her that she'd found a wonderful new lawyer whom she adored.

"You see, the Duchess always loved telling one about her 'finds.' She'd always found the most fantastic person who made the most divine handmade shoes, someone who made the most exciting outdoor furniture—that kind of thing. The Duchess loved to share her 'finds.' She was that sort of person . . . But she certainly never tried to share Maître Blum."

Mrs. Plunket asked me if I'd heard about K. K. Auchincloss and the bracelet? I knew nothing about the whole incident.

Apparently Mrs. Auchincloss quite recently had gone to a sale at Sothby, Parke-Bernet in New York. There she had bought the most beautiful bracelet which was in the shape of two leopards. Later when she was in Paris, the clasp of this bracelet had broken and she had taken it to Cartier to be mended. She had been shocked when they recognized it and told her they had made it for the Duchess of Windsor.

"Does Maître Blum have the right to sell off the Duchess's things?" I asked.

"I suppose she does," Mrs. Plunket said crossly. "Apparently the woman has power of attorney. But if she's going to sell off the Duchess's possessions, why does she have to slip them secretly into sales in New York? The Duchess would probably get much more for them if people realized they were the property of the Duchess of Windsor. I also wish Maître Blum would offer them to the Duchess's friends. We'd adore to have a chance to buy them. No one had more divine things than the Duchess . . ."

I suddenly remembered the way David Pryce-Jones had dropped dark hints about all the things that Maître Blum was up to. Maybe he knew about the clandestine sale of the Duchess's leopard bracelet. Maybe he also knew about other similar transactions that the Maître had conducted. I wondered how Maître Blum herself would justify the secrecy with which she had placed the bracelet on the market. It was possible the Duchess was broke and it was becoming necessary to dispose of her property in order to meet the costs of her heavy medical expenses. Maître Blum, who was so fervently loyal to her, might feel it would be an indignity for the Duchess if it were to become publicly known that her financial situation was now so dire she was reduced to flogging her jewelry.

Mrs. Plunket was rather vague about the Duchess's current state of health. She'd been told that she was in a bad way, but that she was still capable of throwing some of her old tantrums. Apparently she'd always had the most violent temper. "But Wallis only went into her rages when things were done wrong. The Duchess was really wonderful, she was a complete perfectionist." This description conjured up an alarming vision of the Duchess apoplectic and raging despite the pipe that was up her nose.

Mrs. Plunket said the Duchess had been "heaven" in the old days. She always had the most wonderful sense of humor. Like Lady Mosley and Lady Tomkins, Mrs. Plunket stressed how much the Duke had always worshiped her. "The Duchess was his Queen and that was that."

I asked her if she had known Jimmy Donahue. She had known him quite well and he had the most marvelous sense of humor and that's what the Duchess had found so attractive about him.

"What kind of sense of humor?" I asked.

Apparently he had a "naughty" sense of humor. When he dined with the Windsors, he loved to embarrass the footmen by making loud remarks about their genitals. The unfortunate footmen would go scarlet in the face and their hands would shake so much that they nearly dropped all the plates.

Mrs. Plunket remembered an occasion when she herself was gravely ill and lying in a hospital in New York. The head nurse came into her room and said there was "a Madam" who had come to see her. She then showed in Jimmy Donahue who was accompanied by a real madam who ran a brothel and five whores that she employed.

I couldn't see that Donahue's joke was all that amusing and Mrs. Plunket had to admit she would have found it funnier if at that time she had not been so seriously ill.

"But I'm afraid that Jimmy's sense of humor could get quite a bit worse than that," she said.

"How much worse could it get?"

Mrs. Brinsley Plunket felt too shy to tell me. But finally she overcame her embarrassment and she gave me a vivid example.

"Jimmy would be dining at some madly grand dinner either in Paris or New York. It would be black tie, tiaras for the ladies, chandeliers, all that sort of thing. Jimmy would suddenly take his plate off the table and put it on his knee. Then he'd unbutton himself and pull out his cock. You couldn't believe it. He'd lay it out on top of all his food so that you could see it lying on his potatoes and his gravy and his sauces looking like some kind of pink sausage. And then he didn't stop there. He'd start waving to the butler who naturally looked as if he were about to faint. He'd hand the wretched man a knife and fork and he'd say he wanted his meat sliced very fine! Jimmy could be outrageous but I have to admit the horrified expressions on the faces of the people he wanted to shock used to be quite funny and enjoyable to see."

She remembered dining with the Windsors at the Ritz in Paris the night that the Duchess was told that Donahue had killed himself. After dinner the Duchess and Mrs. Plunket had gone off together to find the lavatory which was at the end of a long corridor. That walk with the Duchess had seemed the longest walk she'd ever taken in her life. The whole way she kept wondering if she ought to say something to the Duchess about Donahue's death. Was it heartless not to mention it? Or would it be tasteless to condole with the Duchess after having just dined with the Duke?

"And did you mention his death?"

"No, I lost my nerve."

"Was the Duchess very upset?"

"She must have minded desperately, but she didn't show it. She was immensely dignified. I remember when the Duchess came out of the lavatory having peed, she said to me 'Even that can be a pleasure . . .' That was her sense of humor."

$\mathcal{T}$he day after I lunched with Mrs. Brinsley Plunket I got onto a plane with my mind full of troubling images of the Duchess's leopard bracelet and her suicide lover's naughty sense of humor and I went off to Paris.

The apartment where Maître Blum lived was in the rue de Varenne, the Parisian equivalent of Downing Street. It was just a few doors away from the house of the prime minister of France. I wondered if this was a coincidence.

Maître Blum's building was huge and dark and depressing. Flanked by embassies, it was sufficiently grim and morguelike to seem suitable as an embassy from which the deserted dying Duchess could speak through her spokesperson to the living.

I got into Maître Blum's creaky old elevator which looked as if it were as dangerous as she was reputed to be. I suspected it hadn't been serviced for about eighty years.

I was starting to feel nervous. What would Maître Blum look like? No one had given me any physical description of her. She had always been spoken of as if she were some kind of elemental force rather than a woman. But now I wondered what she would be wearing. Would she have the same superb chic as her employer? The Duchess had been dressed by all the most famous couturiers in the world. She had a personal preference for Balenciaga,

Givenchy, and Mainbocher. Would Maître Blum have a good enough figure to carry off the slim classic lines of these designers? I rather hoped that unlike the Duchess she wouldn't be "Perfection in the exquisite propriety of her appearance." I dreaded her having the Duchess's famed ability to make other women "look like croquet mallets beside a polished arrow."

I also wondered how Maître Blum's apartment would be decorated. Maître Blum's shrewdness, so it seemed, "originally had much impressed the Duchess." But surely there had been other facets of her lawyer's personality which she also found admirable and congenial. The relationship between these two woman appeared to be so intimate. Now the Duchess was ailing, Maître Blum was her only visitor. The Duchess had placed her entire fortune in the hands of this lawyer, who also handled her publicity and dealt with all her correspondence. The Duchess and Maître Blum surely must have more in common than a mutual desire to deprive Lord Mountbatten of his royal swords. Surely there must be some similarity of taste, some kinship of life-styles. I felt it would be interesting to see if Maître Blum's apartment displayed any of the love of flamboyance and luxury that had once been boldly manifested by the Duchess. Wallis Windsor had always been a delight to interior decorators because she favored "the new." If she never became Queen of England, she certainly became queen of the jet set, and as an arbiter of international fashion her innovating dictates had been far-reaching in their influence. To what extent would Maître Blum have imitated her?

A very old and miserable-looking maid with a painful limp opened the door. She looked grumpy, underpaid, and overworked. She showed me into a large, high-ceilinged room which had an uninviting atmosphere.

Although it contained an ample supply of ugly chairs which were dotted around in little arbitrary circles, they were so ill-arranged one had the feeling there was nowhere to sit.

Most people instinctively avoid seating themselves in a position where their back is facing a door. They have an atavistic fear of exposing themselves to a surprise attack. Maître Blum's living room was unique in that it contained six huge doors, so it was hard not to have one's back to one of them.

Nothing in Maître Blum's apartment appeared to have been influenced by the taste of the Duchess. There was no sign of her famous "cunning use of mirrors," nor was there a trace of "le bleu Wallis." The Duchess had a passion for trompe l'oeil. She had a chest which had a realistic rendering of the first crested invitation that the Duke had sent to her. I'd half hoped Maître Blum would have a trompe l'oeil that represented her first invitation from the Duchess, but I was disappointed.

Maître Blum's furnishings were all somber. She had a mixture of equally ugly modern furniture and fake antiques. One got no feeling that the modern furniture was there because she loved "the new." Her living room suggested she was a woman devoid of visual sense. She appeared to have a puritanical horror of color. One shade of dingy brown was superimposed upon some even grimmer shade of lifeless ochre. Everything she owned looked expensive, but no care seemed to have gone into her choice of decor. The Duchess's houses were always cluttered with objects and sometimes her taste was criticized as being too "chichi." This charge could not have been leveled at Maître Blum although she had a jade Buddha on her mantelpiece and a display cabinet which contained a few Chinese plates. If her living room had any theme, it was an oriental one. I wondered if this was due to her husband, the General. Maybe he had fought in Indochina.

Maître Blum was royally late. I became increasingly nervous. I couldn't think what I wanted to ask her about the Duchess, nor could I tell through which of her six doors she was going to arrive. This increased my feeling of unease. She had Chinese ashtrays all over the room; I therefore assumed it was all right to smoke.

Suddenly one of the huge doors swung open and she arrived with such speed she was half running. This was the dreaded "step of the young girl" I'd been warned about.

She seized the only chair where her back could face a wall and seeing that mine was facing a window, with an imperious wave of her gnarled finger she moved me from this advantageous position and made me sit with my back to one of the doors.

She was a small woman. Her bearing was regal. Her face had the cast of an oriental warrior. The cruel set of her mouth gave a ferocity and a distinction to her expression. Her skin had a waxy texture and it was unlined. She had obviously copied the Duchess and had a face-lift. But unlike Wallis Windsor, who had always taken a perfectionist approach to her appearance, Maître Blum had been overexcessive in her use of cosmetic surgery. She'd allowed, or forced, her surgeons to make everything look far too tight. Her eyes had been sewn into slits and they had been given a Chinese-looking slant. They lacked all mobility and she seemed to find it difficult to blink. Her face did not match her wizened little hands, which were those of a crone, and her age was also betrayed by the discoloration of pigmentation, the brown flowers of death that smudged her arms.

"Don't smoke," she said angrily.

I apologized. I felt her Chinese ashtrays were traps that she deliberately laid to lure her visitors into a situation where she could embarrass them.

"I have been in the country," she said. "My husband, the General, is gravely ill."

"I'm sorry," I said politely.

She shrugged irritably as if this remark disgusted her, pursed her lips, and made no reply.

I now realized that she really had been "en voiture" as I'd been told. Her energy was astonishing. It was odd to think of this resolute eighty-four-year-old lawyer speeding down the French highways as she frenetically commuted between the bedside of the diseased old General in the country and the Parisian bedside of the moribund Duchess.

"You understand that I do not want to be quoted," she snapped at me. She seemed to be in a foul temper.

I asked her how she expected me to do an interview with someone who refused to be quoted. Whatever she told me about the Duchess would have to be attributed when I wrote my article.

"It is not necessary for you to say. It's more interesting if you don't say. When people read your article, they will all be trying to guess who you've been talking to." For the first time I saw her give a sly and sour little smile. She apparently liked mystery.

"I understand you are very close to the Duchess," I said.

"We have always had a *relation de chaleur*," she answered.

"A relationship of heat?"

Maître Blum nodded and closed her slitted lids as if she were offering up some kind of prayer of thanks. Although she had a perfect command of English, I noticed that whenever she was asked questions which referred to her more intimate feelings about the Duchess she only liked to express them in French as if she felt that English was a language too unworthy to be appropriate for any discussion of Wallis Windsor.

"The last time the Duchess went out in public, she came here to dine in this apartment," she said.

I didn't envy the Duchess. As everyone had always described her as fun-loving, when she attended her last supper, surely she would preferred to have spent it with someone more sympathetic and amusing than Maître Blum.

I also wondered where the Duchess had been made to sit in this fusty, unwelcoming apartment and hoped Maître Blum hadn't placed her with her back to one of those huge and threatening doors.

And had the Duchess been fazed by all the grim brown-ery of Maître Blum's choice of furnishings? Maître Blum would never have permitted her one single vodka. Wallis Windsor's sharp decorator's eye must have been clear, so-ber, and critical. But maybe the heat of the relationship she'd apparently always enjoyed with her lawyer had been powerful enough to make her lenient. This last evening which she'd apparently spent with Maître Blum had to have been a momentous one in the life of Wallis Windsor. The most worldly of characters, she must have known that she was saying a permanent farewell to the glittering, worldly world as she'd always known it. After that it would be darkness and silence.

"I quite understand why the Duke fell in love with the Duchess," Maître Blum said. "The Duchess is very interesting and she is very interested in other people."

It was remarkable that the Duchess could still be in-terested in other people lying there in her isolation with pipes up her nostrils in her house in the Bois de Boulogne.

"How is the Duchess?" I asked her.

Again she shrugged irritably. "She is not well. But she is in no danger. Her doctors are not worried."

"Can she speak?"

"She speaks every three weeks."

"What does she say?"

"She says good morning and good evening."

The intervals at which the Duchess spoke seemed rather curious and so were the things she said.

"Does her doctor visit the Duchess every day?" I asked.

"The Duchess has doctors," Maître Blum snapped. She

seemed to think I had insulted the Duchess by not realizing she had more than one.

"Does she still have a staff?"

"She has a butler and she has four servants. She used to have thirty-two." Maître Blum suddenly looked very sad. "She doesn't have the hothouse gardeners any more," she murmured wistfully. "Nor does she employ a chef."

"That would be ridiculous." I visualized the Duchess's chef making some delicious feather-light concoction of a soufflé and the Duchess eating it through her nose.

Maître Blum looked suspicious. She obviously didn't like my remark but finally she unwillingly agreed that it would be absurd.

She kept glaring at me with the utmost hostility. She answered my questions with ill-mannered abruptness. Her slanting, unblinking eyes had a snakelike malevolence. She was perverse. If she wanted favorable articles written about the Duchess, she seemed reckless in the way she deliberately tried to antagonize her interviewers.

"I do not trust you," she hissed at me. "I have had many betrayals and now I trust no one."

I had been warned that Maître Blum was a frightening old woman and now I was starting to understand why she intimated the friends of the Duchess. Despite her age, she managed to give the impression that she might be physically dangerous. There was something ruthless and demented in her glinting, paranoid eyes. She was seething with such rage there seemed a danger she suddenly might be unable to control it, that she might spring at me like a prehistoric beast and claw me with her yellow nails.

And why was she in such a towering temper? All this fury was irrational. She had agreed to give an interview. Now she was behaving as if she somehow had been forced to do so against her higher principles.

She was simply dressed in a fawn skirt and sweater. Her clothes were suitable but unmemorable. Apparently her need for one-upmanship took a different form from that of the Duchess. Nothing she was wearing appeared to have been designed by Balenciaga or Mainbocher. She made no attempt to impress by the glory of her clothes. Her hair was snowy white and it was cropped short and neat. But it didn't appear to have been styled by Wallis Windsor's adored René.

"What was the Duchess like?" I asked her. I then wondered if she would be outraged that I had referred to the Duchess in the past tense.

"The Duchess is very dignified. She is immensely dignified. Her favorite word was dignity. . . . The Duchess is very kind. And the Duke was very kind too. The Duke was the soul of kindness."

"In what way was the Duke kind?" I had already been given an example of the Duchess's kindness. But no one had told me much about that of the Duke.

"The Duke used to open the doors of cars to people of no importance."

We had a silence. I wished Maître Blum would offer me some coffee. But with her ungenerous nature I knew it was foolish to hope she would dream of extending any routine courtesies.

"The Duke was kind to the point of self-sacrifice,"

Maître Blum insisted. Her shrewd eyes never left my face
as if she dared me to quibble with this statement.

"Do you feel the Windsors have been unfairly treated
in the books that have come out about them recently?" I
asked.

Maître Blum had a sort of seizure. Her whole body
shook. Her eyes swiveled. She started screaming. "It has
all been lies! It is *dégoûtant*! Everything that has been written about them is *ordure*. It has all been venomous. It has
all been *ragout de cuisine*."

"Do you like Lady Mosley's book?" I asked, hoping
to calm her. "I believe that it is very nice about the Duchess."

Maître Blum refused to answer. She sat there quivering
with anger and glaring at me.

"I understand that it has been suggested that the Duke
and Duchess slept together before marriage. And this is one
of the many lies that has been spread about them." I knew
this would provoke another of Maître Blum's explosions.
David Pryce-Jones had said this was the point she felt most
violently about. Predictably, it instantly set her off screaming again. "That was a dirty falsification! People will write
any sort of *ordure*!"

The violence and tenacity with which she clung to her
improbable theory about the Windsors made me start to
speculate on the sexual orientation of Maître Blum herself.
It was impossible to visualize her lying throbbing with un-
abashed passion and pleasure in the arms of her husband,
the General. Her whole personality was too essentially un-
yielding. It seemed almost obscene to try to picture her in
the nude let alone in some subjugated erotic position. Lady

Mosley had told me that the General had been prematurely aged by his marriage to Maître Blum. Just as the Maître wanted the Windsors to have refrained from any physical activities before their marriage, it was always feasible that she herself had gone much further and insisted on maintaining a nunlike sexual abstinence in all the years that had followed her own marriage to General Spillman. If she'd imposed her old-fashioned respect and reverence for total chastity on this unfortunate military personage, it was conceivable that the pains of his constant frustration had slowly sapped all his *joie de vivre*, and been instrumental in his current decline.

"If the Duchess refused to sleep with the Duke until he married her, does that not make her seem rather scheming?" I asked.

Maître Blum refused to see this. According to this perverse old lawyer, the Duke and the Duchess refrained from all sexual intercourse until they were on their honeymoon.

As the Duke and the Duchess had both been over forty in that period, Maître Blum was making them sound extremely neurotic and peculiar. But she could not be budged on this issue.

It was a delicate subject, and I could see by her violent agitation and the paranoia gleaming like a streetlight in her slanting amber eyes that it was a subject wiser to change.

Did she behave like this when she was in court, I wondered. She had represented Rita Hayworth, Charlie Chaplin, Darryl Zanuck, Walt Disney, Merle Oberon, Douglas Fairbanks, and many other celebrities of her period. She must be extremely able.

Her antics sometimes made her seem clownish but

were they more premeditated than one imagined? Her un-abashed rudeness, her displays of infantile fury, all this glar-ing and shaking and screaming was troubling in a woman of her age. But maybe she wanted to create dismay. There was no restraint in her behavior and maybe her refusal to exert any was extremely cunning. Had she learned from long experience that witnesses became cowed in the face of her naked aggression, and juries could be swayed and made to accept the premises she offered them? If Maître Blum was a clown, she was also a terrifying clown.

Although like all people who are being interviewed, she was temporarily, in a sense, "on trial," her personality was so powerful that she managed to reverse our roles; she gave me the sense that she considered me guilty and an unseen panel would soon agree with her. My crime was a heinous one in the eyes of Maître Blum. She saw me as guilty of insufficient loyalty toward the Duchess.

"You've no idea how much the Duchess is still loved by the people of England. You simply can't believe how many hundreds of letters she receives every day," she told me.

I felt this was very unlikely. But perhaps I was wrong to be skeptical. Many people like writing to celebrities. But could there really be so many balmy English people writing to this living cabbage of a Duchess?

"The Duchess never nags. She never thinks of herself. She never complains. She was always very hardworking. She lived for the poor. She has always only wanted to do good works." Maître Blum drifted in and out of the past and present tense as she recited her pious litany. Her por-trait of this hardworking, selfless Duchess was certainly a fresh and original one. And although it was pleasant to hear that the Duchess never nagged, it was odd that her lawyer seemed to find it surprising.

"The Duchess was adored by all her servants," Maître Blum continued, always scowling at me. "Even the ones she dismissed always tried to come back." She spoke very fast. Her words rattled out like bullets from a machine gun. The speed of her delivery might also be a legal trick for it made it difficult to follow her and gave her listeners little time to query the truth of what she was saying.

"Did the Duchess find it difficult to tip?" I asked.

I knew that the Duke had shocked people on both sides of the Atlantic because he found it impossible to give a tip to anyone who worked for him. Eighty-six pieces of luggage would be carried up to his suite in the Waldorf Astoria and the bellboy would wait in vain for the Duke to fish in his pocket for a dollar. The Duke's ungenerous behavior used to shock because it was not considered princely. I wondered if the Duchess had applauded the parsimonious aspect of her husband's character or whether it had irritated her and made her feel ashamed of him. Now that I was in the presence of her spokesperson I thought I would like this question answered so that I could get a clearer image of the Duchess herself.

"Tip!" screamed Maître Blum. "Why would the Duchess want to tip? Why would she want to demean herself? Why do you want her to tip? You are a jackal!"

She was playing with semantics. I felt certain that she understood the word "tip" in English. She enjoyed pretending that she thought I wanted the Duchess to be upside down with her face buried in the sewage of some manhole while her beautifully shod feet waved desperate high-heels in the air.

"Forget the question," I said.

"I should hope so," she sniffed.

"The Windsors were both so loving," she continued. "They were only concerned with doing good. They cared about sick animals and orphans . . ."

Could Maître Blum be referring to the incident in *The Windsor Story* when Clare Luce suggested that the Duke should make some gesture to help lessen the adverse publicity he kept receiving after the war? Why didn't he adopt a British war orphan to help remind the British public of his love of England?

The Duke had consulted the Duchess, "How do you like the idea, darling?"

"It's silly!" she said. "Who knows how an orphan will turn out?"[1] Operation Orphan was then abandoned like the charitable foundation once discussed with Lord Mountbatten.

"Their charity budget was enormous," continued Maître Blum. "They wouldn't let anyone know how much they spent on hospitals and good causes. They had it kept secret and sometimes they had to refuse to donate as much as they would have liked to, otherwise they would have been submerged with requests."

"They were very rich, I understand."

Maître Blum's whole body jerked as if she had received an electric shock.

"The Windsors were never rich!" she screamed.

"But they must have been quite rich," I insisted. "Is it not true that the Duchess spent 100,000 dollars a year on her clothes alone, before inflation, and that was not counting what she spent on her jewelry and furs?"

"She had to do that." Maître Blum drew herself up proudly and she preened herself. She obviously approved of the extravagance of the Duchess's dress budget. "She only did it for him."

"I imagine the medical expenses of the Duchess must be quite heavy."

Maître Blum looked suddenly despairing. "*Ils sont affreux.*" Her voice sunk to a whisper. Her whole body crumpled over. She held her white head miserably in her hands.

I thought about the Duchess's sold-off bracelet. Maître Blum said the Duchess had never been rich and Maître Blum presumably was an honorable woman. But why was she so insistent on this point? By claiming the Windsors had always been impoverished and behaving so dramatically when she described the grinding burden of the Duchess's current medical expenses, was she giving herself an excuse for the future? If the Duchess were to die and later it was discovered that very little remained of her great fortune, would it seem less odd if one accepted her lawyer's contention that she had never had much money from the start?

Barbara Hutton allegedly died penniless, having given power of attorney to financial advisors. It was claimed that all her money had been dissipated by the costs of the illness that afflicted her in her last years. I wondered how much

Maître Blum was currently paying the Duchess's doctors, and what salary she thought it correct for the Duchess to pay her.

"Is the royal family helping the Duchess to defray the frightful costs of her long illness? Are they aware of her precarious financial plight?"

Maître Blum hesitated. I wondered if she would launch into one of her screaming hysterical tirades against them. But she was unexpectedly restrained. "The royal family inquire about the Duchess's health very often," she said firmly. Whether they had been informed of the Duchess's money problems and whether they were being generous to the unlucky widow of their delinquent relative, Maître Blum refused to say.

"The Duchess is highly intelligent," she told me. She seemed to want to turn to topics which were happier than the Duchess's dire economic situation. Whenever she was talking about the virtues of her employer, her temper improved, her face relaxed, and she started to speak with the tenderness of a mother boasting about her favorite child.

"The Duke was highly intelligent too," she added quickly, as if she did not want to leave him out. She was far less emotional and affectionate when she spoke about the Duke, and she gave the impression that when she praised him it was because he had married the Duchess, rather than for his own intrinsic merit.

"The Duke had one of the best legal minds I have ever encountered," she told me. "The Duke always surprised me. Whenever I submitted any documents to him, I was always amazed by the way he got the point immediately. He always knew how to pick out the vital clause."

"I understand the Duke was very interested in housing, that when he became Hitler's guest in 1937 it was for this reason, although his visit was much criticized and his purpose in making it has often been misconstrued."

Maître Blum twitched uneasily. "The Duke was passionately interested in housing. He only longed to serve. As Prince of Wales, his motto, you must remember, was 'Ich Dien' . . . I serve."

I thought of the Woolworth heir, Jimmy Donahue, and his "naughty sense of humor." When the Duchess became obsessed by him and her husband was suffering horribly, Jimmy Donahue took the unfortunate Duke's motto and had it embroidered on his own pillowcase.

"There is one thing about the Windsors that no one knows," Maître Blum paused dramatically as if she was going to release some earthshaking piece of information. "The Windsors were always ill."

"Always ill?" I was indeed astonished.

"Oui. Ils etaient toujours malades."

This was a brand-new controversial assertion. Bryan and Murphy had claimed that until she grew old, the Duchess always enjoyed "rude good health." But maybe Maître Blum knew better. Maybe the Duchess had told her things that the authors of *The Windsor Story* could never dream of.

I thought of the descriptions I'd been given of the Duchess at the beginning of her love affair. Her first romantic visits to the toylike palace, Fort Belvedere, the Duke handing his guests a machete and asking them to help him chop down rhododendrons. Then the dinners in the evening with the Duchess, her hair sleek and center-parted, seated on his right and smilingly taking an interest in his royal duties. Later the carpet rolled up and the Duke whistling as he danced to his favorite tune, "I want to be-e, a bee in your boudoir   And be-e in your boudoir —all day . . ."

I thought of all the photographs that were taken many years later, the Duke and Duchess caught white-faced and haggard staggering from nightclub to nightclub in Paris, Palm Beach, and New York. There was a seeming frivolity to the way their lives had been spent. But was this being given an extra dimension and poignancy by the fact that under their courageously pleasure-loving exteriors this unlucky couple had always been riddled by disease?

"Many people feel that the Windsors led a rather empty existence after the abdication," I murmured, trying to challenge her. "Is this unfair to them? Would you say that many of the stories spread about them are untrue?"

Maître Blum had another one of her explosions. "All this is lies! All that is malicious slander! It's nothing but filthy tittle-tattle!"

"The notorious nightclub-going of the Windsors, is that completely invented?"

She winced when she heard the word *nightclub*. Maître Blum gave a little scream as if I had stabbed her.

"The Duchess never went to nightclubs. She never went, never, never, never!"

"Never?" I insisted. It was interesting that Maître Blum seemed to have such a violent horror of nightclubs.

When she was a girl, brought up strictly in the French
provinces, had she been taught that "the nightclub" was
the supreme modern evil? Was this why she found it intolerable if anyone suggested that her hallowed Duchess
could have ever set foot in something that she saw as a
final sink of iniquity?

"The Windsors were a very cultivated couple. Is that
how you say it in English?"

"Cultured?"

"Exactly, they were very cultured. They didn't like to
go out in the evening. They liked to stay at home and read
good books and listen to classical music. People were
astonished when they heard their views on art and
literature."

"I've been told that the Duchess drank rather heavily.
Is that another irresponsible untruth?"

She gave another little scream. All my questions now
made her scream.

"The Duchess never drank."

"Did she never drink at all?"

The look in Maître Blum's surgically operated eyes was
getting murderous. With her withered finger she made a
gesture as if she were holding the tiniest possible medicine
glass.

"The Duchess drank maybe this much, once or twice
in her life. And she only drank that much because she was
offered it. *Par politesse*, you understand. The Duchess was
immensely polite and dignified. She had this fantastic
dignity."

Once again she was crooning on about the dignity.

"I will tell you who the Duchess was like," she said. "The Duchess was exactly like Queen Mary."

I remembered a particular photograph taken of the Duchess when she was quite old and frenetically doing the Twist all alone in the center of some nightclub. She looked extremely drunk, rather sad, and also embarrassing. Nothing in this harshly recorded image of her struck me as especially reminiscent of Queen Mary.

"The Duchess never drank," Maître Blum persisted. "That was never the trouble. The trouble was the Duchess wouldn't eat. And that was very wrong of the Duchess."

This was the first time she had said anything critical about her employer, the first time she had shown that on occasion she could get quite angry with the Duchess.

"Do you mean the Duchess suffered from anorexia?"

"Yes, she did." Maître Blum sighed bitterly. "It was all this slimming. She was always slimming."

"I believe the Duchess had a wonderful figure."

Maître Blum's face lit up. At last I had pleased her. She became temporarily almost friendly. Her whole demeanor became transformed.

"Oh yes," she whispered ecstatically. "The Duchess had the most wonderful body. She still has the most fantastic body. You ought to see it. The skin on her body is perfect. It doesn't have a line. She has the lovely, soft body of a young girl."

She spoke with such intensity and passion, I was startled. With the Duchess lying with pipes through her nose in her house in the Bois de Boulogne, it seemed inappropriate that Maître Blum should be raving about her body's loveliness in such an unmeasured and rapturous fashion.

We were not sitting drinking together and exchanging indiscreet late-night confidences in one of the nightclubs she had such a horror of. It was eleven o'clock in the morning and Maître Blum as the Duchess's representative was meant to be giving a sober interview to the British *Sunday Times*.

Yet I realized at that moment that Maître Blum really did love the Duchess, that Wallis Windsor was much more to her than merely a useful world-famous client.

A mystical adoration transfused her face every time that she spoke about the magnificent physique of her employer. Her awestruck reverence for the beauty of the Duchess's body manifested itself in such a guileless and spontaneous manner that I never believed that she was faking it.

Although I felt relieved for the Duchess that there appeared to be evidence that Maître Blum's feeling for her was much more complex than that of the exploitative lawyer, I was troubled for Wallis Windsor on other scores. How often did Maître Blum go to look at her body? Maître Blum had arranged to be the only visitor the Duchess was any longer allowed. It was disquieting to picture Maître Blum making trips to her beautiful house in Neuilly, creeping up the stairs to the Duchess's bedroom, and pulling down the poor woman's sheets in order to gaze at her. Did the Duchess like being inspected in such an intimate way? If she were paralyzed, she could make little protest. And although I had gathered that the Duchess had always been extremely narcissistic, at this last desperate point in her life, would she really be pleased to know that her aged spokesperson was trying to publicize her current physical splendors in a London newspaper?

"And the Duchess's face still looks so beautiful. *Elle est belle comme tout.* Her face has no lines. Her hair and her skin are perfect," Maître Blum continued in the same breathless, adulatory tones.

"The Duchess has this youthfulness, this radiance. The beauty of her soul is shining through her face. It's an inner beauty," she added quickly. "It has nothing to do with face-lifts."

"Did the Duchess used to have many face-lifts?"

The question brought Maître Blum out of her dreamy, ecstatic state. Her angry, suspicious expression returned. She seemed to sense what I was wondering. Was it possible that in the wildness of her desire to exalt the Duchess, Maître Blum was still arranging for this poor wreck of a woman to have face-lifts?

"How should I know," she snapped. "I am only the Duchess's lawyer."

Sometimes Maître Blum maintained her distance and became only the Duchess's humble legal advisor, and sometimes she claimed she had a *relation de chaleur* with the Duchess which sounded to me very hot indeed. Her choice of roles appeared to be dictated entirely by caprice and there was no way of telling which one she would assume at any given moment. All interchange with Maître Blum was therefore enlivened by a constant element of surprise.

And how well was the Duchess of Windsor really looking? The diplomat Walter Lees's description had been a sad one. But he had not seen her as recently as Maître Blum. Was it possible her pipes had been removed and the Duchess had regained the radiance and beauty that her lawyer kept extolling?

If I'd felt certain that the Duchess was still in the same frightful condition that she had been in when Walter Lees last saw her, I'd have felt that it was tasteless to mention that Lord Snowdon was anxious to photograph her. But now that Maître Blum had given me such a reassuring account of her appearance, there seemed no harm in doing so. If the Duchess was looking so marvelous, Maître Blum might love the idea of having her photographed.

"Did you know that Lord Snowdon is very keen to photograph the Duchess?"

Although Maître Blum was such a skilled lawyer, surprisingly she was not cool and she always betrayed her feelings. The shrewd eyes gleamed with excitement. She quivered. This was what she wanted to hear. Lord Snowdon had photographed the Queen of England. In her eyes there was no other figure who would be more suitable to take photographs of the Duchess.

But then her excitement vanished. She looked deflated. The thrilled expression was replaced by a sorrowful one.

"No," she said. She shrugged with a gesture of extreme melancholy. "I'm afraid not," she said. "I'm afraid that will not be possible."

There was a curiously timeless atmosphere in Maître Blum's apartment. World leaders and all international outside events receded until they lost their importance. Within this room with the six huge doors, one became infected by Maître Blum's near-religious belief that the universe was dominated solely by the omnipotent figure of the Duchess.

Yet though I sensed her dominance in this old woman's apartment in the rue de Varenne, I felt I was losing the Duchess rather than getting closer to her. Now she was becoming so dignified, so strictly teetotal and cultured and ever lovely, she seemed more inaccessible to me than before I'd spoken to Maître Blum. As the Duchess of Windsor ascended to an Olympus where she became hedged by her own divinity, her lawyer became increasingly terrestrial.

I noticed that Maître Blum had screwed up her eyes and this increased rather than ameliorated the intensity of her malevolent gaze.

"There is something I want to say to you." Her deep, manlike voice had acquired a new, menacing rasp.

I nodded politely, waiting to hear what she wanted to say.

"If you do not write a favorable article about the Duchess—I will not sue you . . ."

She paused to give her next sentence the ultimate dramatic effect.

"I will kill you."

Maître Blum emphasized the word "kill" and drew it out so that it sounded like "keel."

I gave a nervous reflex laugh. I hoped she would laugh too. But no smile softened the hard, cruel line of Maître Blum's lips. Through their half-closed slits her eyes examined me. She was eager to see my reaction to her warning.

My reaction was confused and rather slow. This outrageous old woman was threatening my life. But surely she was joking. Her threat must have been a mere figure of speech. Maître Blum was a highly respected French lawyer. She was not a movie-type gangster with hired assassins standing ready to bump off those who offended her. Yet I wished she would do something that would indicate she had not meant the terrible thing she had said to me. I suddenly remembered that Maître Blum had tangled with Lord Mountbatten. With a chill, I remembered what had happened to him. I felt Maître Blum was sucking me down into her own morass of total irrationality.

By introducing this note of violence which now lingered like a bad smell in her fusty apartment, Maître Blum had cast a blight on our interview. We were both silent. She sat there crouching in her chair as if she were gathering her strength before she sprang at me. Lady Tomkins had described her as a lioness.

I felt there was now only one question that I really wanted to ask her about the Duchess. Originally I had not intended to put it to her, because I assumed that she would find it agonizingly painful. But she had overtested my tact. She'd made me feel aggrieved and therefore vengeful. I had been perfectly polite and respectful to Maître Blum and I considered that she had treated me abominably. I had arrived at her apartment quite prepared to be civil to her. I'd arrived with an open mind which was all too ready to take a favorable attitude towards the Duchess. I had been continuously patient with Maître Blum despite all her snarling and screaming and other provocations. She had insulted my intelligence by feeding me a steady diet of untruths about the Duchess and I had not made any protest. I had tried to search for the nugget of accuracy which must lie buried somewhere in the bog of her many distortions. But now Maître Blum had gone too far. She finally had compounded all the other injuries she had inflicted upon me by making a terrorist threat on my life.

"Maître Blum," I said. "When the Duchess eventually dies . . ." I had suspected she would find this sentence traumatic, but had underrated the fury with which she would react to it. She had exploded before, but all her previous explosions had been damp fireworks. This was a nuclear blast.

"Don't you dare write anything about that," she yelled at me. She was like a fishwife. She made threatening gestures with her arms.

"But Maître Blum . . ." I didn't feel this menacing old lawyer deserved any mercy. "When the Duchess eventually dies, I must know if she will go to England and be buried beside the Duke in the royal burial ground at Frogmore."

Maître Blum suddenly changed her tactics. She looked as if she were about to cry. It was the first time that I found her rather pitiful. There was something pathetic about the decay of pigmentation that was making brown flowerlike patterns as it crept relentlessly over her aged arms and hands.

"Please don't write anything about that," she pleaded in a sad whisper. "Please, please, please."

Her Achilles heel had been pierced. She had lost all her poise and her bombast. She was a white-haired little old lady who was close to the grave and terrified to face it.

However much Maître Blum deified the Duchess, her

client was not immortal. However much money and energy Maître Blum spent on preserving the Duchess, the terrible day finally had to come when the Duchess would leave the shores of France and go to a place where Maître Blum could never follow her. When the Duchess was laid to rest in the royal burial grounds of Windsor, the tragedy for Maître Blum would be inestimable. Not only would she lose her adored Duchess for eternity, but she would lose her forever to the Duke.

I kept wondering if there was any way by which Maître Blum could circumvent what for her must be this most dreaded impending catastrophe. Could she draw up a will for the Duchess in which she stated that she wished to be buried in France because it was the only country that had been kind to her? This would allow Maître Blum to spend the remains of the Windsor fortune on constructing some magnificent Invalides-type monument that she would consider as a worthy memorial for her client. Maître Blum could also arrange for the Duchess to have an Eternal Flame, and she could spend the remainder of her days tending it. When her own time came, she could be laid beside the Duchess and she and her client would be even closer in death than they had been in life.

This would be one way by which Maître Blum's most pressing problem could be surmounted, but it was doubtful that it would turn out to be feasible. Maître Blum, supposedly, was an ethical lawyer and as such she could not tamper with the Duchess's will in order to suit her own emotional needs and purposes.

The Duchess's destiny had been preordained for her

by the historical events in which she had been the protagonist. When the Duke was dying, he had received a visit from the Queen of England. Bryan and Murphy describe him as "bristling with pipes." He was being treated by Dr. Thin, the same physician who was now treating the Duchess. Despite his tubes, the Duke had been able to kiss the Queen of England's hand. At that solemn moment she had respected her earlier promise to him that the Duchess could be buried at Frogmore.

On the face of it the cards were heavily stacked against Maître Blum. With all her famous ingenuity, and her talent for browbeating and manipulating, it was unlikely she would be able to cow and coerce Queen Elizabeth into allowing her to join the Duchess of Windsor in the royal burial ground.

Maître Blum, on the level, was shrewd and intelligent and mundane. She must know that she was fighting a losing battle. Unless something totally unpredictable occurred, the Duchess eventually would be wrested from her protective lioness's care. Maître Blum seemed to have fused her own identity so inextricably with that of the Duchess that on the day the Duchess died, her lawyer would surely die a little death.

But Maître Blum was a fanatically stubborn old woman. She would not give up easily. She would try to defy the fates. Even if she accepted that ultimately she was doomed to experience the fearful loss of her Duchess, she would still do everything in her power to postpone that ghastly moment. And remembering that the Duchess was being kept alive by medical know-how, I felt this did not bode very well for the Duchess.

"Do you mind me writing that the Duchess is ill?"

I wanted to test the degree to which Maître Blum tried to alter the unpleasant, unalterable fact by denying its reality.

"No! Don't write that the Duchess is ill."

"But won't people find it strange if I make no mention of the Duchess's illness? Won't they wonder what the Duchess is doing with herself? How do I explain why she never appears in public?"

Maître Blum sighed. She still looked miserable. "Yes, I am afraid you will have to say the Duchess is ill. I'm afraid that people know it."

"If I'm to write an article about the Duchess, which friends of hers do you think I ought to interview?"

"The Duchess has so many hundreds of friends. She has so many friends all over the world, it would be impossible to count them."

"Can you give me some of their names?"

Maître Blum couldn't remember one single name. There were too many. She obviously felt that she herself was the sole figure in a position to speak with any reliability on the subject of the Duchess of Windsor.

"The friends of the Duchess have always been the best." She lingered gloatingly on the word "best" and gave a little smile of pride. "The Duchess's friends were amongst the crowned heads of Europe. The Duchess of Windsor has mixed only with the highest and the best."

I suddenly remembered an anecdote that I'd been told about Jimmy Donahue. He had gone to a butcher shop downtown in New York and bought himself a cow's udder. He had cut off one of its tits and stuck it in his fly buttons. He had walked down Fifth Avenue and caused great consternation. Finally someone had called the police. When the cops arrived to arrest him, he took out a pair of scissors and snipped it off.

There was a yawning discrepancy here. How did this jokester figure in the anecdote tally with Maître Blum's worshipful notions of the exalted company the Duchess had always kept?

"I believe Lady Dudley is a friend of the Duchess?"

I was playing it safe. I knew that Grace Dudley was devoted to Wallis Windsor. If I wanted to avoid one of Maître Blum's hysterical tirades I knew it was pure insanity to mention the name of her lover, Jimmy Donahue.

"Lady Dudley?" Maître Blum seemed aghast.

"Yes, Lady Dudley. I understand that Lady Dudley escorted the Duchess to the Duke's funeral."

"Lady Dudley was certainly no good friend of the Duchess!" Maître Blum gave one of her vicious turtle-snaps and sparks of spite flashed from her eyes. My question had not been as safe as I'd imagined. What could Lady Dudley have done to Maître Blum that any mild reference to her existence provoked such an eruption of loathing?

Maître Blum was an exhausting old person to be with. Even if on occasion some of her anger was simulated, her technique of releasing her rage in spurts was still effective for it induced a passivity in her interrogators. I could have asked her to expand on her statement that Lady Dudley was no friend of the Duchess but I felt too drained. There were questions to be asked but she had made me too tired to ask them. And because she had worn me down and sapped my courage, I retaliated by allowing my mind to wander off into realms of purest speculation, where Maître Blum could bring neither lawsuits nor injunctions for all my queries remained unvoiced.

Had Maître Blum longed to accompany the Duchess when she went to England for the Duke's funeral? I remembered the haunting photograph of the widowed Duchess standing in the window of Buckingham Palace looking befuddled by shock and tranquilizers. Did Maître Blum resent the fact that she had not been photographed beside her in the palace window wearing identical black veiling? Did she feel that if she'd been allowed to take her rightful place beside Wallis Windsor the photograph could have then been given an added tragic dimension, a doubling of intensity? Maître Blum and the Duchess could have looked like stricken sisters inseparable in their grief.

The Maître, presumably, would have been intoxicated by every second of the Duke's funeral and all the pomp and ceremony of his service at St. George's Chapel. She would have been dazzled by the glittering cortège which included the Constable and Governor of Windsor Castle in full dress uniform, the Military Knights of Windsor with plumed hats under their arms, the Archbishop of Canterbury with his white miter and black and gold cape. The Duchess had been placed between the Queen of England and Prince Philip. After the hymns and the prayers, Garter King-of-Arms stepped forward in his gorgeous heraldic costume and proclaimed the styles and titles of the late Duke. "Knight of the most excellent Order of the Garter. Knight of the Thistle, Knight of St. Patrick, Knight Grand

Cross of the Order of the Bath and Knight Grand Commander of the Order of the Star of India, Knight Grand
Cross of St. Michael and St. George, Military Cross, Ad-
miral of the Fleet, Field Marshal of the Army, Marshal of
the Royal Air Force, and uncle of our most high, most
mighty, and most excellent Monarch, Queen Elizabeth the
Second." And Maître Blum had not been present. Was it
for this reason that she still harbored such a grudge against
Lady Dudley?

It was quite possible that Maître Blum felt that Grace
Dudley had not offered sufficient emotional support to the
Duchess when she arrived in England devastated by the
Duke's death and had her first confrontation with the royal
family that had always spurned and detested her.

Maybe Maître Blum believed that if she had only been
allowed to be at the Duchess's side, her passionate love and
loyalty would have provided Wallis Windsor with far
greater protection.

But what could Maître Blum have really done for the
Duchess when the Royal Family were standing at the
Duke's graveside in the cemetery at Frogmore? The Duchess started drifting to and fro like a lost, unhappy child.
Would Maître Blum have taken a tight, angry grip on her
arm and been able to keep her still? There had been the
moment later in the day when the Queen Mother took
pity on the Duchess's misery, and although she knew that
Wallis Windsor had always described her not only as a "fat
cook," but also "the Monster of Glamis," she came forward and kissed her. How would Maître Blum have reacted to this generous, if plebeian, gesture? With tears of

gratitude streaming down her face, would she have hugged and embraced the Queen Mother?

What would Maître Blum have done when the dazed, unhappy Duchess drifted up to the Queen and told her she was certain she had seen her face somewhere before? Would Maître Blum have been so mortified by the Duchess's unseemly behavior that her aplomb would have deserted her and she would have remained crushed and silent? Or would she have tried to step in with her notorious eloquence and her lawyer's ability to dissemble? Could she have persuaded the Queen that the Duchess had said something very different?

A lunch had been given at Windsor Castle immediately before the Duke was buried. Even if Maître Blum had attended it, what help would she have been to the Duchess? Wallis Windsor had been seated next to Prince Philip. It is reputed that he turned to her with a bluff tactlessness and he asked her what she planned to do with her life from now on. Would Maître Blum have intervened from across the table? Would she have answered for the Duchess and tried to crush him with some brilliant French repartee? Or would the whole occasion have awed her so that she shrunk back into the role of the Duchess's humble, mouselike lawyer?

It has been reported that Prince Philip, having made a giant gaffe, with even greater insensitivity went on to ask the grieving Duchess whether she planned to return to the United Kingdom now that the Duke was dead. The Duchess, drugged and grief-stunned as she was, still noticed his aggression. She asked him why he was so interested in her immediate plans. "I don't plan to be in England very much," she murmured. "If that's what you are worrying about."

If Maître Blum had been present, would she have let well enough alone? Or would she have been so incensed by Prince Philip's callous treatment of a woman who was just about to go to her husband's graveside that she would have been unable to control herself? Would she have ignored the solemnity of the occasion and thrown a pall on the royal lunch by throwing one of her unforgettable tantrums?

If Maître Blum could have accompanied the Duchess to the Duke's funeral, there was no certainty that her services would have been as invaluable as she now must believe in retrospect. If she'd brought a threat of an injunction, could she really have prevented Cecil Beaton from writing in his diary, "The Duchess of Windsor is now completely gaga"?

I was very quiet while these intriguing speculative questions were going through my head and Maître Blum took this for a sign of weakness. She mustered her forces and promptly went into attack.

"I want to read your article before it's published," she said. I saw that the old menacing expression had come back into her eyes, the same nasty look that had been there when she had warned me what she was going to do with me if she didn't like what I had written. "I want to see your article. I want to amend it."

She was not making a request. She was issuing a command.

"Why didn't you like Lady Mosley's book when it was

so nice about the Duchess?" I was trying to change the subject. I dreaded the amendments she wanted to make on my article.

"Lady Mosley's book is nice. But it is a book '*sans couleur, sans odeur, et sans saveur*'! It says nothing new about the Duchess."

What were the new things that she wanted said? I wondered.

I noticed that Maître Blum was looking utterly exhausted. For a second I felt a little sorry for her. Yet it was all so unnecessary. Why would a woman of her age make herself ill by giving such a combative interview? No doubt she would say she was forced to do it for the Duchess.

I thanked her for talking to me and got up to go.

Maître Blum also rose though the effort was obviously painful to her. Now that I was leaving, she looked anxious. She was clearly worried that she had been too disagreeable to me. At the very last moment she made an attempt to be a little more pleasant. She said she had enjoyed meeting me. She became sickly polite with the cynical, super-gushing politeness of the French *vendeuse*.

"If you will send me your article so that I can amend it . . . I will be delighted to give you any help you want, Madame . . ." There was a sly, evil look in her slanted eyes. "If you will allow me to amend your article, I will help you to write something brilliant. I will help you write something new about the Duchess!"

I started to go out of one of her six doors without answering. I was very keen not to commit myself to showing her the article. If I were to fail in any such commitment

I feared she might sue me for breach of promise. She'd made me suspect that she'd placed tape-recorders in her Chinese ashtrays.

Maître Blum came sidling after me. She seemed suddenly servile, she was still trying so hard to be ingratiating. Her tactics were crude. If she couldn't get what she wanted by using various methods of intimidation, she instantly resorted to bribery. Now she was offering to give me brand-new information about the Duchess. She was dangling one of her dreaded "golden carrots."

She went and got my coat and she started to help me on with it. I disliked her being so physically close. She also conveyed a sense that although she felt this menial gesture should rightly be performed by some footman, she was doing it because she was "kind"—kind in exactly the same way as the late Duke.

Just before I went out of her apartment I asked her one last question.

"Maître Blum, do you think that the Duchess would have made a good queen?"

The rapturous swooning look came back into her face. Her whole expression once again became sentimental and disturbingly erotic. It was quite different from when she studiedly put on an act of trying to look kindly. "Oh yes!" She drew in her breath so that the words came out like a long drawn and wistful sigh. "Oh yes!" she repeated passionately. "The Duchess would have made the most marvelous queen!"

CHAPTER SIX

*I*t was exhilarating to walk in the Paris streets after leaving Maître Blum. I saw people walking arm in arm. They went into cafés. They were smoking. They even ordered drinks. Later they might go to nightclubs . . . Maître Blum would have liked to bring in legislation that would prohibit their activities. Fortunately her power was not yet as absolute as she could make one feel when one was trapped in her presence. There was only one unfortunate whose existence was totally regulated by her astringent dictates. I pitied the poor Duchess of Windsor.

It was intoxicating to see the sky again. I felt I'd been imprisoned in some dark cave and was fortunate to have escaped unscathed. She was like some malignant old spider sitting in her cavern of an apartment spinning out her web of fantasies about the Duchess of Windsor.

Quite suddenly I had the feeling I wanted to find my own Duchess. What had she really been like, this woman for whom a King had renounced his throne? What was happening to her now? How had she managed to fall into the clutches of Maître Blum?

Wallis Windsor still seemed so remote to me that I could only remove the vast distance that separated us by getting technically as close to her as possible. I hailed a taxi and asked the driver to take me to the house of the Duchess.

He didn't recognize the address that I had given him. "But it's the house of the Duchess of Windsor," I insisted hopefully. I felt everyone in Paris must know where she lived. I'd been infected by the unrealistic notions of Maître Blum.

"The Duchess of Windsor?" The driver made a rude French negative gesture. The Duchess meant nothing to him at all. Oh dear! If Maître Blum could hear him say that.

I'd been told that General de Gaulle had once lived in the Duchess's Neuilly house. When I mentioned his name, it had a very different effect. The driver knew the house at once. The Maître would have wanted to sue this man for the subtle insults he kept giving the Duchess.

When I finally arrived at the chateau of the Duchess of Windsor I found it a creepy and depressing sight. The high wire fence that surrounded it resembled that of a prison. So did the great steel gate that sealed off the driveway, for it was riddled with security locks and bolts and alarm systems.

Every window in the Duchess's gray palace of a house was shrouded. Only one had the shutters open. And it was strange to realize that she was lying there in that room, dying slowly behind the only open window. The Duchess of Windsor had become such a legendary figure that she seemed to have passed some eons ago into history with the Duke. She existed in the timeless, spaceless world of books and therefore it was odd to realize she still had a precise and miserable geographical location.

Now that her house had become a house of illness,

peopled by nurses, it seemed all the more desolate because it had once been the setting for so much festivity. It was in this same house that the Duchess once gave her famous dinner parties and the floral decorations on her table were sprayed with Diorissimo to give them added fragrance, and the footmen wore royal livery and the guests all bowed to the quirky laws she established. They accepted that it was "non-U" to serve a tomato which contained a pip. Candles must never be at eye level. Gold jewelry should never be worn in the evening—it had to be platinum.

Looking at the sad exterior of her sealed-off house, I felt my recent interview with Maître Blum had been farcical. If the Duchess was lying there in misery, what use were all the injunctions and lawsuits that her old lawyer kept bringing on her behalf? They were amusing for Maître Blum and they allowed her to display her legal prowess, to exert her hunger for power. But even when they were successful, was the money obtained from them only employed to finance yet another ghastly medical operation? Was this really all that desirable for the Duchess?

And what use was it for Wallis Windsor that her old spokeswoman sat in the rue de Varenne and extolled her virtues while she suffered, cut off from all friends, in the suburbs of Paris? Maître Blum said "il faut respecter la vie." But what sort of life was she giving the Duchess? Five years ago Wallis Windsor had told her best friend, Lady Monckton, that she only longed to be dead and buried beside the Duke at Frogmore. But there she was still alive and interred in this house which had all the gloom of a closed museum.

Lady Tomkins had told me that she believed that the Duchess was being beautifully nursed, that her nurses turned her every fifteen minutes to prevent her from getting bedsores. As I looked at her house, I wondered if they were turning her at that moment.

Her house seemed ludicrously large now that it was occupied only by this lonely old lady who was being turned so often like a piece of mutton on a spit. Would it not be cozier for the Duchess if she were to be moved from the scene of her earlier glory and allowed to endure her living death in some small, warm apartment? But then Maître Blum would want her Duchess to live in palatial splendor to the end. She had seemed agonized by the fact the Duchess could not continue to maintain her former life-style. On one level she longed for Wallis Windsor to retain hundreds of hothouse gardeners. But the careful and parsimonious side of her own nature seemed to be in conflict with the grandiose ideals she set for the woman she loved. She was therefore fortunate that she could justify the grandeur of the Duchess's current accommodation on the grounds that not only was it a suitable one for her famous client, but it was also practical. Thanks to the generosity of the French government, it was free.

On the great iron gate that sealed off the Duchess's driveway there was a sign that warned would-be intruders that the grounds were patrolled by *un chien méchant*. On the top of the gate there were some sharp and nasty-looking spikes to prevent it from being climbed. They provided the only colorful touch in the general grayness of the Duchess's establishment for her spikes had been painted gold. I wondered if they were relics of the days of her lost gaiety or whether Maître Blum had recently authorized their gilding in order to make it clear to the world that the Duchess's residence remained royal.

No sign of life came from the Duchess's house. In the garden, one single, broken down, elderly gardener with the despondent expression of the exploited and underpaid, toiled to improve the garden that it was unlikely the Duchess ever again would see. I wondered what the Duchess's butler did with himself all day in that house. Having once organized the lavish entertaining of the Windsors, surely he must be bored to the point of distraction, shut up in this house to which no one ever came except the doctor, Monsieur Thin, and Maître Blum.

In her autobiography, *The Heart Has Its Reasons*, the Duchess wrote that she "was prey to an unusual number of fears."[1] In particular she had a horror of being alone in the dark. Staring at her house through the prison netting of her fence, I felt that this poor woman's worst terrors must now be realized. If the Duchess sometimes regained consciousness, she must feel that few people were as abandoned as she was, few people had been left so completely alone in the dark.

After leaving the Duchess's house, I went back into central Paris and I telephoned Lady Mosley. I told her that I had just seen Maître Blum and there were certain things the woman had said about the Duchess that I would like to verify. She invited me to have lunch the following day in her house in Orsay. Her house was beautiful. It had a pretentious name, Le Temple de la Gloire, and enemies of the Mosleys who loathed their Nazi sympathies facetiously referred to it as The Concentration of Camp.

It was a shrine to beauty, taste, and style. In the house of these two elderly British exiled Fascists everything was exquisite—the furniture, the flowers, the food, and the wine. They had a magnificent view that looked onto a pearly gray lake. Lady Mosley, like the Duchess, had turned her house into a work of art.

Sir Oswald and Lady Mosley greeted me with grace and friendliness. Lady Mosley looked as ethereal and lovely as usual. Sir Oswald had obviously been ill. He shuffled around with the face of a shrewd old smiling reptile. He was gallant and attentive and had very good old-world manners. He brought me a glass of champagne. I was seated next to him at lunch and he still tried to use the mesmeric charm that had once hypnotized his black-shirted followers and encouraged them to beat up Jews in the East End of London. He had a deep, melodious voice and when he talked, he put his face very close to mine and stared at me so fixedly with half-closed eyes that I felt he was trying to put me in a trance. This was partially successful for as he monologued flirtatiously about the past, his monotone was soporific and I found it difficult to concentrate on what he was saying.

I picked up snippets of anecdotes that started "As I said to Winston," "As I said to Hitler," and then drowsiness set in. Just occasionally he did a peculiar trick which shocked me into attention. For no particular reason his

half-closed eyes would suddenly open like those of a doz-
ing lizard. For a second I saw two rounds of flashing, crazy,
white eyeball. And then his lids came down again and the
beautiful voice continued relentlessly. "As Hitler said to
me, We don't want your British colonies. You can keep
them . . . We don't want a lot of niggers who will only
contaminate our German blood . . ."

Lady Mosley looked a little nervous. Our original misunderstanding that was the result of her deafness had really
never been cleared up. She still hoped I was going to praise
the book she'd written about the Duchess in the *Sunday
Times*. As a result she thought it better to change the subject. She asked me how I'd found Maître Blum. She
laughed when I said I'd not been very drawn to her.
"Many people have much the same reaction. But remember that Maître Blum does love the Duchess."

Sir Oswald then started droning on about the cata-
strophic state of the current British economy. There had
been many recent strikes and he spoke of them with gloat-
ing pleasure. He obviously loved to sit in the comfort of
his beautiful house in France reading about the economic
difficulties that were plaguing the country of his birth.
Every piece of bad news, Sir Oswald read as good news,
for he saw it as proof that he had been right all along.
There should have been appeasement with Hitler and all
would have been well for Great Britain.

He believed that his countrymen were now paying
dearly for having rejected him as their leader. But despite
his ill health he still seemed to have a certain confidence
and optimism. He implied that all was not lost for the

British. Eventually they would come to their senses and he would be recalled from his exile and be elected with honor and glory.

Sir Oswald was a man of immense vanity but listening to him droning on, I felt he was carrying his conceit to the point of lunacy. In the odious event that the British were to elect a Fascist government surely they would choose a younger and fresher leader. Why would they feel the need to recall the services of this self-indulgent, old, reptilian aristocrat? Sir Oswald lived in a bubble. Yet he clearly was loved by his wife and they seemed to be happily married: They had survived imprisonment and exile, and united by their ugly political dream, they were enjoying an old age that seemed more contented than that of most people. The soufflé they served was light as air. It was frivolous like their Fascism.

"The trouble with England now . . ." Sir Oswald said to me. All his statements were delivered with such self-importance they sounded like pronunciamentos. "The trouble with England now . . ." he repeated. He never stopped trying to be hypnotic. I braced myself waiting for some abrasive opinion. But the trouble with England now was that it no longer had any hostesses. "Where are the great hostesses?" Sir Oswald asked with a rhetorical melancholy. "Tell me where are the great hostesses of the ilk of Sibyl Colefax and Emerald Cunard? There are all these lovely, intelligent, young English women but none of them have a salon. And the salon has always played such a vital role in the true life of any country. It really is a tragedy . . ."

I longed for lunch to be over. I felt uneasy and unreal

eating the delicious food of this semisenile Fascist and discussing the dire implications of England's lack of hostesses.
It seemed a very long time until coffee was served and I
went to another room with Lady Mosley to talk about that
most shadowy of figures, the Duchess of Windsor.

I told her that Maître Blum claimed that the Duke had
one of the best legal minds of his generation. She refused
to believe me. "Maître Blum couldn't have said that! You
must be joking! You could have worshiped the very
ground the Duke walked on but you really couldn't say
he had the best legal mind of his generation!"

I then told her that Maître Blum also claimed the
Duchess had been highly intelligent. Lady Mosley said it
was true the Duchess had been clever. She then qualified
this. "Well, she wasn't really clever. But let's say she was
as clever as all our Queens . . ."

She said that the Duchess had always been very vulnerable. Everyone wanted to attack her. They had sneered
at the Windsors for leading an idle and spoiled life. But
most of the British aristocracy led much the same existence. They gave parties, they went to shoots, they played
golf, they bought expensive clothes, and went to chic re-
sorts by the sea. The life of the Windsors had not been
any more worthless and idle than many members of the
upper class.

She also felt it was unfair that the Duchess had been
so criticized for her love affair with Jimmy Donahue. It
was only one brief and unfortunate episode in a marriage
of thirty-five years. That was not bad. Most marriages have
to survive patches of infidelity.

I asked her why the Duchess's affair with Jimmy Donahue had ended. She would only say that Donahue had been very unkind to the Duchess, that she was afraid he had made the Duchess miserable.

She insisted that after the affair was over, the Windsors had settled down and the Duchess had been very nice to the Duke. She had read aloud to him when his eyesight was going. She had been very attentive in his last illness. Once when he fainted, the Duchess had instantly produced his doctor's telephone number from her handbag. The Duchess had always been like that, very efficient and practical. And then she had always been such a wonderful housekeeper. And to the end she had made everything lovely for the Duke.

Lady Mosley clearly identified so strongly with the Duchess that when she was talking about her she often seemed to be talking about herself. She and the Duchess shared a passion for the elegant life-style; in addition, they were both witty and vivacious. Both women felt they had been harshly treated by the British, having been forced to live in France, where they'd spent the rest of their lives beautifully running the households of their notorious and ailing husbands.

When we got back to the subject of the Duchess's illness, she again expressed fears as to what was happening to her. She was still worried the Duchess might be in great pain. She wished Maître Blum wouldn't be so secretive about her condition. When she asked the Maître how the Duchess was, Maître Blum would only say that the Duchess was much the same and she was sitting up in a chair. Lady Mosley would have liked to use her influence to arrange that someone went to see what was happening in the Duchess's house, but she was frightened this would anger Maître Blum. And unfortunately she couldn't do much for the Duchess because her book, *The Duchess of Windsor*, was just coming out. She very much wanted it published in France because the French were so mad on royalty and it might have very good sales. She didn't want to antagonize Maître Blum because she feared she might bring an injunction against her book. As Lady Mosley claimed to have been so fond of the Duchess, I found her attitude jarring. She considered her book on the Duchess more important than the actual Duchess.

"Wallis still has Georges, her butler. At least she still has Georges," she murmured with emotion. "Georges always adored the Duchess."

If the Duchess was shut up in great pain and forbidden to see her friends, I wondered if it was much consolation to her that she still had her butler.

Lady Mosley said that when Georges went on holiday, the Duchess was automatically put in the American Hospital. This certainly was curious. Surely the Duchess no longer needed Georges to bring her mail and vodka on silver salvers. She had ceased to entertain so why did she require an imposing figure in a black tailcoat to open her door. Georges presumably now only admitted Maître Blum and her doctors to her beautiful secluded chateau. Why then did the Duchess have to be put in hospital in the periods when she had no butler? Lady Mosley could give no explanation.

She suggested that I might be interested to meet Maître

Blum's young man. The idea was indeed very startling and intriguing. Did Maître Blum have a much richer life than I had suspected? I would never have guessed she had a young man.

Apparently there was a young Englishman who was studying law with her. His name was Michael Bloch. He was in his twenties. Lady Mosley found it rather peculiar that a young man would choose to study law under an ancient figure like Maître Blum. But that was what he was doing. She made the entourage that controlled the Duchess sound stranger and stranger and I hoped for an opportunity to meet Michael Bloch.

Lady Mosley then complained Maître Blum had treated her very badly over the question of the Duchess's love letters. I knew nothing about these letters and so I asked her to explain. Apparently Maître Blum claimed she owned the love letters of the Duke and Duchess. When Lady Mosley first told the Maître she intended to write a book about the Windsors, Maître Blum said that it was a pity she had not been informed of this a week earlier. If she had been in possession of this fact she would have given Lady Mosley the Duchess's love letters. Unfortunately it was now too late. She had just given them to a French historian.

I felt Maître Blum's behavior sounded very typical. She exerted power by declaring she had these valuable letters in her possession. She tantalized and tormented by waving the lost "golden carrot" of this amatory correspondence which obviously had to become increasingly desirable to Lady Mosley once Maître Blum informed her that it could nearly have been hers.

Lady Mosley had been distressed and she wondered if these love letters really existed. Maître Blum insisted she controlled them, so she had to believe her. But when could the Windsors have written them? They were only ever separated in the period when the Duchess's divorce was going through. And at that point they had telephoned each other every day. As they had spent so much time talking to each other on the telephone, would the Windsors have also written love letters? Neither the Duke nor the Duchess were writers by nature. They were no more writers than they were readers. They read whodunits, they read magazines, and that was about it. Lady Mosley had once lent the Duke of Windsor some book which he wanted to read and she noticed that he'd taken a very long time to finish it. Unwittingly, and without malice, Lady Mosley was destroying Maître Blum's elevated picture of the Windsors with their good books and their classical music, the highly cultured couple.

And what about the Duchess's dignity that Maître Blum seemed to set such store by? I wondered if Diana Mosley who had known her so well would also strip that away from her.

"How dignified was the Duchess?" I asked and she laughed at the absurdity of the question. "Wallis went out and took Twist lessons when she was eighty. I don't know if you call that dignified. Wallis never cared about dignity. That was her whole point . . ."

CHAPTER SEVEN

On my return to London, I told Francis Wyndham that Maître Blum had refused to allow the Duchess to be photographed for the *Sunday Times*. I described the peculiar way that Maître Blum had quivered when I'd mentioned Lord Snowdon was keen to take the Duchess's picture. There had been a delicate moment when she had seemed so stimulated by the proposition that it had appeared she was about to agree. Eventually she had refused, but she had definitely wavered before giving her refusal. If Lord Snowdon personally asked Maître Blum for permission there was therefore still a chance she might relent. He would have to charm her. He would have to flatter her. If he really wanted to photograph the Duchess of Windsor, he might well have to get himself into Maître Blum's favor by first offering to photograph Maître Blum.

A few days passed before I heard Lord Snowdon was still very anxious to photograph the Duchess. A most unctuous letter had been sent off to Maître Blum. It said that the *Sunday Times* was thrilled by the fascinating interview she had given me; that they would like not only to publish a photograph of the Duchess, but to have one of Maître Blum herself. If she would be agreeable, Lord Snowdon would be most honored to come over to Paris to photograph her.

Maître Blum's reply was indecently immediate. It was

also uncharacteristically humble. If Lord Snowdon found her a worthy subject, she would be extremely glad for him to take her photograph.

While the arrangements for the taking of Maître Blum's photograph were being made, I telephoned Peter Coats and asked him if he could tell me anything about the Duchess of Windsor. As the friend of the diarist Chips Channon, the greatest snob-socialite and entertainer of royalty in the thirties, there was a chance he could give me some interesting information as to the current situation of the Duchess.

"Surely you have read my book," he asked me crossly.

I apologized for not having read it. I'd never taken in that he'd written anything, let alone a work he clearly considered to be a classic. I'd not realized that this self-important, silly old character saw himself as a better writer than Henry James. His book had an absurd title, *Of Generals and Gardens*. He told me it contained one of the most fascinating anecdotes ever written about the Windsors. He was amazed that people had not realized this, that it was not more often discussed. When I obtained a copy of his opus from the library, I found the anecdote was as follows:

> On one of the many sunlit holidays I spent in Venice in the fifties, there was much entertaining for the problematical Duke and Duchess of Windsor, and one evening after dinner I found myself sitting next to the Duchess, and she told me a curious story. I admired a really magnificent brooch she was wearing on the shoulder of her dress—a baroque

pearl set in enamel, and small, many-colored jewels, and I asked her its history. She paused for a moment, as if considering, and then launched forth, in her pleasant Southern voice:

'When the Duke and I were in the Bahamas, his brother Prince George was killed in an air crash. We were both very upset. I naturally wrote to Princess Marina, but I felt I must write to Queen Mary, Prince George's mother, too. Well, as you know, I was never on good terms with my mother-in-law. But in spite of that, I decided to do the conventional thing and send my sympathy: I took a lot of trouble over my letter. It was in the middle of the war, and communications were difficult and slow. But, to my surprise, within a few weeks, I received a reply. It was a packet containing this brooch, and with it was a card, written in Queen Mary's writing, saying, "At the time of your marriage my heart was too full to think of wedding presents, but I hope that you will accept this now. It belonged to Charles I." '

I have often thought of this story and wished that I had an opportunity of confirming it. Neither the Duke nor the Duchess mentions the incident in their books *The Heart Has Its Reasons* or *A King's Story*, and I cannot think why, as everyone comes out of the story well. Perhaps I imagined the whole thing—and yet the wording of Queen Mary's message has a ring of truth.[1]

This anecdote had a pleasantly topsy-turvy quality. Fantasy and wishful thinking had mingled in this unlikely little vignette to a fairy-tale degree. But I was relieved to learn that people were not discussing it with the fervor Peter Coats demanded. The parsimonious and unrelenting Queen Mary was made to have a brainstorm and behave totally out of character. Jewelry shone with such brightness and power in Peter Coats's sentimental anecdote that it healed the historical rift between the Duchess and the royal family. I decided that I would copy out this picturesque passage from *Of Generals and Gardens* and check on its veracity. It seemed like an excellent example of the dreams the Duchess inspired and it would be curious to have it vetted by a rival dreamer. I would take this nonsensical piece of writing to the multidoored apartment in the rue de Varenne and I'd show it to Maître Blum.

I decided I would take Maître Blum one other text. I wanted a good excuse to see her again. This vituperative old lawyer with her lioness's passion for Wallis Windsor had started to haunt my imagination. I felt that being given the privilege of spending time with Maître Blum was like being offered a free ticket to a mesmerizing theatrical performance.

The legendary French actress Sarah Bernhardt was reputed to have such histrionic genius that she could pick up a telephone directory and read out a list of the names and addresses it contained. Instantly her listeners would start to laugh and weep in turns. When the Maître started to speak about the Duchess of Windsor, I felt her powers were not dissimilar.

The Duchess of Marlborough had just written her autobiography under the jaunty title of *Laughter from a Cloud*. She describes a visit that the Windsors made to her English country house in 1946.

> The Duchess arrived with a jewel case which was no ordinary affair. It was a trunk in which she had many of H.R.H.'s fantastic collection of Fabergé boxes and a great many uncut emeralds which I believe had belonged to Queen Alexandra. The Duchess liked jewels very much, though this is rather an understatement as she was continually having them reset, mostly in Paris. One of these priceless baubles had only just reached her, a vast sapphire which she had converted into a bird of paradise by Van Cleef and Arpels. But the butler's prudent suggestion that this trunkful of things surely to be found in an Aladdin's cave should be put in the strong room was rejected by the Duchess. Her jewel case, she said, would remain, as it always did, under her maid's bed![2]

Reading this page I tried to guess what Maître Blum would think of it. To the casual reader the behavior of the Duchess might seem show-off and unattractive. Why did she have to travel around lugging this great trunk containing the Crown jewels and enough treasure to fill Aladdin's cave? Was her love for her own jewelry so great that she could not be parted from any of it for even a short period? The Duchess's zany need to tote along all the fabulous royal gold Fabergé boxes when she went off to spend a weekend in the English countryside seemed even more bizarre. What did she hope to do with all these irreplaceably precious objects when she was a guest in someone else's house? At least she could wear some of the Crown jewels and display them. But Maître Blum might construe it all differently. Would she feel that it befitted the wife of a dethroned emperor to travel with just such panache and style? Would she give one of her rare but tender approving smiles and say, as she'd said of the astonishing sums of money that the Duchess spent yearly on her dress, "The Duchess had to do it. She only did it for him"?

And then the Duchess's decision to leave the trunk under her maid's bed seemed to have a fecklessness that verged on lunacy. What interpretation would Maître Blum give to that? Could she stretch a point and see it as evidence of something unworldly in her client, something that refused to stoop to mundane care for her possessions?

Before Maître Blum was given the chance to palm me off with any unrealistic explanations of her client's questionable behavior in this incident, I asked John Richardson to explain. He'd known Wallis Windsor and he reminded me that the Duchess had been born in the American South and all her life she had retained what he described as "a Southern side." In the South, it had apparently been a common practice for rich families to hide their gold and silver under the mattresses of their servants who were housed in misery in the slave quarters. It was thought that the most voracious robber would never dream of searching for anything of value in such a degraded spot.

On being given this explanation I wondered if I would dare to bring it up with Maître Blum. Would she like it? Or would she loathe it so much she would consider it actionable?

During the Windsors' visit to the Duchess of Marlborough, not surprisingly, the great trunk of valuables was robbed. The Duke and Duchess went up to London and returned to find that thieves had broken into the house by climbing up a white rope which they'd hooked onto the windowsill. The Duchess of Marlborough writes:

> The thieves left the white rope with the hook hanging from the sill while they proceeded to get at the loot. Much of this they left, including the collection of heavy Fabergé gold boxes, on a tray on another window-sill where I found them. Either they had forgotten them or this was not what they had come to get. Some of the Duchess's jewels, which they took, were not even mounted. The detectives found something like eighteen odd earrings scattered over the Sunningdale golf course but, much to her fury, not one pair . . . The Duchess was in a bad way. She wanted all the servants put through a kind of third degree, but I would have none of this, all of them except for one kitchen maid being old and devoted staff of long standing. By the following night the Duke was both demented with worry and near to tears. The Duchess started the next day with a grim face and wearing on her dress about the only jewel that remained to her. Just before we all went

out for a little stroll she said, "David, put this brooch
in a safe place." On our return he could not remember where he had put it! He thought the most
likely place was the room he was using for sorting
the papers he had fetched from Windsor. There he
ensued a frantic search, but to no avail. When it was
time for bed the Duchess and Eric [her husband,
Eric Dudley] went upstairs; it had been a grim day.
The Duke said he was going to continue the search
although he looked grey with worry and exhaus-
tion. I was desperately sorry for him, and anyhow I
would have stayed to help him in his search, hoping
at least to find this one remaining jewel to which
the Duchess appeared attached. We stayed up most
of the night; he obviously feared to go up to bed
empty-handed. I made endless cups of black coffee
while the Duke went through his papers, which he
seemed convinced was the likeliest place. At about
5 A.M. by some miracle we found it, under a china
ornament. Never have I seen a man so relieved. He
was still ashen in the face, but he rushed upstairs.[3]

I felt this portrait of the Windsors might be sufficiently
provocative to arouse some interesting reactions in Maître
Blum. This old lawyer made such claims for the dignity of
the Duke and Duchess. Would she be able to see any con-
spicuous dignity in the Duke's role in this incident? One
of the Duke's mistresses, Thelma Furness, was once asked
if she had ever loved him and she answered that she
couldn't because he was too abject. And certainly there

was abjectness rather than dignity in this picture of a tearful and ruined Duke sitting up all night drinking black coffee because he was too terrified to go to bed and tell the grim-faced Duchess that he couldn't find her jewel.

In this description of the robbery the Duchess's character seemed to come through not so much as lacking in dignity, but rather as lacking in niceness. Yet her lawyer, no doubt, would find means to condone her favorite client's behavior. I therefore telephoned Maître Blum and asked if I could come to see her after she had been photographed by Lord Snowdon. I explained that I had just read two published items about the Duchess that I found perturbing. I wanted to show them to her and find out if they were true. Maître Blum was not rude to me. She seemed to find my request quite normal, even praiseworthy. As she spent her life fretting herself into a state of apoplexy over things that kept coming out in print about the Duchess of Windsor, she seemed to take it for granted that everyone else did the same.

Maître Blum agreed to see me an hour after her photograph had been taken. She needed a little time to repose herself. It was going to be a tiring day for Maître Blum but she sounded very excited about it. Lord Snowdon and a senior editor from the *Sunday Times* were flying over to Paris with the sole purpose of taking her photograph. She was then going to be consulted about two controversial passages about the Duchess which, for all she knew, with a little luck, might easily turn out to be actionable. All this activity clearly stimulated her. She seemed to feel that in some way it all resounded to the greater credit and glory of her Duchess.

CHAPTER EIGHT

When I got to the rue de Varenne for the second time, Maître Blum had already been photographed. Her mood was very different from the last time that I'd seen her. She seemed exalted and she was much more mellow. She had put on a little lipstick for the photograph. I would have expected her to disapprove of makeup just as she disapproved of nightclubs. She was wearing a long gown. But although she had made a great effort to look resplendent for the photograph, I'd sustained a fantasy which was disappointed. I'd hoped she would get so carried away by the whole occasion that she would dazzle us all by wearing some of the Duchess's fabulous jewelry.

I wondered if Lord Snowdon had managed to persuade her to allow him to photograph her client. Her self-satisfied demeanor made me guess that he had failed. Once Lord Snowdon had taken Maître Blum's photograph, would she see any real need for him to take one of the Duchess? She had been photographed with a lot of fuss and false sycophancy exactly as if she were the Duchess of Windsor. In Maître Blum's desire to fuse her identity with Wallis Windsor there seemed to be an element which longed to supplant her. It had been an important occasion for this old lawyer. She had been the Duchess for the day. As a result her temper was much improved.

"What a charming man Lord Snowdon is," she crooned. "I could tell at once that he was *un vrai artist.*"

A young man was hanging around in Maître Blum's apartment. She introduced him as Michael Bloch. "Michael is your compatriot," she said. "Michael comes from the North of Ireland. Both of you come from Great Britain's worst trouble spot."

She managed to make this introduction subtly insulting. She seemed to see us both as tainted by the province from which we came. She made it sound as if she saw both of us as potential "trouble spots."

I watched him closely. It seemed to me that he had a very shifty manner and a weak, vicious mouth. On that occasion I noticed that he had a nervous habit of wriggling his whole body and then fluttering his eyelashes and gulping. He treated Maître Blum with such deference one felt he must be playacting. Whenever he referred to her he called her "my Master," which to me sounded totally ridiculous in English.

"Lord Snowdon has just taken the most beautiful photograph of my Master," he told me in a whisper. Michael Bloch was dressed up in an amazing boating blazer that was decorated with broad red and white stripes. It would have been a suitable costume for a chorus boy in some Hollywood musical based on an Edwardian romance. In his buttonhole Michael Bloch had a bunch of lilies of the valley.

Maître Blum kept ordering him about. She clearly liked his flattery, but her attitude towards him had a petulance. She chided him continually and gave him various impatient directions, making proprietorial gestures with her brown-flowered hands.

Maître Blum then asked me to read her the extracts that I had brought her. She told Michael Bloch to sit down and pay close attention. Not only was this young man being trained in law by this old woman, she was training him to be as obsessed as she was by the Duchess. I started to read the extract from *Of Generals and Gardens*. In a querulous voice she interrupted and she ordered Michael Bloch to take down the title of the book, the author's name, and the name of its publisher. Bloch bowed and got out a notebook. With his eyes lowered to denote he recognized the solemnity of his task, he wrote down all the facts she wanted. Later presumably, Maître Blum would order herself a copy. She and Bloch would then study it in depth to see if it contained material on which she could sue on behalf of the Duchess.

The extract from *Of Generals and Gardens* sounded extremely pointless and flat when read aloud. However, Maître Blum listened with electric interest. Was this because it mentioned a jewel she hadn't known existed? After I had finished reading Maître Blum turned to Bloch. "We must ask Georges if he knows about Charles the First's brooch." It seemed odd that the Duchess's butler should be the expert on the Duchess's jewelry.

"Do you think this anecdote is true?" I asked Maître Blum. She hesitated. She obviously would have liked to have said it was true. As a dream about the Duchess, she approved of it. But as a lawyer she was loath to commit herself to any statement that the Duchess had been given the baroque pearl of Charles I. She told me she would try and find out about the jewel. She would check with Georges.

When I read her the extract about the robbery from *Laughter from a Cloud* Maître Blum liked it much less. If she hadn't been in such a mellow mood after the photograph, I think she'd have thrown a tantrum.

"It's all lies! It's all lies!" she hissed at me. "The Duchess never owned one single jewel belonging to Queen Alexandra!" The amber light of paranoia had come back into her eyes. I asked her why she thought the Duchess of Marlborough had written that they were Queen Alexandra's jewels. What would be her motive in lying about this? With all her legal training Maître Blum seemed nonplussed. She was unable to give me a plausible answer. Michael Bloch tried to come to her aid.

"The Duchess of Marlborough is a very old woman," he said hopefully. "The Duchess of Marlborough's memory has probably gone."

I was interested that Maître Blum was so incensed by the suggestion that her client possessed Crown jewels she didn't seem to care that both the Duke and the Duchess cut very sorry figures in this description of their robbery. But why did the jewels matter to her? If the Duchess had been given royal jewels by her husband, why should Maî-tre Blum feel this rebounded to the Duchess's discredit? The Duchess was the rightful owner of these jewels. It was not as if she had stolen them from Queen Alexandra's safe.

Although many of the Duchess's Crown jewels were

stolen, quite a few, presumably, had not been in the trunk. And the Duke replaced the stolen ones with money obtained from insurance and he bought the Duchess new jewels worth $100,000. When the Duchess's wily old lawyer so emphatically denied that her client had ever owned any Crown jewels, was she worrying about the future? Once the Duchess died, would the British royal family want to know the whereabouts of these ancient royal heirlooms? As the Duchess had no heirs, and she had been so careless with her royal possessions, would the royal family feel they not only had a claim to any original gems that remained, but even a claim on their replacements?

Later, because Maître Blum had not seemed straightforward on the subject of the Duchess's jewels, I checked the facts with the Duchess of Marlborough. She had not lost her memory. She had total recall. She was no more senile than Maître Blum. "Of course all the jewels that were stolen from my house were royal jewels," she said. "The Duke told me they were royal jewels. That's why he cried so much the night they were stolen."

While Maître Blum and I were quibbling in an unsatisfactory manner about Queen Alexandra's jewelry, the telephone rang in her apartment. Maître Blum made an imperial gesture with her gnarled hand and ordered Michael Bloch to answer it. He went next door with a self-important expression on his face. When he came back, he seemed very excited. It was Lord Longford, Lady Mosley's publisher. "He wants to speak to you, my Master."

Maître Blum looked triumphant. Michael Bloch and his Master exchanged glances. They both smiled. The old woman made no effort to conceal her greed and her sense of power.

"You can speak to Lord Longford, Michael. You can tell him our demands."

"Yes, my Master." Michael Bloch bowed and strode off looking self-consciously bold and ruthless.

"I was so frightened it was going to be in the press," Maître Blum said to me. "Day and night the journalists keep telephoning. The press give me no peace. Whenever the Duchess goes into the American Hospital, they telephone me day and night. They want to know what's wrong with her."

Maître Blum quite suddenly seemed to forget she was giving a press interview and she became naively confidential. She told me that it was always a problem deciding how best to palm off the press. She invariably said that the Duchess of Windsor was in hospital with appendicitis. Maître Blum often worried that the press might not be satisfied with this statement. Maître Blum had claimed the Duchess of Windsor was in the hospital with acute appendicitis too many times before. She feared the journalists might find it odd if they were told the Duchess's appendix was being continually removed.

It was disquieting that Maître Blum seemed to want my sympathy because the burden of the lies she loved to tell sometimes became unbearably heavy.

"I 'ate the press!" she said. Without the *h* Maître Blum's hatred sounded ominously devouring.

"They all want the Duchess to die!" Maître Blum's fury sent her whole body into spasm. "Why does everyone want her to die?" Her voice rose with this question and became the screech of a seagull.

Then she collapsed. She seemed overcome. When she next spoke it was in a pathetic, quavering tone. Her eyes became misty. She repeated her question in such a weak whisper, it was as if Maître Blum were herself expiring. "Why does everyone want the poor Duchess to die?"

We had got back onto the subject that Maître Blum could never come to terms with. She was able to tackle most delicate matters that concerned the Duchess of Windsor. She bluffed her way out of them either by dissimulation, general arm pulling, gangster-style life-threats, or the bringing of lawsuits. But any reference to the possibility of the Duchess's death seemed to bring Maître Blum face to face with her own extinction.

"But the Duchess is not going to die!" Maître Blum regained all her crazed liveliness. She leaned forward excitedly. Her eyes flashed, her chin jutted to express her defiance and the volcanic force of her determination.

"Her heart and lungs are perfect! The Duchess is going to live to be a hundred! Her aunt lived to be a hundred. Everyone in the Duchess's family lived to be a hundred!"

The Duchess of Windsor's spokesperson was lying again. Or to be fair to Maître Blum, she was embroidering on the truth. Certainly the Duchess's aunt, Bessy Merryman, had lived to be a hundred. But why had Maître Blum forgotten the fate of the Duchess's father? The sickly Teakle Warfield entered hospital a few months after the Duchess's conception. He never set eyes on his one-day-to-be-famous daughter. Snapshots of the infant Duchess crawling were held up to him as he lay on his deathbed. There was good reason for Maître Blum to overlook this unlucky American. His lungs had not been perfect. He had died of tuberculosis at the age of twenty-seven.

And while Maître Blum kept predicting the Duchess was going to live to be a hundred, I kept thinking about Teackle Warfield. If Maître Blum planned to keep the wretched woman alive for umpteen years only some genetic flaw in the Duchess's metabolism could save her from a truly hideous future. Imagining all the baroque royal pearls that were being sold to pay for the Duchess's life without death, the constitution of the Duchess's father seemed more and more important. If he had passed on any hereditary physical weaknesses to the Duchess, he had done more for his unseen daughter than he ever could have dreamed of. The frailty of Teackle Warfield's constitution now seemed to be the Duchess of Windsor's only hope.

Michael Bloch reappeared. When this young man became excited, he had the trick of sticking out the tip of his tongue and holding it clamped between his lips. His tongue was very red. As he stood in front of Maître Blum with the end of his scarlet tongue protruding, she became impatient with him and as she was so keen to hear about his conversation with Lord Longford, she seemed to forget that the Duchess must one day die.

"What did Lord Longford say, Michael? Don't just stand there. *Mais voyons* . . . Did you tell him your demands? What did he say?"

"I told him your demands, my Master."

Maître Blum smiled. It was rare when this old woman

gave one of her surgically constricted smiles. It always came as a shock.

"How did Lord Longford react, Michael? But don't just stand there. What was his reaction?"

"Lord Longford was not at all happy when he heard your demands, my Master."

"I'm quite sure he wasn't." Once again Maître Blum gave one of her shocking smiles. "Did he agree to meet my demands, Michael?"

"Yes, my Master, Lord Longford agreed to meet your demands."

The old woman was showing off. She obviously loved appearing mysterious and sinister. She was holding Lord Longford up for ransom and behaving like a ruthless kidnapper in a grade B Hollywood movie. Her ludicrous little charade was being overacted for my benefit.

"How is the Duchess?" I interrupted Maître Blum while she was sitting there like an old cream-fed cat, still pretending she had scored a world-shaking financial triumph over Lord Longford. I hoped to bring her back to reality. Sometimes Maître Blum could go into pipe dreams in which she believed her "demands," her lawsuits, and schemes for her client had more importance than the current state of the Duchess.

"The Duchess is talking. *Elle parle tout le temps.* She never stops talking. She talks and she talks," her lawyer told me.

This was new. The Duchess sounded in much better health than when I'd last seen Maître Blum. At that point she'd only given utterance every three weeks. But what was the Duchess talking about? It seemed indelicate to ask her old lawyer.

The Duchess had once been renowned for what some called her "wisecracks," others her "wit," and Maître Blum, her "mot juste." Alexander Woolcott had made her wit sound like wine. He claimed it didn't travel. I'd been given various examples of her humor. John Richardson, the writer and art critic, once took her back one evening to the Waldorf Astoria. They had been to a party and it was late and the Duchess was unsteady on her feet. When they got to the elevator he therefore asked if she would like some help up to her room. The Duchess smiled and said she didn't need any help. She had two black gentlemen waiting for her upstairs in her bedroom, and they would take care of her. The Duchess liked to startle. By the two black gentlemen she only meant her pugs.

In the period just before the present Queen of England was crowned, the Duchess was asked if the Duke would attend her coronation. "Why should he go to her coronation?" the Duchess of Windsor is reputed to have said. "He didn't go to his own."

Then there was her condescending comment on John F. Kennedy. "In a litter of nine, one of the pups tends to turn out O.K."

Her witticism when she was once playing bridge in a foursome with the Duke was somewhat better. "My King doesn't take any tricks," the Duchess said. "He just abdicates."

When she was asked why she had no children, she said that the Duke was not "heir-conditioned."

When Maître Blum said the Duchess of Windsor never stopped talking, could the Duchess still be talking in this vein? And who listened to the unfortunate woman now? There were her nurses, and there was her butler, and there was Maître Blum. But it was unlikely that a French butler would appreciate her particular kind of wisecrack. And surely Maître Blum would have to be horrified by the risqué nature of the Duchess's humor. How could even Maître Blum manage to persuade herself that the ribald mots justes of the Duchess ever could have come from the lips of the straitlaced figure she longed for her to resemble. How, in all truth, could they resemble any of the utterances of the pompous and regal Queen Mary?

It was therefore terrifying to imagine the Duchess bravely wisecracking through her pipes while Maître Blum stood silently by her bed frowning with puritanical disapproval.

"Do you find it encouraging that the Duchess is talking so much?" I asked the old lawyer. "Do you feel that the Duchess might still make a full recovery?"

She drew herself up and she threw out her chest as if she were taking unto herself the strengths of her client.

"It would not surprise me. With a woman as astonishing as that—anything is possible!"

Michael Bloch had been very quiet while Maître Blum was speaking about the Duchess's potential recovery. His lids were lowered as if he were praying and he wore a "thanks be to God" expression.

He suddenly turned and asked if I knew that his Master was a very brilliant novelist. His attitude towards Maître

Blum was oddly similar to the old lawyer's attitude to the Duchess. He seemed petrified that some of Maître Blum's accomplishments and virtues might be overlooked.

"She writes under the name of Suzanne Blum!" Bloch seemed to linger lovingly on her name just as his Master's voice always lingered on the name of the Duchess.

"She has written seven novels," he said. "All of them have been highly acclaimed here in France. Many important critics consider *To Know Nothing* to be her masterpiece . . ."

I told Maître Blum I'd love to read it. This was certainly true. What sort of novels would this unusual old woman write? Would they contain any Cinderella fantasies about a poor little girl who makes good and becomes a Duchess?

Maître Blum told Michael Bloch to fetch me a copy of *To Know Nothing* from her bedroom.

She then became very cross with him. He sometimes seemed to bring out the worst of the bully in her nature. She told him to hurry up. He knew where the book was. What on earth was the matter with him? When she became irate he seemed to become paralyzed and to dither and become slower in taking action. She then had to scold him much harder both in English and French, for she seemed to expect this young man to run with "the step of a young girl" to get me a copy of her novel.

When he finally fetched it, she handed me *To Know Nothing* with a certain disdain. It was as if her huge vanity was only partially immersed in her book. I felt she'd have much preferred to have proudly handed me a novel that had been written by the Duchess.

"Are you still writing novels?" I asked Maître Blum. She shook her white head impatiently and her body gave a little jerk of anger. Of course she had stopped writing recently. She was far too busy for that! She had far too much to do for the Duchess!

At first I felt her statement seemed absurd. What was there for Maître Blum to do for the Duchess of Windsor? Presumably Dr. Thin, her physician, and her nurses coped with her medical requirements.

No doubt Maître Blum subscribed to various international press-cutting services, and if the Windsors were mentioned in the newspapers in any capacity—even in error, such as in some reference to the products of Windsor and Newton, the British manufacturers of paint—inevitably, she would be sent their clippings. This might well take up a certain amount of time for she'd have to peruse each item to see if they presented her with any opportunity to sue on behalf of the Duchess. Then there were all the books of fashionable memoirs that kept coming out all over the world. Maître Blum would have to read the whole lot, word by word, for they too might easily contain some unfavorable and actionable memories of the Duchess.

But all the same, why did Maître Blum really have to give up writing her novels? The Duchess's name cropped up quite rarely in print in recent years, more rarely than Maître Blum, on certain levels, would like.

On the other hand, someone had to choose the Duchess's nightdresses and that person was most certainly Maître Blum. She must know all about the Duchess's old passion for exquisite lingerie and would therefore take this duty very seriously. The Duke with his "kindness" had once treated this task as a major part of his life's work and Maître Blum would be all too happy to seize the dead man's role and derive huge joy from superseding him. It was not inconceivable that she bought her client some new and perfect nightdress nearly every other day. If she took hours choosing the Duchess's bedtime attire, and her brown-speckled hands lovingly, but critically, fingered hundreds of silk and satin and *broderie anglaise* items of nightwear, this activity would eat into her working day.

Then there were the visits she made to see the Duchess. And there was no telling how long she liked to remain with her client. If one thought about it seriously, maybe Maître Blum really didn't have all that much time to write her novels.

"Are you going to sue Bryan and Murphy for writing *The Windsor Story*?" I asked her. I had taken for granted she would sue. The portrait of the Duchess of Windsor given by the two American journalists was extremely unfavorable and spiteful. I'd still not been told what punitive legal steps she was taking.

The question made her do one of her violent jumps. It was puzzling that Maître Blum, whose reputation in the international law courts was so "cool," had not yet learned to control her physical reflexes. Certain questions reacted on her like stimuli placed on an old Pavlovian dog. She could be made to twitch on demand.

Maître Blum looked at Michael Bloch and they exchanged glances. The yellow war light was back in Maître Blum's eyes.

Maître Blum was obviously loath to tell me what she planned to do about *The Windsor Story*. If she announced she was going to sue this book, Bryan and Murphy could be warned of her impending suit and she would be deprived of all the malicious relish that she would get from a surprise legal attack.

Instead of answering about her suit, she went off into a hysterical diatribe against Bryan and Murphy. All the mellowness that Lord Snowdon's photographic visit temporarily had given her vanished. As on the first occasion that I'd seen her, Maître Blum became immoderate. She called Bryan and Murphy vile slang names in French which sounded so derogatory and abusive I couldn't understand them.

"Bryan and Murphy didn't even know the Duchess!" she hissed with hysteria. "How would a great woman like *la Duchesse* know men like that?"

"But Maître Blum, surely Bryan and Murphy helped the Duchess to write her own autobiography. How could they have helped her if they had never met her?"

This question maddened her even more. She saw it as a direct assault on the Duchess.

"A woman with the brilliant intelligence of the Duchess never needed help with her autobiography! Why would the Duchess of Windsor need any help?" she screeched at me.

When the Duchess of Windsor's spokesperson lied, she was unlike most liars. She did not seem to want to deceive. She had a regal contempt for deception, just as she had a regal contempt for the truth. It was as if she saw herself as above both truth and deception and saw them as commodities only suitable for "people of no importance."

Maître Blum took facts and she reordered them and skillfully wove them into a world of her own invention. She was as inviolable as Freud when he said that he didn't want to hear any data if it didn't fit in with his theories.

It was Maître Blum's ability to restructure cold fact that had enabled the childless Maître Blum to give birth to her unique and most original child creation, a music-loving and hardworking, intellectual Duchess of Windsor.

The Duchess created by Maître Blum was a Jewish Duchess in the sense that, despite her unenviable current condition, she'd been made the very embodiment of her lawyer's superego. It was unlikely that there has ever been a Duchess like her. Once one had accepted the Maître's premise that her creation had more validity than the real Duchess of Windsor, nothing Maître Blum said about her could be called a total falsehood.

Since Maître Blum had taken over the Duchess of Windsor, she had pumped new life into this living vegetable and infused her with her own vigorous and puritanical qualities. There was a selflessness in the way Maître Blum had poured so many of her own virtues into this eighty-four-year-old invalid.

Maître Blum would hardly have been chosen to be legal representative of the world's five leading film companies if she had not been a woman of brilliant intelligence. In addition to her legal skills, she was also an acclaimed novelist. One only had to meet her for five minutes to know Maître Blum was very hardworking. Naturally she resented the insinuation that the Duchess to whom she'd given so much of her unusually clever mind would be incapable of writing her autobiography without help.

Maître Blum looked extremely healthy. Her own heart and lungs were probably perfect, and since emotionally she had donated her own strong organs to the Duchess, she saw no reason why the Duchess should not live to be a hundred.

When she said that Wallis Windsor never drank or went to nightclubs—from Maître Blum's point of view— even this was not really untrue. Since the Duchess of Windsor had come under her control—since in Maître Blum's eyes, the Duchess had come into her fullness— Wallis Windsor was a reformed creature. She certainly no longer drank one drop of vodka from a silver mug, nor did the poor woman set foot in a nightclub.

"Did you know my Master's husband, Monsieur le General, is gravely ill?" Michael Bloch asked me. He self-consciously put on a sad, solemn expression.

"I'm so sorry to hear that. Where is the General? Is he in the country?"

"We had to move him to Paris. We have put Monsieur le General in the American Hospital." Michael Bloch was suddenly using the royal "we."

Maître Blum gave him an irate glance that told him to shut up. She didn't seem to want him to talk about the General. We were not gathered in her apartment to discuss such trivia as the plight of her husband. We were here to give our full and undivided attention to the Duchess of Windsor.

I wondered if Maître Blum would visit the General after I left. There was a certain pathos to the image of this neglected eighty-year-old military figure who was lying deathly ill and unvisited in the American Hospital while his indomitable wife was not only photographed in the Duchess's stead by Lord Snowdon, but then went on to give a press interview about her adored Duchess.

"When will your article on the Duchess be finished?" Maître Blum asked me. Her slanted, unblinking eyes challenged and threatened. I feared she might repeat what she would do to me if she didn't like it.

I was too cowardly to tell her that I had not written a line of the article. The Duchess that Maître Blum had presented to me was far too eccentric to write about. She did not tally with any facts which were elsewhere on the record about her. Maître Blum could dotingly describe the current glow and beauty of her unlined body, but if I were to do the same, any sensible reader would think I'd gone insane.

"You know I want to be shown your article before it's published. You know I want to amend it."

Her eyes were greedy and excited. She couldn't wait to have her version of the Duchess in print, particularly as it now would be illustrated by photographs of herself. Her emendations would presumably all be flattering adjectives. If I were to write that the Duchess was still beautiful, Maître Blum would amend that and make me write that the Duchess was not only still ravishingly beautiful, but she had retained all her intellectual and artistic interests—that she was still dedicated to good works and continued her life-long battle to improve the lot of the downtrodden and the needy, that in particular she continued to devote herself to ameliorating the unsatisfactory housing conditions of the German worker.

I could only feel that my article once Maître Blum got her brown-freckled hands on it, once she had amended it to her satisfaction, was going to be a very unsettling piece of writing indeed.

This time when I left her apartment she made no effort to help me on with my coat. She didn't even command Michael Bloch to display a single grain of the "kindness" she had so admired in the late Duke. She was bored by me. I felt she was even rather bored by the Duchess. She only wanted to be left in peace so that she could think about the splendor of her own photographs as taken by Lord Snowdon.

CHAPTER NINE

On returning to London after my second visit to see the Duchess's lawyer, I telephoned Lord Longford. "Do I understand you have been having some trouble with Maître Blum?" I asked him.

I was curious to find out what sum the Duchess's lawyer had obtained for her client. Maître Blum and Michael Bloch had made it sound enormous.

At the very mention of Maître Blum's name, there was an explosion from Lord Longford. "Trouble! That old woman's middle name is trouble. Maître Blum must be losing her marbles. She is really quite outrageous!"

He then explained that Lady Mosley's book on the Duchess was being published that week. Maître Blum had threatened to bring an injunction against it. The book contained a photograph of the Duchess for which Maître Blum was asking to be paid four hundred pounds in order to allow it to be reproduced. If she wasn't paid this sum, she intended to prevent publication of the book. She had waited for the book to go into print before throwing her firebomb. Lord Longford found her request monstrous. "Four hundred pounds for one boring, rather bad photograph! Can you beat it! Maître Blum says we are abusing the Duchess's copyright. But it is absolute rubbish. The Duchess doesn't even own the copyright of this photograph. But I've given in. I've agreed to pay Maître Blum.

I can't afford to have any trouble when the book is coming out. The old bitch knows that. It's really blackmail!"

Maître Blum as usual had triumphed on behalf of her client. The Duchess of Windsor would be paid four hundred pounds. But when I heard about Maître Blum's success, it all seemed so sad and paltry. Maître Blum sank in my estimation. She appeared petty and small-time.

I now knew more about the Duchess than when I'd first met Maître Blum. From everything that I'd heard or read about Wallis Windsor, she could be criticized for the scale on which she once lived, but it could certainly never be decried as puny. When I was informed of the degradingly tiny sum of money Suzanne Blum had just obtained for her client, a rush of miscellaneous information which I'd obtained about the Duchess started going through my mind. The Duchess never became a Queen but she had done her best to live like a Queen. She and the Duke had once traveled with insouciance through a war-torn Europe taking with them no less than 222 suitcases, and that was not counting all her extra hat and jewel boxes. Their entourage was enormous, it resembled an unaffiliated army, it included so many maids carrying lapdogs that belonged to the Duchess. When the Windsors arrived at stations, journalists were sent to meet them in order to get photographs of Wallis Windsor's monumental pile of luggage.

The Duchess deeply loved her pug dogs, and the Duke, with the "kindness" that Maître Blum ascribed to him, used to walk them for her. The abdication had aroused such fraught and hostile feelings that the Windsors became paranoid about their worldwide unpopularity.

They therefore set a great store on loyalty. Their pugs for this reason were very important to them. They had heard that the pug is the dog that is reputed to be the most faithful to man. Rather mischievously the Duchess had given one of her favorite pugs the name of "Captain Townsend" after the man whom Princess Margaret had loved and been forbidden by the royal family to marry. Soon after her marriage to the Duke, Wallis Windsor had formed a collection of Meissen china pugs which was by far the largest and most valuable in the world.

In the thirties she had also formed a collection of Aubusson carpets and tapestries so immense that she was unable to house it and had to store it in a warehouse in the Parisian suburbs. She once hopefully, and in retrospect, sadly, regarded this collection as an insurance that would guarantee her a comfortable old age.

Alec Guinness remembers meeting the Duchess at a party in Paris, and as an actor he had never forgotten the theatrical impact of her amazing yellow diamond. He was unable to take his eyes off it. He describes it as having looked like a huge and delicious, gleaming candy. He was seized by a childish longing to eat it. The Duchess was wearing a simple black Mainbocher suit and not one other piece of jewelry on that occasion. Alec Guinness still praises the Duchess's stage sense. She was quite aware that her yellow diamond had to be worn alone otherwise all the force of its dramatic impact would have been lost.

For the Duchess once owned innumerable other diamonds and if she had been less restrained and subtle she could have bedecked herself until she glittered like a

Christmas tree. Her most valuable solitaire was one of fifty carats and it was described by New York gossip columnists as the "Dookess' Big Ice."

She also collected priceless rubies from Burma and Ceylon. She acquired many aquamarines because at some point she had been told they were her birthstone. The Duchess was always keen to have some very good reason for the jewels that were in her possession. Later when she read in women's magazines that some astrologers believed that pearls—while others maintained that moonstones—were the valid birthstones for June, the month of her birth, the Duchess solved the problem this conflicting news presented by obtaining extra sets of pearls and moonstones, in addition to a few new sets of aquamarines.

The Duke was always begging the Duchess to wear opals because he felt they suited what he called "her elusive and complex personality." But opals are meant to bring bad luck and the Duchess was superstitious and she did not consider her husband's fanciful vision of her character as a sufficiently good reason to include these unlucky stones in her collection.

So many of the Duchess's jewels were once legendary. Her favorite single piece was her diamond pin that represented the feathers of the Prince of Wales crown. Her most intricate tiara was the one designed for her by Van Cleef & Arpels. It was unique, for it was reversible and could be worn on certain evenings as a tiara, on others as an extraordinary necklace.

In June 1944 an article on the Duchess appeared in the *American Mercury*:

The Duchess gives the impression of terrific neatness, not a hair out of place, not a line awry. Her nose never shines. Her slip never shows. She looks like a period room done by a furniture house, a room in which nobody lives comfortably. Figuratively speaking, there are no ashes on her rugs, no papers lying around, no blinds askew. To give a real picture of the Duchess, I must describe her clothes. In them—it sounds harsh, but it is true—a large part of her personality resides. And she spares no effort to put it there. She has lost none of her flair for style. It had become one of her prime passions. She is proud to be called the best-dressed woman in the world. It is a profession with her. She enjoys setting the style. She has launched many fashions. The vogue for high-necked evening gowns, for example, may be traced directly to her—she wears them because of her flat-chested and boyish figure.[1]

The columnist admits to being harsh, but even if her charge was true and the personality of the Duchess did at one point reside for the most part in her clothes, at least they were splendid and she managed to make them just as fabled as her jewels. Long before her illness, long before she was "Blumed," the clothes of Wallis Windsor were treated as works of art. Many are still housed in the Metropolitan Museum in New York. There were her full-length sable, her blonde otter, her broadtail jacket—all designed for her by Maximilian, the famous New York furrier. She used to wear the jacket beneath her reversible, mink-lined Burberry raincoat.

Even her shoes were fought over by all the major museums in Europe. She bought them like a fetishist, on one occasion purchasing fifty-six pairs. Then there was her passion for exquisite lingerie which Maître Blum was very probably continuing to honor. Again it was the verve and extravagance with which she acquired it that made the Duke beg to accompany her whenever she went off on a spree to buy her underwear. When the salesgirls were doing up the Duchess's parcels, her husband, with all the kindness Maître Blum so admired as his prime quality, liked to help them. When they snipped off bits of extra string and threw them away, the Duke used to pick them up and put them in his pocket. "I save string," the dethroned emperor would say. "One never knows when one may need it."

In her villa at Cap d'Antibes the Duchess's bath used to be made of pure twenty-two-carat gold. In April 1938 *The New York Times* reported that "a burglar recently hacked a sizable chunk out of the Duchess's bath-tub."

Soon after the abdication, the house in East Biddle Street, Baltimore, where she had lived as a child was turned into a museum. It contained a life-size wax figure of the Duchess curtsying to two life-size wax figures of George V and Queen Mary. Visitors could pay to see all her furnishings including the pre-gold, very ordinary bathtub she was meant to have used as a girl. A businessman from New Jersey tried to buy up the contents of her house including the bathtub. He intended to form a Wallis museum in his own state.

This matter was considered to be of such gravity that it was brought before the aldermen of Baltimore. The

Duchess's museum had become one of the greatest tourist attractions in the city's history. After much solemn discussion and deliberation the city fathers refused to let the Duchess's furnishings go.

Rumors then spread that most of the contents of the Duchess's museum were bogus. The only authentic thing in the house which could be proved to have been used by the Duchess in her girlhood was an old stove on which she had once made fudge.

The curator of the museum was confronted by these rumors. Her defense was curious. She said that the museum was never meant to be a peep show. It was meant to be something much more important. It was intended to be a shrine to the Duchess.

Maître Blum was perhaps the only living human being who could have understood and applauded the curator's astonishing reasoning. But the lives of Maître Blum and the Duchess had not yet made their unlikely collision.

The attendance at the Wallis museum dropped disastrously once visitors started to feel they were being made to pay for the privilege of staring at a bathtub that commemorated the Duchess, rather than one in which she had genuinely lain.

But even if her museum had failed, Bernard Shaw still wrote that the Duchess had given the British monarchy the greatest jolt in history. She made the phrase "Wallis Blue" pass into the language so that it became like "Chartreuse Green" and "Burgundy Red." "Wallis Blue" was the same color as the ribbon of the Noble Knights of the Garter. And even if her "elusive and complex personality" sometimes became almost unfindable, it was so obscured in the haze of rumors about her Mainbocher suits, her Prince of Wales plume pins, and her suites at the Waldorf Astoria, the style with which the Duchess of Windsor had lived her strange life might not have always been commendable but at least it always had a largesse.

But that was all long ago.

Recently I'd been made to watch Maître Blum making her absurdly dramatized "demands" on behalf of the Duchess. Now when I heard about the pathetic four hundred pounds, and thought about the glee Maître Blum had shown me after having scored what she saw as a major coup for her client, I found it inappropriate. Maître Blum pretended that she wanted to exalt the Duchess, but in truth, I felt that she was really demeaning her. The heir to an empire had given up his throne for this "complex" American. As a siren Wallis Windsor had been a figure who had changed historical events more drastically than any other woman in human history. Now at the end of her life, it seemed humiliating for the helpless Duchess that Maître Blum with her *petit bourgeois* greed should be trying to extort piddling little sums like four hundred pounds on her behalf.

And why was the Duchess in such dire need of four hundred pounds? Why did Maître Blum threaten to suppress a book in which the Duchess was presented in a uniquely favorable light in order to extort such a pointless little pittance?

And what had happened to the Duchess's solid gold bathtub? Could such a hefty and sensationally precious object have just melted without a trace? The burglar had only

taken a sizable chunk of it. If the Duchess had been reduced to inexplicable penury, would it not be to her interest to hack out another chunk and place it in Sotheby's?
Even the sale of a couple of Meissen pugs would bring her
in more than Maître Blum could hope to raise from the
copyright of some dull photograph.

Lady Mosley had been one of the Duchess's closest
friends and if she had been in any state to make financial
decisions Wallis Windsor would presumably have allowed
her to use the photograph totally free of any measly little
charge. Not only was the Duchess being segregated from
those who had been fond of her but in her sad and supine
position she was being made to blackmail someone who
had always regarded her with affection. The stricken
woman was being forced to blackmail her friend from her
bed without her knowledge. The whole incident seemed
shady and distasteful.

After discovering the small-time level on which Maître
Blum was prepared to make battle for her client, I learned
from the editors of the *Sunday Times* that Maître Blum had
refused to allow Lord Snowdon to photograph the Duchess
of Windsor.

When they had arrived at her apartment, Maître Blum
had been both ingratiating and sweet. She had not let Lord
Snowdon see any of the belligerent aspects of her character
that she had shown to me.

Michael Bloch had been there with his Master wearing
his embarrassing striped blazer. He had not worn a bunch
of lilies of the valley in his buttonhole; he had worn a rose.
Michael Bloch seemed to be determined to get himself

photographed with his Master. Lord Snowdon had taken an instantaneous and allergic dislike to Bloch and made desperate signals to Francis Wyndham to get this intrusive young man out of the room. This had been quite difficult for Michael Bloch was all dressed up in his blazer and his rose buttonhole and he kept hovering round Maître Blum making suggestions as to where she ought to sit to look her best.

He had tried to make suggestions about the lighting. As a brilliant and professional photographer, Lord Snowdon had not been grateful for Bloch's artistic ideas. He'd found them impertinent and infuriating.

Finally Francis Wyndham had managed to get the unwilling Michael Bloch to go into another room. He then had to make conversation with him while Lord Snowdon photographed Maître Blum with the hope of persuading her to let him photograph the Duchess.

Francis Wyndham had asked Bloch if he recently had been to visit the Duchess. Bloch had said Maître Blum allowed him to visit the Duchess's house every Saturday. "That's my treat!" he'd said.

When asked if he found it a depressing experience to go to the house of a dying old woman, Bloch appeared puzzled. He seemed to Francis to have been thrilled to get so near to the pipe-fed Duchess. However, Bloch expressed sadness that the Duchess of Windsor's house no longer had any flowers.

Francis Wyndham had asked Michael Bloch whether he had actually seen the Duchess. The young man had claimed that Maître Blum wouldn't allow him to accompany her when she went into the bedroom. "When I have my treat, I sit in the Duke's study." That was all that he was prepared to say.

I wanted to know how Maître Blum had behaved when she was with Lord Snowdon after her photograph had been taken. Had she been dignified? This seemed very important. After all, she was representing the Duchess.

Apparently Maître Blum had been only fairly dignified. She had sat in her chair looking regal and aloof. She had said that she loved cats much better than she loved any human beings. She had uttered this chilling statement with quite a lot of dignity.

In the kitchen at the back of her apartment, her battered and abused-looking maid had started cooking a chicken for lunch. Maître Blum had been very upset when its odors started floating into her living room. She had started glaring at Michael Bloch as if she blamed him for these mundane smells which she saw as totally unroyal in the house of someone who was representing the Duchess of Windsor.

Apparently, Maître Blum had only lost all dignity when she was shown slides of herself. Francis Wyndham described her as having behaved like a member of some savage and backward tribe. She became crazily overexcited once she saw her own image. It was as if she never before had heard of the existence of the camera. As she had legally represented a plethora of Hollywood stars and Hollywood studios, her lack of sophistication in regard to photography had been all the more disquieting.

Awestruck, she had kept gazing at these slides, which

in truth were so dark and fuzzy and tiny that no one but herself could have made them out. She had gasped that they were *belles comme tout*. They were "true works of art." They were *magnifique*. They were "exquisite." She'd used every possible word of French and English praise.

Then Maître Blum had made Michael Bloch admire them as well, and when he held them up to the light he had seemed just as overwhelmed by these shadowy slides as she was.

I was dismayed to hear how Maître Blum had behaved when her picture was taken. I'd just spoken to a journalist who'd been present when the Duchess posed for the very first photographs that were taken of her after the abdication.

The journalist had been amazed and impressed that the Duchess had been so competent and professional. She told the photographer to stand where she wanted him to stand. She explained precisely from what angle she wished to be photographed. She accepted that her nose was too long and she knew the ways to shorten it. She directed all the lighting men for she was very precise as to how she wanted herself lit. The Duchess kept shifting and reshifting the folds of her skirt so that the line of her costume would show to its best. She had been as poised and experienced as any movie star. As usual the Duchess had looked immaculate on that occasion. Her hair had been superbly arranged and she was wearing some perfect dress. She had also worn a pair of spotless white gloves. She had always liked to wear white gloves although she was frequently criticized by the leading French couturiers for doing so.

They claimed that white gloves were old-fashioned. But the Duchess was stubborn and she'd always known better than they did. She had always been aware that her hands were not her best feature. Cecil Beaton had always described them as "utilitarian looking."

After the lighting men had satisfied all her requirements for the taking of her first post-abdication portrait, the exhausted cameraman was just about to click the shutter. Suddenly, with an imperious gesture, the Duchess signaled him to stop. She clapped her hands. At that moment the door burst open and, like a genie, in rushed her maid. With great tenderness she took off the Duchess's perfect white gloves. She then put on an even more snowy white and perfect pair.

Since I heard this account of one of the Duchess's photographic sessions, Maître Blum's unsophisticated behavior over the slides seemed all the more depressing. The Duchess had not allowed herself to become shamingly overexcited by the beauty of her own transparencies. Maître Blum was a woman who loved to upbraid, but now she herself deserved reproach. Representing herself as the Duchess's "vicar on earth" during the visit from Lord Snowdon, it was Maître Blum who had let down the Duchess.

Once Lord Snowdon had failed to get the desired permission from the lawyer, the *Sunday Times* was in a position where they had financed his trip to Paris only to find themselves in possession of some highly expensive but pointless commissioned photographs of Maître Blum. Some sort of text was therefore needed in order to justify their publication. Maître Blum could persuade herself that her own portrait was just as interchangeably valuable as any photograph of her client, but the British public was not likely to share her rarefied opinion. None of the timeless mystique and glamor of the Duchess had really dusted off on her lawyer. Those who had retained an old romantic fascination for this woman who had created an historical world-famous upheaval would have been riveted to have been allowed to get one last glimpse of her as seen through the camera lens of Lord Snowdon. There was no such a universal desire to be given a last glimpse of the forbidding face of Maître Blum.

On the basis of my two interviews with her difficult lawyer, I knew it would be impossible to write any form of sane article on the Duchess of Windsor. To do that I would have to go much further than Maître Blum was prepared to take me. I would have to speak to many more of the Duchess's contemporaries, and interview those who were more reliable in their estimation of her personality.

It was therefore suggested I return to Paris and interview the old lawyer about her own life. Her career had been very remarkable quite apart from her climactic and emotionally charged involvement with the Duchess. If a straight profile of Maître Blum could be written there would be some reason to publish her photographs.

Another letter was dispatched to Maître Blum. It said that her own photographs had come out so beautifully that if the *Sunday Times* were to publish anything about the Duchess, they would like to include them. Would she therefore consent to give me one more interview? They felt that any article would be enriched if she would agree to give me as much information as possible about her own uniquely distinguished career. Would she also send them some old but beautiful photograph of the Duchess?

I felt this last request was very important. Maître Blum was unpredictable. Although there were moments when she seemed to need to outshine the Duchess, one could easily misconstrue her complicated feelings on this issue. Maître Blum had other moods in which her own self-respect was so intertwined with that of her supine client that any slight to the Duchess was experienced like a knife blow cutting through her own belly. It was therefore vital she be asked to provide a photograph of the Duchess for only then could Maître Blum feel entitled to grant an interview about herself. Even if her own true motives were on an unconscious level obscured to herself, she must never be allowed to have the feeling that she was being asked to leave the Duchess out.

While I was waiting to hear if Maître Blum would give me a third interview, I telephoned Countess Mountbatten, the daughter of the late Lord Mountbatten. As Maître Blum had put an end to the charitable trust he had tried to set up for the Duchess, I thought it might be intriguing to hear what he had felt about the Duchess's ancient lawyer.

On hearing Maître Blum's name, Countess Mountbatten became so agitated she sounded close to tears. "Oh, it's the most ghastly business! Daddy minded about it all so much. That lawyer has got all those lovely things. I can't tell you how many she's got. You'd never believe what wonderful things the Duke and Duchess used to have. And all of them royal. All the Duke's Sèvres snuffboxes were stamped right through with the royal arms! Nothing has been returned of course . . ."

"I believe that Maître Blum also has some of the royal swords?"

Countess Mountbatten gave a heavy, upper-class sigh. "Oh, my dear, I'm afraid it's very much worse than that," she whispered mournfully. "That frightful old woman's got the royal insignia and the regimental drums."

Later feeling a little vague as to the meaning of "insignia," I looked up the word in the dictionary. The definition was curious: "emblems, tokens, significant of anything." What would they signify to Maître Blum? For some reason it was nice to think of her having the regimental drums. I wondered if her neighbors in the rue de Varenne were sometimes disturbed by slow, rumbling peals at night, as this eighty-four-year-old lawyer sat frenetically beating the royal drums.

After my conversation with Countess Mountbatten, I had a coffee with Lady Tomkins. The ex-ambassadress was brisk and tweeded and garrulous. She was interested to hear that I'd met Maître Blum. What had I thought of her? Didn't I find her rather splendid? Wasn't it wonderful that there was someone to take care of Wallis? She'd certainly never expected that the poor Duchess would last so long. Five years ago her husband had received instructions from the Palace telling him what to do if the Duchess died. As British ambassador he was to travel with the Duchess's coffin and escort it to the burial ground at Frogmore, Windsor. Since then four other British ambassadors had been given the same instructions. Their terms as diplomats had expired—but the Duchess had not.

It was strange to think of all these changing ambassadors who had vainly waited to travel with the corpse of the Duchess of Windsor. The current British ambassador in Paris presumably was now doing the same. When the Palace gave their morbid instructions they had not counted on the tenacity of a certain wily old party sitting in the rue de Varenne. They had not guessed with what a violent force and resolution Maître Blum respected "la vie" of the Duchess.

Lady Tomkins wondered what would happen when the Duchess finally died. All the guests that attended her funeral had to be personally invited by the Queen. It was unlikely the Queen herself would attend. Conceivably, Prince Charles might go. He'd always liked his renegade great uncle and had been fond of the Duchess. Just in order to preserve good form, surely some member of the royal family had to appear at the Duchess's funeral.

She assumed Lady Dudley and Lady Alexandra Metcalfe would be invited. But she didn't know who else would be asked. So many of the Duchess's friends were dead now. She herself wasn't sure she wanted to go to Frogmore. She'd prefer to slip into the local church and say a prayer for Wallis.

The Duchess of Windsor, in her time, had given so many spectacular and envied parties. It was therefore ironic that her funeral at Frogmore was now being seen as this notorious hostess's last important party. Already jealousies and speculations were arising amongst her old surviving friends and acquaintances as to who would manage to attend it.

"Don't you ever feel a little worried about the Duchess?" I asked her.

"But the Duchess has Maître Blum," she said. "Maître Blum is a very efficient lady. I'm sure she is beautifully cared for."

"Have you ever tried to find out how she is?" I asked.

Lady Tomkins could not be ruffled. The Duchess was in excellent hands. Maître Blum had taken over the Duchess's household soon after the Duke had died, and she had gotten rid of all the servants who were cheating her. In that period the Duchess once said she felt that her household was like a ship without a helmsman. The Duchess was therefore very lucky.

Wallis Windsor's other friend, Mrs. Brinsley Plunket, was also interested to hear that I'd met Maître Blum. She wanted to be told everything the old lawyer had said about her client. I'd warned her that Maître Blum was not the soul of accuracy on the subject of her protégée, but when she heard Maître Blum's claim that the Duchess never drank, Mrs. Brinsley Plunket gave the loudest snort of impatience and disbelief.

"Oh, really! I can't believe it! How could Maître Blum have told you that! I remember both the Windsors tumbling about. One simply didn't know which it was the most important to hold up first! And anyway—how would Maître Blum have known if the Duchess drank? Maître Blum was only her lawyer, after all. None of us drink when we go to see our lawyers . . ." She quickly qualified this statement. "Well, maybe we do if we know they are going to tell us very bad news about our finances. But when we are with our lawyer obviously we drink in a rather different way . . ."

Mrs. Brinsley Plunket said she was very worried about a roll of tweed she had given the Duchess very soon after the death of the Duke. It was the most "divine" tweed from Galway. The Duchess had been thrilled by it. However, it had saddened her for she complained she no longer had the money to have it made up. Her advisor had told her she was far too poor to buy any new clothes.

"And was Maître Blum her advisor?" I asked.

"Exactly," Mrs. Brinsley Plunket muttered grimly. "At that point her advisor was Maître Blum."

She remembered the French couturier Hubert de Givenchy had been very distressed when the Duchess suddenly stopped going to him. He saw it as treachery and assumed she was being dressed by some other designer. But in fact the Duchess was no longer being dressed by anyone. She was much too frightened of Maître Blum.

"Was the Duchess someone who could be easily frightened?" I asked.

"You could easily frighten the Duchess about money. The Duchess never really knew how much she had. She was that sort of person . . ."

Mrs. Brinsley Plunket was still very concerned about her roll of tweed. As the poor Duchess wouldn't need it any more she was very keen to try and get it back. Did I think she could write to Maître Blum and ask her to return it?

There seemed to be no harm in her trying. The Duchess's bale of missing tweed formed a melancholy image. I thought of Maître Blum sitting in the rue de Varenne and I doubted Mrs. Brinsley Plunket would succeed in retrieving it. The tweed had probably gone the misty way of Queen Alexandra's emeralds, the solid gold bathtub, and the drums and the royal insignia.

"Don't you think that the Duchess's situation seems rather awful?" I asked.

"It couldn't be worse."

"But can't any of her friends do anything for her? Can't they at least find out her condition?"

"Nothing can be done. What can anyone do with Maître Blum? The Duchess now belongs to that awful old character." Mrs. Brinsley Plunket spoke as if the Duchess were a dog and Maître Blum were her owner. She was more optimistic about getting back the Galway tweed than she was hopeful about getting news of the Duchess.

"At least the Duchess still has Georges," she said. "At least Maître didn't get rid of him. Georges was magic in the old days. He really adored Wallis. I think he was probably homosexual but he was married and his wife was called Ophelia. He used to love kneeling in front of the Duchess and putting on her slippers. He was always doing devoted little cozy things like that. I'm sure that Georges must be taking the best care of the Duchess. I'd be much more worried for the Duchess if I didn't know she still has Georges."

Later that same week, I was shown some photographs of the Duchess. Hugo Vickers, the talented young British biographer, owned some pictures that had been taken three years ago by Spanish paparazzi. They had made a raid on her house and by using long-range lenses had managed to take shots through the window.

The photographs shocked me. The Duchess looked pitiful. Her tiny shrunken body was being lifted by a nurse. Her legs were cigarette-thin and they dangled uselessly. Her hair was tied tightly back in a knot. Her head lolled helplessly on her chest. There was a close-up of her face and she looked a little like a Chinese mandarin, but more like a dead monkey. Her famous azure eyes were closed slits, and they had the same slant as those of her lawyer.

It was bizarre that the Chinese theme that had always threaded through the legends of her jewelry, her coolie-style mink capes, and even her sex life, once again had emerged on her deathbed. In earlier photographs the Duchess had never looked Chinese. Since Maître Blum had formed her close liaison with the Duchess had she managed to stamp her own Oriental cast of feature on her client? Or was it the other way around? Had her adoring old lawyer so passionately admired something elusive and un-western in the dying appearance of the Duchess that she had decided to emulate this quality? Was it an accident that Maître Blum now looked half-Chinese?

When I examined the photographs of the paparazzi I understood why Maître Blum had refused to allow the Duchess of Windsor to be fashion-photographed by Lord Snowdon. The Duchess was no longer recognizable as a woman. Her hands, which had once been criticized by Cecil Beaton as "utilitarian-looking," were frozen by paralysis and had the look of the embalmed paws of a marmoset.

Yet this was the radiant talkative creature that Maître Blum kept telling me about. And these photographs had been taken three years ago. Presumably the Duchess's appearance had further deteriorated in the years that followed.

Yet Maître Blum still found this dead-looking fossil of a marmoset beautiful because it was the remains of the Duchess. "Home to me is where the Duchess is," the late Duke of Windsor used to say. And Maître Blum seemed to feel exactly the same. Technically she inhabited her apartment in the choicest *quartier* in Paris. Emotionally she lived with the Duchess in her huge gray house in the Bois de Boulogne.

For those who were not under its spell, the sexual allure of Wallis Windsor had always been seen as an enigma. Cleveland Amory in *Who Killed Society?* quoted from the diary of someone he tactfully described as "a prominent American lady who married a distinguished British title." Written in 1936, the diary of this anonymous lady shows she feels all the fury and venom that springs from bafflement.

March 22nd, 1936

London is seething with gossip about the new King and his blatant exploiting of his mistress, Mrs. Ernest Simpson and her 8th rate husband always on tour.

Everyone seems to have a new disease "Simpsonitis" and "sucking-up" to dear Wally is the thing to do. Emerald Cunard heads the list as the biggest horses ass, then Duff Cooper—it really strikes me as being ludicrous, all this toadying is all so temporary, one never knows when Mrs. S. will be "out" and some new horror "in."

In another entry a few months later, the same anonymous lady wrote:

> July 18th, 1936
>
> If I ever made a mistake in my life, I did when I said that "Queenie" Simpson would be "out" and a new one "in." I'm afraid that when a man reaches 42 (as our monarch is) and if he loves a plain woman, his own age—it is a thing that will last . . . Rumor has it our dear Monarch wants to marry her —he had given her Queen Alexandra's jewels . . .

> December 8th
>
> Every minute counts now—Baldwin motoring down to Fort Belvedere spending hours with the Royal . . . (pardon my French). Members of the Royal Family visiting him, trying to persuade him to use his mentality—instead of pouting that he wants his "Wally." It's too much! The world is in a frenzy—and he bull-headedly wants to marry that . . . Mrs. Simpson.[2]

It was the plainness of the Duchess that seemed to enrage the American lady of British title. Her irritation with it is expressed in the dots that replace the abusive words she would have liked to apply to Mrs. Simpson. And the

Duchess's appearance was always under attack. Her figure was considered too flat-chested and bony, her nose and her chin too jutting. Not only her hands were sneered at. Her feet were said to be too big and flat and she was therefore uncomfortable in high-heeled shoes. It was also said that the Duchess's body was too stiff below the waist; her arms and torso were supple, but an unbecoming rigidity in her lower body was all too evident when she danced.

The Duchess's physique was always dissected with this relentless cruel attention because it never gave any obvious clue as to why her husband adored her with such a passion. If she technically had been more beautiful, her public might have found it easier to comprehend the willingness of the King to renounce the British Empire for her sake.

When I was shown the photographs taken by the Spanish paparazzi I found it difficult to understand why Maître Blum was so enthralled by the Duchess's beauty. But remembering that the nature of the Duchess's spellbinding powers had never been understood in the past, it just seemed easier to accept that the same mysterious hold that had once gripped the Duke now gripped the otherwise tough and worldly Maître Blum. *The Heart Has Its Reasons* was the title of the Duchess of Windsor's autobiography. If one asked why Maître Blum had formed such a fierce erotic attachment to the Duchess's seemingly ruined body, the Duchess's title seemed all that could be said.

Maître Blum gave a very quick and affirmative reply to the request of the *Sunday Times* that she would give me a third interview about her own life. The news that her Snowdon photographs had come out beautifully seemed to have acted like fertilizer on the monumental vanity of this unusual old lawyer. She obviously was all too anxious to have her photographs further embellished by an accompanying text that would give full credit to various astonishing aspects of her noble character, amongst which would be included her saintly devotion to the Duchess of Windsor.

However, a passion for paradox seemed to be at the very core of Maître Blum's nature, and she'd never been a woman who liked to make things easy for those with whom she had any dealings. While she agreed to give me a third interview in which she announced she would be happy to give me information about her long and distinguished career, she also warned the *Sunday Times* she would not be prepared to speak about herself. Maître Blum was such a "Mary, Mary . . ." She adored to be "quite contrary." How could any journalist be expected to write a serious profile of a figure who would only consent to grant an interview on the understanding that nothing about her life be disclosed, let alone printed? Could there be more logic in her apparent lunacy than I could perceive? Did she feel that nothing in her illustrious career had any importance until the moment when she'd made herself the sole legal representative of the Duchess of Windsor? Was she planning to speak to me only about the wondrous aspects of Wallis Windsor, because she felt the Duchess was her life and nothing else about herself was worth discussion? I would only discover once I was with her again in Paris and she had me with my back to one of her six huge doors.

CHAPTER TEN

*B*efore returning to Paris in order to write this problematical profile of the Duchess of Windsor's lawyer, I read her novel *To Know Nothing*. If Maître Blum was not prepared to divulge any facts about her background I hoped that her fiction would give me certain insights into the inner workings of her "complex mind and personality."

The dust jacket of *Ne Savoir Rien* was studded with rave reviews. After I had finished it I was puzzled as to why it had been so widely acclaimed in France. I mentioned this to Francis Wyndham and he reminded me that Maître Blum was legal representative of the entire French press. He suggested that as Maître Blum represented every single publishing house in France, she might tend to get good reviews.

Maître Blum's novel was distinguished by its extreme snobbishness and its total lack of humor. Almost all her characters were excessively well-born. She made a laborious point of their long lineage. One of her protagonists traced his descent back to the Plantagenets.

Maître Blum's fictional creations were cardboard people. She allowed them no real life. Only the trappings of their *haut* French bourgeois existence were acutely observed. Her characters lived in the grandest *quartiers* of Paris. They had exquisite taste in furniture and pictures.

They frequented the most important salons. They were received by *tout Paris*. Like Maître Blum's "Duchess of Windsor" they loved classical music. They sat in the best box when they went to the opera.

In life, Maître Blum was too regally arrogant to care if she was believed when she made her various statements. The same sublime contempt for her readers was all too evident in her fiction.

Maître Blum's novel was a murder story. There was a frightening violence in Maître Blum's fantasies and this emerged very strongly in her creative writing. If she didn't like one of her characters she killed them off in a moment of vicious caprice. When she had delivered me her death threat she'd already demonstrated her uncontrollable impulse to cause the instant death of anyone who displeased her. This ruthless desire to annihilate any opposition had also colored all her erratic tantrums and her insensate diatribes against the authors of all books about the Duchess. But when the heroine of *To Know Nothing* decides to murder her husband, it causes total consternation in Maître Blum's readers.

Nothing that previously has been established about this woman suggests she would be capable of resorting to such lethal action. On the contrary, Maître Blum has taken care to describe her as extremely "well brought up" in the French *haut bourgeois* tradition. She is beautiful, well-mannered, and loving. She has fantastic taste. She is dignified and courageous, and of course, she loves the poor. She has all the virtues that Maître Blum ascribes to the Duchess of Windsor. Before she commits her murder, Maître Blum's heroine is so perfect in her respect for comportment and decorum she is really not unlike Queen Mary.

Maître Blum does not deign to give any psychological buildup to explain why this paragon of aristocratic French womanhood turns overnight into a cold-blooded murderess.

As Maître Blum was such a brilliant lawyer, I had expected that her fictional plots would be worked out with immense finesse and skill. I assumed they would be tight as one of her legal briefs.

In *To Know Nothing* Maître Blum's plot was not only careless, it was risible. Maître Blum's lack of interest in her own credibility stood her to very poor account in her novel. When her previously saintly heroine commits her dark deed, she successfully murders her husband in the most unlikely manner. She slips some Nembutal into his brandy. The unfortunate, lamblike man innocently gulps it down. He then falls dead on the spot.

To Know Nothing was intended to be a realistic novel and in Maître Blum's murder, her abrupt departure from realism was all the more chilling coming from the pen of a woman whose life had been devoted to the pursuit of true fact.

Maître Blum, who had officiated in so many trials and spent so many decades in the law courts, most certainly should know how many sleeping pills are needed in order to cause the death of a full-grown man. Anyone who has ever pulverized a Nembutal tablet is aware that its contents are acid and unpleasant in the extreme. For Maître Blum's heroine to kill her husband in the fashion she described, the victim's husband would have to be totally moronic not to notice his glass of brandy tasted funny. If it were to contain the required death dose, it would be as thick with sleeping tablets as a soup.

As Maître Blum had agreed to let me write an article on her life while at the same time refusing to tell me anything about it, I asked my editor if he could arrange for her to be looked up in the files of the *Sunday Times*.

As Maître Blum had always been internationally eminent I assumed there must be a lot of material about her. Quite apart from my journalistic need to obtain some basic facts about this unique old woman, I had become personally curious to find out what her career had been like.

It then transpired that it would not be at all easy to pick out any information from the filing system of the *Sunday Times*. To get what I wanted, many researchers would have to be employed, and time and money spent.

Maître Blum would have been enchanted if she had known what had happened. Symbolically, it was astonishing. Despite the distinction of her long career, Maître Blum had no individual file in the archives of the *Sunday Times*. By some suitable, yet eerie stroke of fate, Maître Blum had been filed with the Duchess.

Her life was therefore unfindable. The Duchess's file had the immensity of that of Jackie Kennedy, the Queen Mother, and the Princess of Wales. Few women have ever received more publicity than the Duchess. For years and years everything she did, every article of clothing she had appeared in, was made into a leading news story by the international press. And somewhere in this great ocean of frivolous news-cuttings, the impressive and hardworking life of Maître Blum lay buried.

As there was no time to employ researchers to extract Maître Blum from her client's overwhelming files, I realized the basis of my article would have to be drawn from the unpromising interview she intended to give me. I had been told that there were references to her in the autobiography of the American composer Virgil Thomson and as I had so little information about her I obtained a copy. Virgil Thomson described meeting her on an ocean liner when he was traveling to the United States from France just before it was invaded by Germany.

> My warmest friend on board was a woman lawyer, Suzanne Blum. She knew that her safety lay in leaving France, being Jewish and also prominent. And yet she worried over where her duty lay, to leave, or not to leave, her aging mother. Being by now a practiced hand, through long experience of Blitzstein, Kirstein, Grosser, and the Stettheimers, at comforting Jewish emotional indecision, sweetly, firmly I assured her she had done right. So friends we became, and friends we have remained.[1]

I found this anecdote depressing and its whole tone as recounted by Virgil Thomson was chillingly facetious and unpleasant. Later in his book he went on to describe how Maître Blum managed to get him awarded the Legion of

Honor and this provided his readers with some explanation as to why he found her such a delightful character.

He also described returning to Paris after the war was over and becoming what he blithely called "involved with the *collabos*." In particular Virgil Thomson became a friend of a man called Bernard Fay, who had been condemned to life imprisonment, seizure of property, and national degradation for his pro-Nazi activities.

"I essayed what little power I could wield," Virgil Thomson wrote with a boastful modesty. "It was Suzanne who helped the most, for she was legal counsel to a ministry. And it was she, unless I am in error, who procured his removal from the Île de Réy, an island fortress where his health was being injured, to a prison hospital on the mainland near Le Mans; and it was from this easier situation that a year later he escaped to Spain."[2]

I knew nothing about Bernard Fay, but Maître Blum's reasons for wishing to aid him seemed more than murky. It occurred to me that perhaps she was not being quite so eccentric as I'd previously thought when she agreed to have her profile written, just as long as she didn't have to speak about her life. David Pryce-Jones had warned me that even if she appeared clownish, one must never forget that she was a very terrifying clown.

CHAPTER ELEVEN

When I arrived at the rue de Varenne, Maître Blum was sitting in her six-doored living room with Michael Bloch. He was not wearing his blazer.

Once again I was struck that Maître Blum had furnished her apartment in a way that was calculated to make one feel acutely uncomfortable. She provided chairs only because it was correct as a wealthy lawyer to do so. But by their arrangements she conveyed that it irked her that convention forced her to provide her visitors with something to sit on. Disliking human beings so much more than cats, Maître Blum would have much preferred to make humans stand.

Maître Blum was in one of her most fiendishly angry moods because she had not yet received any copies of Lord Snowdon's photographs of herself.

"Mr. Wyndham promised he would send them immediately but I have received nothing." She muttered furiously.

This was not my fault. But Maître Blum didn't care if she was unfair. I apologized all the same. My apology did not placate her and she glared at me with the utmost hostility.

"Mr. Wyndham tells me that the photographs Lord Snowdon took of you are very beautiful." My sycophancy only partially pleased her. I knew I hadn't massaged her vanity enough.

"Mr. Wyndham has not sent the photographs as he promised." Her voice growled with peevish discontent. She had a genius for making one feel awful.

"I wondered if you would tell me something about your life?" I said nervously.

"I 'ate to talk about myself!" By dropping the *h* of hate she made the word sound particularly menacing and voracious.

I'd flown from London to Paris to see her and now it seemed I'd wasted my time. This perverse old creature was going to do exactly what she had threatened. She was going to give me an interview in which she teasingly refused to speak.

If I were to persuade her to talk to me I knew I had to blackmail her with her own photographs. Obviously she was violently anxious to get them published. The photographs had to be dangled just as she loved to dangle "golden carrots."

"As the photographs have turned out so beautifully, Maître Blum, it would be a pity if the *Sunday Times* cannot use them. I think they will only do so if you tell me something about yourself. You know what newspapers are."

I expected her to see through my heavy ploy and I waited for it to madden her. But her self-love was so immense that it made her naive and it allowed her to be manipulated. I saw a look of real horror come into her angry eyes. Obviously it had never occurred to her that there was any danger her photographs might not be published. She had taken for granted that the British public would hunger to see them for she regarded them as even more unique than mere reproductions of her own image; they were reflections of her as the intrepid and devoted custodian of the Duchess of Windsor.

She hesitated before answering. Her crafty legal brain needed time to readjust her exact position. If she were to concede, she had to make her concession with dignity.

"I 'ate to talk about myself," she repeated. Then her face softened and took on a strange, sentimental expression. Her eyes became moist. "But I love the Duchess so much," she whispered. Her voice choked as she said the word "love." "I love the Duchess so much I would prefer that you write about me—rather than you write about her. *Je vais me sacrifier pour la Duchesse*—I am prepared to sacrifice myself for the Duchess!"

She was shameless. She looked manic. It thrilled her to pretend that she was crucifying herself for her Duchess.

"Where were you born?" I asked. It seemed better to quickly start the interview while she was still burning in the fires of her own martyrdom.

"I was born in Niort."

"Niort is in the west of France," Michael Bloch interrupted.

"Is it a village?"

"Niort is a French provincial town." He reprimanded me.

Maître Blum told me that her father had come from Alsace. "He was *de bonne famille*," Michael Bloch came beeping in. Apparently her father had fled to France as a boy to avoid becoming a German National.

"He arrived in France with nothing but the pack on

his back," Maître Blum said. "My father then opened a store which became successful, but he was a very great intellectual. Our house was always filled with poets and painters and writers."

Maître Blum told me the names of the artists who had once frequented her father's house but they meant nothing to me.

"I was brought up in the usual way," she said. "I was made to learn to cook, to do embroidery, and play the piano. I was taught everything stupid . . . Nothing useful . . . My family wanted me to do nothing but have babies —which I would have 'ated . . .'"

She spoke with fury, as if the imposed expectations of her parents had traumatized her. She became much more sympathetic when she started speaking about her own background. Her pain and her old frustrations seemed real and she was more interesting than when she became incensed on behalf of the Duchess of Windsor. It was intriguing to think of Maître Blum as a brilliant little girl entombed in the provinces and forced to do embroidery. And the babies that her family wanted her to breed were not pleasant to imagine. Who could visualize what it would be like to be Maître Blum's baby? The only figure who had taken on this dangerous role was the hapless Duchess of Windsor.

She told me that when she first announced her intention of becoming a lawyer, her family had been appalled. "You cannot imagine the scandal I created! In those days there were no careers open to women in France. Women could be maids, they could be nurses, they could be couturiers. And that was about it. No well-brought-up woman was meant to work. That was considered a disgrace. You couldn't believe the horrible disgrace it was considered!"

She spoke with great passion. Her struggle had been admirable. She had broken through the stifling conventions of her time. As a girl from the French provinces without money or contacts it was a huge feat that she had managed to break into the legal profession. Around the turn of the century when this woman had been born, the odds against her achieving her ambition must have been overwhelming. But through her intelligence and drive she'd overcome the prejudices and snubs she must have received, and she had risen to be one of the world's leading lawyers.

"Did your family continue to disapprove of your life and your career?" I asked her.

She smiled with cynical disgust. "My family became very proud of me. But only once my name was in the papers."

She had graduated from the University of Poitiers in 1921. Her talents were noticed by Joseph Paul-Boncour, who was one of the most eloquent and distinguished law-yers of his time. She became his legal assistant and worked with him on all his most important cases. "Paul-Boncour was one of the most wonderful men in the world," she told me. "He represented the crowned heads of Europe and he represented the little man down the road. That's where I acquired my experience."

It was peculiar to hear Maître Blum expressing her approval of a human being who was not the Duchess. "Crowned heads" always seemed to figure very highly in

Maître Blum's praise. She had claimed the Duchess only mixed with them. While these "crowned heads" were dining with the Duchess and eating her marvelous food by the light of candles which were never at eye level, it was fascinating to think that all the time they were being legally represented by Maître Blum's mentor, Paul-Boncour.

Maître Blum said that she was one of the first woman lawyers ever to appear in court. "No one trusted women in those days. It was said that women had voices which were too high-pitched to carry any authority . . . It was said that no jury or judge would be capable of taking the high-pitched squeakings of a woman seriously. It was felt that any client who put their life in the hands of a woman lawyer would be committing suicide . . ." Maître Blum made a gesture with her gnarled hand that indicated she was slitting her throat.

"C'est ridicule," she continued. "But it was thought that women were such feeble, stupid creatures that they were incapable of standing up to any aggression from the opposition—that if they were challenged or cross-questioned they would break down before the judge and cry. In those days people thought that women were born with no brains.

"Nobody believed that a woman could ever master all the complications of the law. Nobody wanted to be represented in court by a chimpanzee . . . That was the attitude of the times . . . So I was lucky that I was taken under the wing of a marvelous and powerful man. Paul-Boncour protected me. If it had not been for Paul-Boncour I would have met with all the usual prejudice."

"Is it still difficult for a woman to have a successful career as a lawyer in France?" I asked.

"The general attitude towards women lawyers has improved. But it is by no means perfect."

She said that her feminism had been expressed by her life. She had been too busy to sign petitions and manifestos and go to feminist meetings.

Maître Blum was a famous novelist, and also a leading international lawyer. Having carved two brilliant careers for herself, she seemed to view the women's movement with a lofty contempt as if it were little more than a refuge and excuse for those who were not hardworking. It was alarming to imagine the rudeness with which Maître Blum would treat some naive young feminist who was unwise enough to come round to the rue de Varenne hoping to get a petition signed. What would happen to this unsuspecting figure if she chose some inopportune moment when Maître Blum was just setting off with Michael Bloch to pay a visit to the Duchess?

I asked Maître Blum about her first husband. He apparently had been a famous lawyer and he had worked in the French branch of Allen & Overy, the law firm that represented the Windsors.

Michael Bloch murmured that Maître Blum's husband had been a great wit, that he had been famous in Paris for his "bon mots."

I asked her about her present husband, the ailing General. He, too, apparently was a wit. Maître Blum seemed to need this quality in those she was close to. She claimed that he was very humane. In the course of his distinguished military career he had been loved even by those he had conquered.

"General Spillman subdued Southern Morocco," Maître Blum said. "And he subdued it humanely."

She said that the General was a great intellectual. He was a man of immense courage. He had once been the victim of an assassination attempt in North Africa. "*Il a perdu son épaule.* How do you say *épaule* in English?" she asked Michael Bloch. She tried to use him as an interpreter but he looked baffled.

"Shoulder?" I said. "The General lost his shoulder?"

"Yes," Maître Blum said. "The General lost his shoulder. But even his assassin grew to love him."

She gave me a very curious picture of the General. I wondered if it was possible to lose a shoulder without losing an arm. The assassin presumably was arrested by the French army and must have gone on loving the General from some cell.

"That is enough," Maître Blum said. "I've said all I have to say."

She hated to give. Now she seemed to feel she had given too much. In fact the data she had given me was rather sparse. She had been born in Niort. She had married two witty and distinguished men. She had studied law with Joseph Paul-Boncour. This hardly provided the basis for a very interesting profile.

"Could you tell me a little more, Maître Blum? Can you tell me about some of your famous cases?"

"I will not talk about my cases!" She was getting angry again.

"My Master will not talk about her cases," Michael

Bloch said mournfully. He seemed accustomed to resigning himself to her willful nature.

"But if she doesn't talk about her cases, I cannot write a profile on her."

"Maître Blum has had an immensely distinguished legal career. She has represented many illustrious clients," he said.

"I know that Maître Blum is very famous in France. But I will be writing about her for an English audience. The English know very little about her. Therefore she must give me more details about her distinguished career and her cases."

Michael Bloch insisted that Maître Blum was very famous in England. This was only true in the sense that she had made herself rather famous as the explosive defendant of the Duchess. When the TV series "Edward and Mrs. Simpson" was first released, Maître Blum had denounced it in such a fiery fashion in the British press that its producer, Verity Lambert, said the Thames Television ought to have paid Maître Blum for the priceless publicity she had given the show.

"If Maître Blum will not give me more material, I really cannot write the article." I got up and thanked her as if I were leaving. Maître Blum's lynxlike eyes were scrutinizing me to see if she'd gone too far. She loved to tease, but now she was once again becoming anxious about the publication of her photographs.

"Wait!" she ordered. Maître Blum rushed off next door. For a woman of her age it was remarkable the speed at which she could move. She returned with a huge photograph album which she placed at my knee. When I opened it I saw that she had painstakingly pasted in all the newspaper-clippings that reported her various legal battles. I just read the headlines: STRAVINSKY IS OPPOSED BY THE CELEBRATED LAWYER SUZANNE BLUM.   SUZANNE BLUM DEFENDS JACK WARNER.

The album looked fascinating but she gave me no time to read it. Up she came and she seized it back from my knee. Then she went into a corner and sat herself down and started to look through it. As she gently turned its pages her face was suddenly transfused by exactly the same tender, sentimental look which always came over it whenever she mentioned the Duchess. The album was a partial record of her life and when she surveyed the news items that recorded her past, she acted like a doting mother to her own past and she gazed down at it with all the devotion of a woman admiring her infant in the pram.

This driven old woman was a Narcissus, and her press-cuttings were her pool. When her name started getting in the papers, she had overcome the disapproval of her straitlaced French *petit bourgeois* family. Then she became spokesperson for the Duchess of Windsor and managed to fuse her own publicity with that of her client so that her pool had extended its boundaries to a point where its waters appeared limitless. Maître Blum could now gaze into them with total satisfaction. If Maître Blum's mother had been alive to see what her daughter had accomplished, Maître Blum's mother would have been very pleased.

Maître Blum suddenly came out of her doting reverie. She snapped the album shut and gave a big sigh. She jumped to her feet and ran off through one of her six doors, taking her album with her.

"Where has she gone?" I asked Michael Bloch.

"I think Maître Blum considers the interview finished." He looked embarrassed.

"But Maître Blum gave me no time to read the album. Surely she is coming back."

"I don't think that Maître Blum will be coming back." He spoke as if he were a specialist on Maître Blum's erratic behavior.

"But she still hasn't given me enough material to write a profile on her."

Michael Bloch nodded sadly. He shrugged with the despair of someone accepting the unpredictability of the forces of nature. He invited me to go and have a drink with him in a café in the rue de Varenne.

"What do you think of Maître Blum?" he asked once we had ordered some whiskeys. "Isn't she an amazing character?"

"She certainly seems rather amazing. But she hasn't been very helpful with the article."

"Maître Blum is a curious person. For a woman of her fame and accomplishments she is astonishingly modest. Did you know she is still practicing at the Paris bar?"

I'd not realized this; I'd assumed her only client was the Duchess of Windsor.

"Naturally the Duchess takes up more of Maître Blum's time than any of her other clients." Michael Bloch bashfully lowered his eyes. "Maître Blum's relationship with the Duchess is very special."

He then paused tactfully. "Maître Blum's relationship is of a romantic nature . . ."

He was clearly unwilling to tell me more about Maître Blum's involvement with the Duchess. He'd been indiscreet about Maître Blum and now he appeared to regret his remark and was anxious to change the subject.

"Isn't it sad about the General's ill health?"

"Very sad. But I know very little about him. I've been told he is terrified of his wife."

"Maître Blum should have been the General," he said. "Don't you think Maître Blum would make a superb general?"

"I suppose she would." I never thought of it. But in fact it was quite easy to imagine Maître Blum commanding her armies. I hoped she would be as humane as her husband.

"Maître Blum told me that the General lost his shoulder. Is his arm crippled?"

Michael Bloch hesitated. "I don't know why Maître Blum told you that. It surprised me very much when I heard her telling you that."

"You mean there's never been anything wrong with the General's shoulder! You mean Maître Blum made the whole thing up!"

I was quite seriously astonished. The lawyer's young admirer was clearly not at all fazed by her. He simply accepted that Maître Blum, like her Creator, moved in mysterious ways. He admitted that although he'd met the General many times, he'd never noticed there was anything the matter with his shoulder.

"But why does Maître Blum want to make me write that her husband, the General, lost his shoulder when he never lost it?" I asked.

"My Master worships the idea of superhuman courage," he answered.

"So Maître Blum enjoys the idea that her husband endured the loss of a shoulder with a courage that was virtually superhuman."

"That's it," he said. "You've got it."

"And the Moroccan would-be assassin, the one who went on loving Maître Blum's husband long after he'd made a failed attempt on his life; can you tell me more about him?"

"My Master never discusses her private life with me," Michael Bloch said firmly. He knew that the earth of our conversation was becoming exceedingly boggy.

"But you live in Maître Blum's apartment?"

"My Master has given me that honor," he agreed, and his eyelids lowered with pride and modesty.

"You have met General Spillman many times and yet neither Maître Blum nor her husband has ever referred to the assassination attempt?"

"When my Master told you about the attempt on the General's life, it was the first time I have ever heard her refer to it."

"Don't you find that strange?" I asked.

Michael Bloch insisted I must remember that his Master was a woman who lived in a different era from the one which we both currently inhabited. Her values were very different.

I wished he would refrain from calling Maître Blum his "Master." When he was in her pulverizing presence, it was just possible to accept that he saw a need to address her in this manner. But now we were both talking in an ordinary French bar. We were both English-speaking, we both came from the North of Ireland, Maître Blum was not eavesdropping, and Michael Bloch's mode of referring to the Duchess's lawyer was starting to grate like a nail file on my nerves.

"Do you feel that Maître Blum's values are superior because she was born in a different era?" I asked him.

He felt that they were immensely superior. Maître Blum was very puritanical because her upbringing had been old-fashioned and straitlaced but she was capable of being quite lenient. In some ways she could be almost modern in her thinking.

He insisted that Maître Blum never objected to any hints that the Duke of Windsor was a homosexual. She never sued if any such insinuation appeared in print. I found this rather perverse of Maître Blum. But then she was a character of many complexities. If the Duke had been a homosexual, maybe she felt this somehow made the Duchess even more marvelous and dignified and superhumanly courageous for having married him. It could also be a device by which she removed the unfortunate Duke as a serious rival. Maître Blum wanted the Duchess to have been a virgin on her wedding day. Quite conceivably in fantasy she went even further than that. It was possible she wanted the Duchess to be a virgin now.

I asked Michael Bloch where he came from. How had

he first met Maître Blum? He said that he was born in Ulster, that his family came from Armagh. He had recently been writing a biography of the English hostess Sibyl Colefax. He found references to the Duchess of Windsor when he was going through various papers connected with his project. He'd contacted Maître Blum, knowing her to be the Duchess's spokesperson, because he wanted to verify certain information. He had visualized Suzanne Blum as a young woman. In the letter he wrote he had addressed her as "Miss Blum." She had not liked this at all. She still often chided him and reminded him of his mistake. He said that his Master could be a bit like an elephant. There was a saying that an elephant never forgets.

When he had gone over to Paris to see her, they had immediately felt very affiliated to each other. Now he was studying law with her. He adored his life in Paris with her and she had allowed him to move into her apartment. He had become so close to Maître Blum that she often invited him to stay with her in her *propriété* in the French countryside.

I asked him what Maître Blum's propriété was like. Was it a château? Surely Maître Blum had to live in a castle.

This guess was quite wrong. It turned out Maître Blum did not live in a château. But she lived in a house that looked on to a castle. You could see a château if you looked out of any of her windows.

When I heard this it seemed very fitting. For in a sense the Duchess was some kind of castle for Maître Blum. And although the old lawyer sometimes seemed to forget it, she herself had not made the King of England leave his throne.

When the Duke made his famous abdication speech in which he explained that he had given up the Crown because its burdens would be too heavy "without the help and support of the woman I love," the English-speaking world had stood still for seventy seconds. Millions of people had wept as they listened on the radio. Even in New York cars and taxis had pulled onto the side of the road because their drivers had started crying to the point that they could no longer see the road through their tears. H. L. Mencken had said that the Duke's speech was "the greatest news story since the Resurrection." Yet at the historical moment when the Duke spoke of "the woman he loved," he had not been speaking of Maître Blum.

Nor had he given Maître Blum Queen Alexandra's jewels. King George VI had never deprived Maître Blum of the right to be called "Your Royal Highness." International hostesses had never fretted over their dilemma as to whether or not they should address Maître Blum as "Ma'am" and curtsy to her when they shook her hand. It was unlikely that Maître Blum had ever fallen in love with a figure as dissolute and disloyal as Jimmy Donahue who spread rumors all over the New York homosexual grapevine that no one "gave a blow job like the Duchess," and then ruined his tribute by adding "sleeping with the Duchess is like sleeping with the Ancient Mariner."

Maître Blum's life had been long and varied but never had she been voted the world's best-dressed woman several years in succession. And it was doubtful that with her anal character she'd ever bought fifty-six pairs of shoes at a time.

Then last, but much the most important, Maître Blum was not lying in misery in a gray palatial house on the fringe of the Bois de Boulogne. In reality, rather than dreams, Maître Blum was not the Duchess of Windsor. She only looked from a metaphorical peephole on to the Duchess. It was therefore agreeable to learn that in the French countryside Maître Blum had chosen to live in a situation that typified so much of her life.

"Don't you think that Maître Blum is a very good-looking woman?" Michael Bloch asked me.

I agreed she looked very striking and this seemed to delight him. I thanked him for the drink. I was getting claustrophobia in his company.

As I went out to look for a taxi he came rushing after me, looking flustered. "For God's sake will you make Mr. Wyndham send Maître Blum the copies of her Snowdon photographs. If she doesn't get them very soon there is really going to be hell to pay!"

CHAPTER TWELVE

Once I got back to my Paris hotel, I thought about Maître Blum, and I felt annoyed. Her behavior during the interview had really been infuriating. By placing her interesting album on my knee and then instantly grabbing it away before I'd had time to look at it, she had behaved very much as she had behaved to Lady Mosley over the matter of the Duchess's love letters. It was disgusting that Maître Blum could get such joy from any opportunity that gave her the power to disappoint.

And then there had been the General's lost shoulder. I could not easily forgive her for that. Michael Bloch claimed Maître Blum had a special relationship with the Duchess. Maître Blum often became unreliable when speaking of her client, but it was just possible to excuse her on the grounds that she was emotionally biased. But no one had ever told me that Maître Blum had a special relationship with her husband. She had not the slightest excuse for telling me lies about the General's shoulder.

I even wondered if her statement about her husband had not been defamatory, whether some other lawyer should not sue her on General Spillmann's behalf. Maître Blum had tried to sue *The New York Times* for printing that her husband was retired and it appeared that under French law she had correct grounds to take this surprising action. Surely a shoulderless General would be a figure far less reassuring than a retired one. He wouldn't be able to take proper control of his gun. The more I thought about the untruth that Maître Blum had told me, the more irritated I got.

It seemed to me that Maître Blum had been profoundly silly. By wreaking havoc with the interview she had acted against her own interests. I cared very little whether or not her photographs were published. If she made it impossible to write her profile, it caused me little distress.

I was starting to feel far more interested in trying to put emotional pressure on the recalcitrant and over-nervous friends of the Duchess in order to persuade them to force their way into her house so that it could be ascertained precisely what Maître Blum was doing to her.

Ever since I'd been told about the Maître's obsessional admiration for superhuman courage I'd begun to wonder if the Duchess had been allowed any adequate and appropriate painkiller since she had been "Blumed." When the Maître had arranged for the Duchess to have the series of ghastly operations that Lady Mosley had described to me, had Maître Blum stinted on her anesthetic?

I had the suspicion that Maître Blum might abhor the idea of all pain relievers just as much as she loathed vodka. She could say that they were not at all advisable for the Duchess's blood pressure.

Michael Bloch had claimed that her feelings for the Duchess were of a romantic nature, but Maître Blum appeared to be excessive in all things, and I felt that the very force and intoxication of her romantic feelings might easily be proving disastrous for their recipient. They could lead to her imposing her own ideas of perfection on her love object. They could allow her to demand a display of superhuman physical bravery from the Duchess when Wallis Windsor had never claimed to possess any such courageous qualities.

Even if the Duchess sometimes failed in the aspirations Maître Blum set for her, even if she sometimes howled all night like a wounded animal, and screamed aloud for painkiller, there was no one likely to report it. Her house was too sealed and isolated. It was guarded like a fortress. Her lawyer was a master of the art of intimidation. If the Duchess was to display the most miserable signs of human frailty, Maître Blum would be in a perfect position to see that they were hushed up. She seemed to derive great pleasure from hushing up any aspects of the Duchess's character which she saw as detracting from the glory of the woman whom she'd made her idol.

And even if the Duchess was in a state of coma, which was very likely despite her lawyer's claim that she was still talkative, there was no certainty that she was immune to any feeling. I'd remembered once seeing a boy who had suffered head injuries from which he was never to recover. When I visited him he was lying in hospital with the inevitable pipes up his nose. He was in an apparent coma but every time his tubes were changed the procedure appeared to agonize him and tears would start rolling down his cheeks. The boy had devoted relatives and friends who became increasingly frantic and distressed by the sight of his soundless weeping. They begged his doctors to give him painkiller. At first the medical establishment treated them dismissively and they were told that his tears were "merely reflex" and they were not a sign that the patient was suffering. His relatives were stubborn and they continued to pester until his doctors weakened and they gave him some analgesic. The moment the boy was given painkiller he ceased to cry and he no longer seemed to suffer any further physical discomfort. This phenomenon gave credence to the idea that while there is life there can always be pain.

If the Duchess was enduring a timeless agony which she was unable to articulate, Maître Blum had seen to it that she had no one able to make any fuss and special pleadings on her behalf. Her doctors would be professionally obligated to employ every modern medical method in order to prolong her life. And the Maître would always want her Duchess to courageously endure. The Duchess had conquered the love of the Prince of Wales. She had conquered world fashion. But her conquests had never been military. If Maître Blum was asking her to die a soldier's death it seemed monstrously unfair.

Maître Blum seemed incapable of sustaining any idea without allowing it to become an *idée fixe*. At the moment she was obsessed by the publication of her photographs by Lord Snowdon. If this was comic it was harmless. But some of her other obsessive ideas might not be so innocuous.

There seemed to be only one interesting question worth asking her. For whatever reasons, romantic or otherwise, was she being downright cruel to the helpless wreckage of a woman I had seen in the photographs of

the Spanish paparazzi? As there was not the slightest like-
lihood she would answer it with any honesty, I saw little
point in having any more dealings with her.

And then there had been her death threat. Originally
I had laughed it off as one of the ravings of a becrazed
old woman. But now that I had received more and
more evidence of the ruthlessness of which she was capable, I was starting to wonder if it might not be foolhardy
to disregard her warnings. If she'd always been enraged
by everything that appeared in print about the Duchess,
quite regardless if it was sickly flattering, she might take an
even fiercer stance against the idiot who tried to write
about her.

I thought about all the felons that Maître Blum most
probably had aided. She must have many contacts in the
French underworld. Any dubious figure who had been
spared from the consequences of his criminal acts by her
brilliant legal representation would owe her an inestimable
favor. I had no wish for Maître Blum to arrange to see that
I was "subdued" in the same way that her husband, the
General, had subdued the inhabitants of Morocco. It
wouldn't help me if she were to do it "humanely."

In a mood of revulsion against her, and in a mood that
was marred by cowardice, I telephoned Maître Blum, and
inevitably it was Michael Bloch who answered. I told him
that as Maître Blum was clearly not anxious to cooperate,
I had decided to abandon the whole idea of writing her
profile.

Michael Bloch sounded extremely stuttery and upset.
Although the Snowdon photographs were not mentioned,

it was clear that their publication was in grave jeopardy. I was glad I wasn't sharing an apartment with Maître Blum and I didn't envy Michael Bloch.

He said he would speak to his Master. He would try to persuade her to be more flexible about releasing information on her cases. He would speak to me after he had conferred with her.

Michael Bloch telephoned me again all too quickly. Maître Blum and I were locked in a clash of wills. In our pointless little battle my strengths and powers of blackmail were for once stronger than hers. I realized with little pleasure that I seemed to be winning. If she had suddenly agreed to cooperate, I recognized with dread that I was going to end up writing her profile.

Michael Bloch said that he would soon be going to England. Once I got back to London he'd bring round some old newspaper-clippings that would give me some information about Maître Blum's most famous cases.

Soon after I got back to London, I read in the papers that the Duchess of Windsor had been admitted to the American Hospital. Maître Blum would have been pleased to see that the Duchess could still make the British headlines.

I decided to telephone Maître Blum to ask her what was wrong with the Duchess. If the Duchess had been in pain all these last years maybe she was at last going to be released and nature was finally going to triumph over the resources of science.

Maître Blum was not at all reassuring on that count. She said that there was nothing wrong with the Duchess.

She needn't have really gone to the hospital at all. She was only having tests.

Lady Mosley had told me that the Duchess was always put in the American hospital when Georges, her butler, went on holiday. Maître Blum's calm attitude towards the present hospitalization of the Duchess suggested that the seeming crisis in her health was caused by nothing more serious than Georges' desire to take a trip to the Greek Isles or the South of France.

"How is the Duchess?" Once again I asked Maître Blum the same useless question. She gave me such an exalted answer. She sounded more demented than she'd ever seemed before.

"The Duchess is magnificent! *Elle parle, elle parle.* She never stops speaking! She is beautiful like you cannot imagine. She is covered with flowers!"

It was a very strange picture and not entirely reassuring. The Duchess was talking her head off in the American Hospital in Paris, her butler was swimming in the blue seas of some sunny seaside resort, and the Duchess was being covered by flowers either by Maître Blum or by Michael Bloch.

"Will the Duchess's will be published when she dies?" I was risking a blast and predictably I got one.

"The Duchess's will is never going to be published!" Maître Blum's voice rose in a scream of anguish. "If I have anything to do with it, the Duchess's will is never going to be published. Never, never, never . . ."

Soon after this I received a telephone call from Michael Bloch. He was speaking from Paris. "General Spillmann has died!" he gasped.

This was indeed shocking news. The General must have taken up some small but vital part of Maître Blum's prodigious energies. This dynamic old woman now had nothing at all to deflect her from devoting her entire life to the resuscitation of the Duchess of Windsor.

Michael Bloch said that Maître Blum was being very brave. In the last days of the General's life there had been all the usual agonizing questions and decisions as to whether certain medical procedures should be applied or not.

I asked if Maître Blum was being almost superhumanly courageous. My question was intended to be provocative. Michael took it as a serious query and nodded agreement.

Bloch had never seen anything like the funeral that Maître Blum had given her husband. Maître Blum was now swathed in black veils and widow's weeds. She had pulled down all the blinds in the rue de Varenne and now she was sitting there like Electra. She had arranged for all her stationery to be ringed with a thick band of black. Michael Bloch said that he would soon be bringing me a bunch of Maître Blum's news-clippings.

After hearing about the General's death, I felt I ought to speak to Maître Blum. Maybe Maître Blum was genuinely very sad about his loss. I had never seen her with her husband. Their relationship could have been much warmer than I give her credit for. Admittedly, Maître Blum still had the Duchess of Windsor. But it was obscure how much companionship and support the Duchess, at this point, could give anyone.

I reached Maître Blum by telephone. I muttered that I was sorry to hear the news. Maître Blum merely grunted. "I still have not received my Snowdon photographs!" Her tone of accusation was just as snarling and belligerent as ever. Her impatient grunt was the only reference she made to her bereavement. It seemed that Maître Blum could go through the Valley of Death and keep her preoccupations and her priorities intact.

The following day an obituary of her husband appeared in the London *Times*. The death of obscure French generals can often go unmentioned in English newspapers. General Spillmann's obituary was therefore some kind of triumph of string-pulling on the part of Maître Blum. The tribute was written by Michael Bloch, but the ink of his Master's mentality flowed from his pen.

"No one who met General Spillmann . . . can fail to have been struck by his simple dignity and extraordinary perception of human affairs."

It was reassuring to see the speed with which Maître Blum's pet themes emerged within the very first paragraph.

There was the Duchess of Windsor's "simple dignity." It was nice that Maître Blum had extended the same tribute to her defunct spouse. And there was the Duchess's "extraordinary perception of human affairs." I believed that Maître Blum would be happy to claim that Wallis Windsor retained just such astonishing intuitions even now.

Michael Bloch's obituary of the late General continued in a pleasantly predictable vein. Like his wife, the General was *de bonne famille*, hailing from a notable old German Protestant family.

The General's mother had become the Baroness Fabvier; she had been a famous beauty and an intimate friend of Proust.

Later I looked up General Spillman's mother in George Painter's *Proust*; I found no mention of her there. I have since checked with various Proustian experts and no one has yet traced her. Her close friendship with Proust can therefore still be questioned. There remains the doubt that it may resemble the General's lost shoulder.

Michael Bloch's obituary for Maître Blum's husband meandered on like a country stream. It described how the General had served at St. Cyr and in the First World War. In 1920 he had set off for Morocco, which "he perhaps loved and understood better than any of his countrymen." Autocratically, General Spillmann had apparently believed that France was "history's guest" in Morocco.

Maître Blum's dead husband was also depicted as "a profound student of the native civilization." When General Spillmann had led the Goums against the savage tribes of the interior, according to the obituary the "tribesmen often came to love their sympathetic conqueror."

Michael Bloch's tribute movingly concluded with the information that when the General had married Maître Suzanne Blum, the Duchess of Windsor's advocate, the charm and wit of the couple had made them among the most popular people in Paris.

Not long after I'd read his obituary, Michael Bloch telephoned me from London. He'd arrived with a large envelope of press-cuttings from Maître Blum. Where would I meet him so that he could give them to me? I suggested the bar in the Carlton Tower Hotel in Cadogan Square. That seemed as good a place as any.

Michael Bloch sounded horrified. The Carlton Tower

bar was not nearly private enough for a meeting of such a confidential nature. There would be other people there. We might be overheard.

I insisted we meet in the bar of the Carlton Tower Hotel. He was only going to hand me over some old press-clippings. I became stubborn because I found Michael Bloch's attitude annoying. He capitulated but in the gravest possible manner. He repeated that there was great risk in our meeting in the spot I'd chosen. But if I insisted, there was little he could do.

I was the first to arrive at the Carlton Tower Hotel. There were other people in the bar, just as Michael Bloch had feared. They were mostly cigar-smoking American and Iranian businessmen who were talking very intently about deals, transactions, and dollars. It seemed most unlikely that Maître Blum's press-clippings could distract such prosperous figures from the subjects that all-absorbed them.

Eventually Michael Bloch appeared clutching a fat yellow envelope. He nervously viewed the American and Iranian businessmen. When he sat down he surreptitiously passed me the yellow envelope under the table. Later when I looked at it, I saw it had an inscription written in Michael Bloch's hand: "Master's Clippings."

Michael Bloch announced that he was in a jubilant mood. He had just got an advance from Weidenfeld and Nicolson. They wanted him to write a book about the Duke of Windsor in the Bahamas.

"Hasn't the Duke in the Bahamas been fairly well covered already?" I asked.

He admitted that many people had written on the

subject. "But none of them have been sufficiently pro-Duke."

When I heard about Michael Bloch's project I nodded politely. I still wondered if he would find his task as easy as he now seemed to think. How could any serious "pro-Duke" book be written about the Windsors' stay in the Bahamas?

Maître Blum claimed that *Ich Dien* (I serve) dominated the Duke of Windsor's aspirations. Once he married the twice divorced Wallis Simpson, the Duke was given little opportunity to carry out his Prince of Wales motto.

The Duke was allowed to govern the Bahamas by Winston Churchill who was loyal to him in an old-school-tie fashion. Churchill had been a friend while the Duke was Prince of Wales. After the abdication, the Duke and his American wife with their pro-Hitler sympathies became an acute embarrassment to the British government. The Duke was of royal blood but by his defection he found himself in a netherworld where he was no longer seen as royal by his own country and yet he was curtsied to in New York and turned into an American royalty. He was treated as an emperor whenever he took the Duchess to the Colony Club and the Waldorf Astoria.

As Prince of Wales, the Duke of Windsor had enjoyed immense popularity in Great Britain. He was handsome and blond and he seemed a perfect figure to fill the role of a glamorous prince. He made various attempts to behave more democratically than his parents, George V and Queen Mary. He joined the army and made friends with British servicemen. Just before he abdicated, he toured the mining villages in Wales and he was upset by their desperation and poverty. It was then that he gave his famous statement which made him regarded as a working class savior. He made the famous remark "something must be done."

Even if the Duke's folk-hero popularity while still Prince of Wales was spurious, it existed. Many accounts written in that period describe him as possessing "magic." Lady Diana Cooper told me that there was nothing more touching than the sight of his "young golden head" moving through the crowds.

The Duke of Windsor's popularity was one of the factors that caused unease for it was seen as a threat to his brother, George VI, the current British monarch who had succeeded him and was much less golden-haired, and a shy and stuttery, far less dashing figure. The Duke was therefore never encouraged to return to England, nor was he offered any posts by which he could serve his country in an official capacity.

The governorship of the Bahamas was the one exception. Winston Churchill offered it to him only because Great Britain was at war and he felt that it was highly advisable to remove the controversial Duke and his divorcée wife as far from Europe as possible. At that particular point in history the honor of being allowed to govern the Bahamas was not one that was fought over in English diplomatic circles. The islands had little strategic military value for the British. When the Duke was offered the Bahamian governorship, he was being insulted by his countrymen and the Duchess recognized it more clearly than he did.

She knew that her husband had been offered a dud post. The Windsors still accepted the only official position that was offered to them. Although the Duke had renounced the throne, he was not willing to renounce all forms of power. The European conflict had made it difficult for the Duke to know in which country he could set up a royal-type residence suitable for the wife he regarded as his rightful Queen. Hitler had rejected his offer for his services. The Duke accepted the governorship of the Bahamas as a very last resort.

Winston Churchill had yet another well-considered reason for trying to make the Windsors move to a far-flung British colonial outpost. In wartime the diplomatic rulers of Britain's colonies could not expect to be received by the royal family as they were in times of peace. If it had not been for the war, the Duke of Windsor could have demanded that as a governor general he and his wife be invited to Buckingham Palace. Winston Churchill was wily enough to know that under wartime conditions the Duke could not create any unpleasantness on this delicate issue.

In the midsummer of 1940 the Duke of Windsor and his wife arrived in Nassau to take up their duties. They had deliberately constricted the amount of luggage which they brought with them. As the Duke's homeland was suffering heavy German bombardment, it was thought tactful that Britain's governor general should keep a low profile. When the Windsors drew into the Nassau harbor, only fifty-seven pieces of baggage and all the dogs were carried down the gangplank. They brought with them only two cases of champagne, two cases of gin, and two cases of port. The rest of their belongings were shipped secretly and separately.

The Windsors had hardly unpacked when they learned that Buckingham Palace had issued orders that the Duchess was not to be called "Your Royal Highness." Nor was the Duchess to be curtsied to. When the Duke heard that his wife was to be refused these protocol honors he became hysterical. He was going to see "that she damn well got them—every single one of them!"

In the first dinner of welcome given by Sir Frederick Williams-Taylor, the waiters brought the platters of food to the Duke before they served the Duchess. The Duke was as good as his word. He instructed them angrily to "serve the Duchess first." The waiters obeyed him but the guests were made to feel uncomfortable.

The Duchess very soon grew to hate the Bahamas. She felt it was an insult that her husband had been asked to govern "these godforsaken islands." She described her post as "St. Helena—1940 style." With her passion for beautiful interiors she was appalled by the state of the Government House. The woodwork was riddled with rot and termites. And the Duchess described the dining room as looking like a "ski-hut in Norway."

The Duke sent an angry cable to the minister for the Colonies: "Impossible to occupy . . . it will take at least two months to make it habitable."

While I was wondering how Michael Bloch would write his "pro-Duke" book I assumed he'd have to take a position pleasing to feminists and plead that from the very beginning of his governorship the Duke had always put the concerns of the Duchess first.

Once the Windsors settled into the Bahamas, Michael Bloch might find it harder to make a very impressive case for the Duke's handling of his responsibilities. It could be argued that the Duchess took over her position in a more memorable fashion than her husband.

Wallis Windsor totally redecorated Government House, in a modernistic style with occasional Regency touches. She introduced New York wallpapers and she painted one room exactly the same shade of her favorite face powder.

She transformed what had once been "an awful old barn." She furnished it with low, glass-topped cocktail tables, open cupboards that displayed Sèvres china, and she dotted it with bamboo chairs. She filled the house with so many tropical flowers, it seemed like a garden.

She hung her own portrait by Brockhurst over the mantelpiece and placed a photograph of her mother-in-law, Queen Mary, on the Duke's desk. In this photograph Queen Mary looked extremely grim and at her most forbidding. "Can't we get a better picture of Mother?" the Duke once asked her. "No," the Duchess told him firmly, "that is the best one, dear." She wanted her husband to be reminded that he'd lost little that was desirable when he'd forfeited the affections of his family.

The door of Government House was an eyesore. This provided a challenge for the Duchess. It was venerable and she was advised not to replace it, for it had withstood many hurricanes. She surmounted this problem with her usual panache. She arranged to have its upper half covered with a black glass panel on which, in white, there was printed her husband's motto *Honi soit qui mal y pense*.

The Duchess revitalized Government House at a cost

of 21,000 dollars, including 1,500 dollars for a new dining room table which she made dazzling with very intricate floral decorations and non-eye-level ivory-colored candles. The House of Assembly had only assigned her 6,000 dollars as her wartime budget. She ignored these financial considerations. When she was criticized, she explained to the press "I must make a home for him. That's why I'm doing this place over; so we can live in it in comfort as a home. All his life he has traveled, and a palace to come back to is not always a home."

When Princess Alice, Countess of Athlone came to visit her cousin, the Duke of Windsor, she overcame her royal prejudice and she praised the Duchess's efforts. She grudgingly admitted that Government House in the Bahamas had been much improved by the Duchess.

Seeing herself exiled like Napoleon, for she was unable to make many visits to New York because of the war, the Duchess found it hard to create a perfect tropical wardrobe. She therefore arranged for fitters and seamstresses from New York to be flown to her. Inevitably Mainbocher sent her an envoy, and so did Hattie Carnegie. The star fitters of these great dressmakers arrived with silk and shantung and tulle. They brought with them great rolls of voile, linen, and piqué as well as plaster busts of the Duchess. They tried their dresses on these busts in the upper rooms of Government House because the Duchess had her duties to perform and it was understood they must not waste her time with fittings.

Meanwhile the Duke played golf. He also did what he'd originally done when he first flirted with the Duchess at Fort Belvedere—after dinner he played solos on the Scottish bagpipes. Lady Diana Cooper had always complained that the Duke of Windsor loved to torture his guests with these instruments. "No one could quite tell if he was playing horribly out of tune, like it sounded. The Duke always cheated a bit because we'd have known if he'd tried to entertain us on the violin."

The Duchess of Windsor was president of the Bahamian Red Cross. She therefore had to prepare accommodations and facilities for the victims of British and American torpedoed ships. She was informed she would have to help four thousand wounded seamen. As the only Red Cross building on the islands had been burned to the ground, the Duchess of Windsor converted an abandoned casino into a hostel for the survivors. "Aren't I the busy bee?" she laughed and then added with poignancy, "But I wish it were somewhere else . . ."

The Windsors, meanwhile, frequented the choicest nightclubs in the Bahamas, the Emerald Beach and the Porcupine.

If Michael Bloch was trying to write a "pro-Duke" book I could only assume that Maître Blum would insist that this be the fact she would consider the most important to be swiftly edited and eradicated. It was at these clubs that the Duke made a great friend of a wealthy Swede called Axel Wenner-Gren. Before the outbreak of war this man had been very close to Goering. Mr. Wenner-Gren owned fish-canning and real-estate interests in the Bahamas. He provided employment for a thousand local workers. When I was speculating as to how Michael Bloch would write his "pro-Duke" book, I wondered if he would use this fact to justify the Duke's friendship with this dubious figure. It would tally neatly with Maître Blum's insistence that the Duke's controversial visit to Hitler was inspired by his concern for the German worker.

Mr. Wenner-Gren provided jobs on a depressed island but he had lucrative business sidelines. He manufactured armaments. He was therefore placed on the blacklist of the U.S. Department of State. The Duke of Windsor was soon forced to sign a warrant that expelled his friend from the Bahamas although he had received endless hospitality on the enterprising Swede's yacht.

It was possible that Michael Bloch with all fairness could say the Duke had bad luck with his friends when he was governing the Bahamas. Sir Harry Oakes, another self-made millionaire who was also very close to the Duke, was murdered. The Windsors had been Sir Harry's guest in the period when the Duchess was revolutionizing Government House. At the time the Duke was very much criticized for his handling of the case. But now it seemed he had Michael Bloch to defend him.

Instead of bringing in Scotland Yard to investigate the murder, the Duke called in a detective from Miami whom he'd once employed as a bodyguard. The Duke's detective was not very effective. The crime was never solved and Sir Harry Oakes's murderer is still at large.

There were many rumors that the Duke of Windsor could have cleared up the murder case if he had chosen to. Some thought Sir Harry was the victim of various gangster figures who were anxious to establish casino rights on the island and the Duke was a party to these interests. The whole case still remains murky and, seeing Michael Bloch wriggling and furtive in the Carlton Tower bar, I was curious as to how he would clarify it.

There is only one rumor that could explain the Duke's refusal to bring Scotland Yard into the Oakes investigation. The Duke is meant to have received a warning from the Mafia. They advised him not to seek justice for the murderer. If he did so, they threatened to slash the face of the Duchess. The Duke was besotted with his wife. He therefore might be excused if he was cowardly and mishandled his duty over this matter.

After we had ordered drinks, Michael Bloch suddenly informed me that Maître Blum had given him access to the Duke of Windsor's letters. I asked if he'd been given any of the Duchess's love letters. He sadly shook his head. She paid him only in letters that the Duke of Windsor had written from the Bahamas. Maître Blum enjoyed exerting total control and the irregular coin with which she paid this young man could not give him much of a feeling of financial independence. If Michael Bloch were to go out to eat in a Parisian café, the waiters would hardly be overjoyed if he fished in his pocket and tried to pay for his meal by waving some crumpled and boring letter from the late Duke.

I wondered if the Duchess's butler, Georges, was paid for his services in the form of Windsor correspondence. Maybe he insisted on some more solid form of remuneration. I knew it would be useless to ask Maître Blum that question.

I asked Michael Bloch if he had seen the Duchess's love letters. He claimed that Maître Blum had shown them to him. He described them as very "lovey dovey." Lady Mosley had doubted they existed because the Windsors were so rarely apart except for their period of enforced separation when the Duchess was getting her divorce from Ernest Simpson. Michael Bloch cleared this matter up. The love letters were notes that the Duke liked to slip under the Duchess's bedroom door. They didn't sound very interesting, but Michael Bloch maintained they were going to "change the face of the abdication." Later I asked Lady Mosley if she believed this might be true. The absurdity of this possibility astonished her. "Nothing is ever going to change the face of the abdication! The abdication was the abdication—and that was that . . ."

As we sat drinking in this London hotel, Michael Bloch once again implored me to treat Maître Blum's press-clippings with the utmost secrecy. I told him that I failed to see why Maître Blum's packet had to be treated as a confidential item of a highly explosive nature.

He then became embarrassed. But after much nervous coughing, he gave an answer. All his seemingly neurotic terror about the yellow envelope was then explained. As a lawyer, Maître Blum had taken a legal oath similar to the Hippocratic oath that is taken by doctors. She had sworn she would never make use of her clients in order to seek publicity for herself, and thereby promote her own career. I had thought Maître Blum was being perverse when she refused to tell me anything about her famous law cases. Her behavior at that point had been totally correct.

I'd also misjudged Michael Bloch when he insisted on such secrecy when he handed me Maître Blum's news-clippings. Maître Blum was breaking her oath by giving them to me, and if it were ever to be discovered, Maître Blum could be struck from the French legal bar. For Maître Blum, the whole issue was one of a colossal gravity. Driven by her reckless longing to get her Snowdon photographs into the newspapers, Maître Blum was risking disgrace and the ruination of her long and eminent legal career. And for the old lawyer it was even more serious than that, for she was risking the loss of the only thing she seemed to care about in the universe. If she were struck from the French bar, Maître Blum might actually lose the Duchess.

While I was trying to imagine what such a loss would mean to Maître Blum, Michael Bloch interrupted my reverie saying that he had to go back home to telephone his Master.

After Michael Bloch had left, I went home and read Maître Blum's press-clippings. The newspaper items that she had sent me represented what she saw as the high points of her long life and her selection was therefore interesting. The first cutting I looked at startled me. It was a fashion drawing of Maître Blum, a head and shoulders outline that depicted her oriental profile. She was wearing a white tippet. Underneath it there was a caption which read "The celebrated lawyer Maître Blum wears a white ermine stole when she attends galas in Paris."

For years Maître Blum had handled the Duchess of Windsor's publicity and dealt with the international press

when she was representing her Hollywood clients. One
would have expected her to have become worldly. Yet she
seemed to have remained an innocent. There was something very unsophisticated in the way she was so proud of
this idiotic and pointless clipping.

The effect of the fat packet of press-clippings Maître
Blum had sent to me was depressing. Time had browned
them, just as time was browning her hands. For in the
jumble of old news reports there lay buried the impressive
Maître Blum. There was an account of her suit in which
she won one million dollars for Warner Brothers. There
was the case an enraged Stravinsky had brought against
Paramount when they turned *The Firebird* into a sentimental waltz. He was opposed in court by Maître Blum and
suffered a predictable fate. He was awarded a farthing's
damages.

There was also an account of the vast alimony that
Maître Blum obtained for Rita Hayworth when she got
her divorce from Aly Khan. There were the cases of Coc-
teau and Sartre—their triumphs because Maître Blum had
been on their side. She had been chief witness at the wedding of the clarinetist Sidney Bechet. Merle Oberon had
got married to Sir Alexander Korda in Maître Blum's
house. Presumably both these figures were rewarding her
for the invaluable legal services she had afforded them.
Maître Blum had arranged to get Douglas Fairbanks divorced and remarried with such speed that she became
known in the Paris press as "Cupid."

There was the report of a case in which a dancer at
the Paris Opera had sued for injuries incurred during her

work. The dancer had been directed to throw herself backwards into the arms of the chorus. When she had done so the chorus had failed to catch her. As a result she had taken a flat fall and sustained a horrible injury to her spine. She had been lucky enough to have Maître Blum representing her in court. She was awarded heavy damages after Maître Blum had risen to her feet and with her habitual eloquence made the ringing statement "In every sense my client has been let down."

Looking through the aged lawyer's clippings, which were dotted with many of the most famous names of her era, one got the impression that those who had Maître Blum legally behind them had always won. For those who had been opposed by her, it seemed to have been total disaster.

Representing the vast financial concerns of Paramount, Warner Brothers, and Metro Goldwyn Mayer, Maître Blum came looming out of her news-clippings like a giant Portia quite invincible in her flowing black lawyer's gown.

Then running alongside the mighty torrent of her legal success, there was the steady stream of her triumphs as a novelist. For included in Maître Blum's packet were all the full-length reviews that had acclaimed the publication of her seven books. Rarely had I seen the novels of any writer treated with quite such enthusiasm and reverence. When a distinguished French critic said she had written *un veritable coup de Maître*, his praise compared to the others was lukewarm.

Her dynamic career had been interrupted by the war when she had been forced to flee to New York to escape the Nazis. In an interview she had given many years later, there was a pathos to a statement that Maître Blum had made: "I realized then I would have to start again." In the same interview she made another announcement that showed the domineering side of her nature. Maître Blum said she only ever wanted to be known as "Maître." She'd then added "even my husbands have called me that."

Having forged such a successful career against the opposition of her family and the society of her time, it must have been despairing for Maître Blum to find herself in the United States without any legal practice. But with courage and resourcefulness she had obtained an American degree. While the Duchess had spent her exile in the Bahamas painting rooms in Government House the same color as her powder puff, Maître Blum had spent a much more exacting exile surmounting the problems of obtaining a degree in an unfamiliar language and doing valuable work for French refugees.

And yet where did all this fit with the fashion drawing of the white ermine stole that she seemed so proud of? And where did it fit in with an even odder page from the French newspapers that Maître Blum had included with her cuttings? When I first read it, I was baffled. I searched and searched the newspaper print, but I couldn't find Maître Blum's name. Yet presumably she had to be mentioned somewhere. The more I searched, the more I failed to find it. I had just decided there had been an error when she had sent me this page, for it contained nothing that had anything to do with her. Then exactly as in those puzzles you find in children's books where you are expected to pick out the hidden figure of a rabbit or a toy drum that has deliberately been concealed within the confusing lines of a greater landscape, Maître Blum suddenly jumped out of the page. I then couldn't understand why I'd failed to see her earlier. I'd been searching for her name in the newsprint and I'd not noticed that in the page she had sent me there was a picture of Queen Elizabeth that had been taken during a visit she had once made to France. The Queen was attending a Paris soiree and she was wearing a fur and a tiara. And behind her was a tiny little white blob of a person whose face had escaped the proper focus of the camera. This blurred and tiny person was craning forward in desperation, trying to get herself into the picture, and she was gazing at the Queen with rapt adoration. And dismal as it was to realize it, this background figure who was pressing herself up to the Queen was none other than Maître Blum.

If something as abstract as disloyalty could be photographed, this old press picture had made a good attempt to capture it. What had happened to Maître Blum's notorious role as the fearless defender of the Duchess of Windsor in her traditional feud with the British royal family? After all the distress Maître Blum had caused her late husband, the humane General Spillmann, when she kept denouncing the royal family for their cold treatment of her client, the moment that the Queen arrived in Paris, it seemed that Maître Blum was prepared to be a turncoat and transfer her adoration.

Maître Blum must have tenaciously elbowed through hundreds of guests at the soiree in order to get as close to the Queen of England as she had managed. She had got herself so close that she had made herself almost invisible for her body had blended into the Queen's fur. And Queen Elizabeth seemed totally unaware that Maître Blum was so near to her, that the Duchess of Windsor's lawyer was gazing up at her with slobbering love and wonder.

Maître Blum obviously took great pride in her presence in this photograph. Maître Blum's life had been much longer and more distinguished than that of many women of her generation. Yet her genuine achievements seemed to have given her little sense of accomplishment, it was as if they had totally failed to give her any feeling of identity.

She had chosen to live in a French country house that looked onto a castle and thereby she could continually peep at it through her window. She was quite rich enough to have bought herself some French château which she could have inhabited. But she seemed to feel more comfortable peeping at castles rather than owning them. Every day of her life in recent years she went to the house of the prostrate Duchess of Windsor and crept into her bedroom in order to gaze at her.

Maître Blum could have moved in with the Duchess and made her beautiful historic house in the Bois de Boulogne her own.

As she had been so consummately successful in cutting off the Duchess from all interfering outside sources, there was no one to make any protest; there was not a soul to prevent her from taking an action that might seem to lead to the fulfillment of her most cherished dreams.

Maître Blum could have thrown out all the Duchess

of Windsor's decorative and distinctive furniture and replaced it with her own ugly, uncomfortable, forbidding
possessions.

She could have painstakingly ill-arranged her own hid-
eously fake antiques so that every trace of the legendary
and welcoming atmosphere the Duchess had created was
destroyed and visitors would have trembled, feeling only
the chill of an ambience that reflected the most dour and
inhospitable side of Maître Blum's nature.

The old lawyer could have set up a cot beside the
Duchess's bed and day and night she could have listened
to all the talking which she claimed Wallis Windsor did,
and whatever intimate conversations she entertained with
the Duchess she could have kept as a hugely royal and
personal secret.

But Maître Blum had not chosen to make these seemingly sensible arrangements even though she could have
been spared from so much tedious commuting as she strug-
gled to the bedside of the Duchess and had to endure endless ennui as she sat gridlocked in the asphyxiating fumes
and horrible honking of the Parisian traffic.

Yet despite all inconvenience to herself she had chosen
to remain in her dingy apartment in the rue de Varenne
where she was near to the French prime minister but not too
near him. In some ways Maître Blum could be quite a
wise old woman. She recognized that sometimes too much
proximity can make moth holes in the sails of romance.

Another significant item she had sent me in the yellow
packet was a clipping Maître Blum had painstakingly cut
out from some old French gossip column. It listed the

names of the diners at a fashionable restaurant in the South of France. At one table there had been Prince Aly Khan dining with Princess Soraya. At another table there had been Maître Blum dining with the local prefect of police.

In Maître Blum's terms, she would seem to have been dining at the wrong table. But she clearly didn't see it like that. She had felt it was worth sending me the cutting. For Maître Blum, presumably, it had tremendous interest for it displayed her once again in her favorite position of dazzled onlooker to a glamor that was always at a certain remove from her. The local prefect of police most probably had a very difficult and unrewarding dinner when he'd supped with Maître Blum that night. Her attention must have kept wandering away from him as she swooned over the sight of the prince and the princess.

She would have been bored to the point of distraction if the unfortunate man had tried to regale her with any matters he might rightly consider to be of professional interest to her.

When Maître Blum had been given such a unique opportunity to gaze from close quarters upon a couple of "crowned heads," surely she'd have responded with all her brutal genius for expressing rudeness if the prefect of police had tried to make her listen to any matters of local and legal importance.

Reading Maître Blum's press-cuttings one got the impression that her values were totally askew. The Duchess of Windsor would always be a legendary figure, but only because of the inherited position of the man she had managed to marry. The Duchess had arranged to have spectacular floral arrangements on her dinner table, she'd much improved Government House in the Bahamas, and she'd set many dress fashions, but otherwise her achievements were negligible. Maître Blum had made herself celebrated and world famous and feared entirely through her own drive and intelligence. Whether one liked her or not, Maître Blum existed as a hugely forceful and unique personality in her own right. There was no obvious need for her to lavish her adulation on a woman who had achieved her fame only through marriage—particularly at a point where this woman had virtually ceased to exist at all.

Even if one found Maître Blum's character harsh, ruthless, and abrasive, it would be patently unfair to say that her personality resided "mainly in her clothes." This had been the critical charge leveled against the Duchess, yet Maître Blum herself seemed disquietingly anxious to place her own personality there. Why else did she want it on record that she had once worn a white ermine stole when she attended galas in Paris?

The late Duke of Windsor had always seen his wife's character as "elusive and complex." As I studied the press-cuttings I felt that the very same adjectives would be far more apt if applied to Maître Blum.

CHAPTER THIRTEEN

Once I'd finished the contents of the yellow envelope, I thought about these two old ladies, Wallis Windsor and Suzanne Blum. They were both women in their eighties, but apart from their advanced age what else did they have in common? Did they share any similarities of personality traits and mutual experiences? They were born on different sides of the globe. They had been brought up speaking different languages. Maître Blum, being far more able, was to achieve an excellent command of English, but the Duchess, after spending years in France, failed to pick up more than a smattering of French.

Yet once their very different lives had made their unlikely collision in old age, they had formed this very special symbiotic relationship in which they were totally dependent on each other. Wallis Windsor owed her life to Maître Blum, and Maître Blum had fused her identity with the Duchess to such an intense degree that she seemed to feel that her own life had little emotional validity apart from her role as the sole custodian and adorer of Wallis Windsor.

On the face of it, it was easy to think that the Duchess could have hardly found a figure less suitable to represent and cherish her once her health started to fail than Maître Blum. Wallis Windsor had been loved and admired by many in the past because she had such "pep and infectious gaiety." It was unlikely that Maître Blum would see the possession of "pep" as a valuable human characteristic. And the whole notion of "infectious" gaiety seemed to be so foreign to Maître Blum that it was hard to believe she would see it as desirable.

"It was my private judgement that when I was being good I generally had a bad time and when I was being bad, the opposite was true,"[1] the Duchess of Windsor had blithely written in her autobiography. Maître Blum would have liked to have sued her for making such a statement.

"No one has ever accused me of being an intellectual," the Duchess of Windsor also wrote. Maître Blum would have liked to have taken out an injunction to prevent her from writing that too.

And yet Maître Blum had told me that she continued to have this "relation de chaleur" with Wallis Windsor, when the whole point of the Duchess was not a point one would expect her to see.

As I tried to discover any bond of experience that Maître Blum had shared with the Duchess, I could only see that there were certain similarities in their upbringing.

Maître Blum, brought up in the provincial village of Niort, and Wallis Warfield, brought up in the provincial American town of Baltimore, were taught from birth that their only function and purpose in life was to make a good marriage. Both women came from struggling and impoverished families who were obsessed by an aching nostalgia for the old, lost days when they'd had position and money and glory. Maître Blum had told me that her father was "de bonne famille," and that although he had to open a shop when he came to France as a refugee from Alsace, he was an "intellectual." Maître Blum's family valued learning much more than that of Wallis Warfield.

But although the parents of Maître Blum valued intellect in the abstract, they seemed to have seen it as an attribute only desirable in the male. They had apparently done their best to crush the intelligence of their unusually brilliant daughter. They had pushed the frying pan and the broom and the embroidery into her hand and instilled her with the pernicious belief that she had only been put on this earth in order to make some man a good wife.

The social attitudes from which Suzanne Blum and Wallis Warfield had suffered were all too common in the era in which they were born. The girls of the family were only meant to devote their minds to achieving skills which were seen as most likely to attract rich husbands. They were taught that cleanliness and thriftiness and virginity were the only qualities required of them. Daughters were viewed rather like investments. Money had been sunk into their upbringing. Since their birth, their food and clothes and other sundries had been paid for. The family felt entitled to expect repayment for the debt which was owed them. The popular method by which daughters were expected to fulfill their filial appreciation was by the making of some mythical and marvelous "match."

Although the constricting, destructive pressures that had been placed on Suzanne Blum and Wallis Warfield when they were young girls were far from unique in their epoch, these paralyzing expectations were imposed on Wallis and Suzanne with an unusual severity because they both came from families who felt that they had "come down in the world." Both Maître Blum and Wallis Windsor had been made to feel that not only was it their duty to restore the lost fortunes of their impoverished mothers by the making of lucrative, brilliant marriages, but they were expected to make restitution for all the misery and shame that their mothers had endured when they had been forced to battle with the pain and ignominy of penury.

The Duchess of Windsor was brought up to be a Southern belle. When her young father, Teakle Warfield, died, the Duchess was still a small baby. After his death her mother, Alice, was left virtually penniless. She led a miserable, knockabout life bringing up her child on the charity of her wealthier relations. First she moved in with her mother-in-law, a severe, old, snobbish woman who sat in a rocking chair, wore widow's weeds, and read the Bible. "How will you ever grow up to be a lady unless you learn to keep your back straight?" this stern figure kept asking Wallis. The Duchess's mother was also insistent that her daughter grow up to be a lady. If Wallis Warfield used a swear word when she was a little girl, her mother washed her mouth out with soap.

Writing of her mother's unhappy situation in that period, the Duchess said:

Few jobs of any kind were then open to women, and these few were for the most part closed to women of gentle rearing. My mother had been raised in the manner of a young Southern lady; that is to say, she was completely but charmingly uneducated except in the decorous graces. Like most Southern women, she was a wonderful cook. She could also sew. Until I went off to boarding school, all my clothes were made by her.

Living a parasitic, impecunious life and bringing up her child on the financial handouts of relatives, the Duchess's mother clung more and more to the idea of "gentle rearing." If Wallis was ill-mannered, her mother spanked her with a hairbrush. From infancy Wallis was trained to be a gracious and suitable wife for some unidentified rich and well-born man. Alice Warfield herself had not married for money. Feeling that she had ended badly, she was terrified her daughter might repeat her mistake.

Although the State of Maryland never seceded from the Union, the sympathies of its leading families still lay with the Confederates, and not being technically Southerners they clung all the more tenaciously to the Southern dream. They loathed Yankees more than most true Southerners. They had an even more fanatical worship of exquisite manners and good breeding and the old, gracious, Colonial life-style. After the Duke of Windsor abdicated, he gave an interview on the radio. He was asked what nationality he saw himself. His answer was surprising coming from a former English king. He said that he saw himself as a Southerner. The extent of his identification with his wife is curious and it is made all the more so because he was identifying with the dubious identity which was imposed upon the Duchess by the Baltimore society in which she was brought up.

"To be a Southerner was a matter of life-and-death importance," the Duchess wrote of her early life in Maryland. Poverty-stricken and yet clinging desperately to the coattails of respectability, Wallis and her mother were in a very undignified position in Baltimore with its rigidly aristocratic ideals. As a child, Wallis never really had a home. She was constantly moving and she was always in the humiliating position of the orphan who is taken in for care. Later when Wallis became the Duchess of Windsor, she spent most of her money and energies in creating spectacular houses and providing her guests with every refinement of comfort and luxury. Even her enemies always granted that the Duchess was an "excellent housekeeper."

The Warfields saw the Duchess's mother, Alice, as their social inferior. As she and her child were totally dependent on this family, she had to put up with their slights and their patronage and take everything she could get from them.

For a long time Wallis was dressed in secondhand clothes which were sent to her mother by relatives living in England. Sewing was one of Alice's few accomplishments and she did her best to see that Wallis was as neatly dressed as possible. She altered her handed-down skirts. She made her dresses to suit the current fashionable style. She darned Wallis's stockings. But the Baltimore society in which Wallis was brought up saw darned stockings as contemptible. Compared to the rich girls with whom she was sent to school, Wallis was made to feel uncomfortably aware that her clothes were shabby.

While Alice and her daughter were living with old

Mrs. Warfield, Wallis's uncle, a banker, whom she knew as "Uncle Sol," was living in the same house. He fell in love with Alice Warfield. Old Mrs. Warfield's sense of propriety was offended. She was shocked and dismayed that her living son should become attached to her dead son's widow. She therefore asked Alice and her child to find other accommodations.

Wallis and her mother were forced to move to a genteel family hotel. Alice Warfield made children's clothes and sold them to support herself and her daughter. She felt hopeless and miserable. She saw herself as a social pariah. Understandably Wallis had a horror of the period when she lived in the seedy Baltimore hotel. She had all her meals alone with her mother and day by day she had to contend with her mother's unlifting state of self-deprivation and near-to-suicidal depression.

Remembering the lowest point of her childhood, the Duchess of Windsor was to write much later:

For the first time I came to know loneliness as loneliness can only be known in the excruciatingly sensitive perceptions of childhood. There is no way, in my opinion, of explaining how a child is able to sense the unhappiness and despair of grown-ups; but the phenomenon occurs—I experienced it. A shivery feeling comes, as when on a crisp fall day the sun is momentarily obscured; and the tenuous apprehensions that now assailed me took the form of a dread of being left alone.

Uncle Sol sent Alice Warfield small sums of money from time to time. But the amounts were erratic depending on his whim. Sometimes the sums were fairly generous and sometimes they were too small to pay the hotel bill. "The ever-shifting contribution complicated things for us," the Duchess of Windsor wrote later.

Alice Warfield, despite her state of financial desperation, was determined that Wallis should go to the best Baltimore schools. She was not particularly interested in Wallis's education, but she considered it essential that her daughter meet the children of Baltimore's leading families. She believed that fashionable schools were vital rungs on the ladder that would lead Wallis to make a good marriage.

Wallis's mother managed to move into the house of another relative, Mrs. Bessie Merryman, and Wallis was able to go to a good school. But once again, a young and potentially talented girl was made to feel humiliated.

Alice Warfield was an excellent cook and she then tried to turn this to some advantage. She opened a boardinghouse, but her ideas were too ambitious to be practical. She behaved in Southern grand style, and she served her guests with prime sirloin steak, elaborate pastries, soft-shell crabs, and terrapin stew. This lavishness was not economically viable and her boardinghouse very soon had to close.

Alice Warfield then married an impecunious figure called John Rasin. He was a coarse, ill-educated man who never did a stroke of work and sat around the house all day smoking. In Baltimore he was known as the "Seedless Raisin." "Mother adored him, of course," wrote the Duchess of Windsor. "I often wondered what she saw in him. But that was before I'd learned what an all-out, cap-over-the-windmill infatuation can do to you."

Although Alice Warfield's financial situation was not improved by her marriage, and she was still forced to scrimp and battle and worry, she still tried to live in the carefree style of a Southern lady. She and her husband would get up very late and they would then breakfast together. He would be unshaven and wearing his bathrobe. Alice Warfield would be wearing a chiffon negligee as she served him quail and champagne. Her mother's passion for extravagance and luxury had a very strong influence on the future Duchess.

Despite her marriage, Alice Warfield kept some kind of emotional hold over her brother-in-law, Uncle Sol. He paid for Wallis to be sent to one of the best boarding schools in Maryland. Its motto was "Gentleness and Courtesy are Expected of the Girls at all Times." There she showed that she was quick-witted and had a "twenty-four-hour memory." It also turned out that Wallis was hopeless at all mathematics. She couldn't understand them and they made her cry. This inability to do any sums was to affect her much later in life.

Maître Blum had a very shrewd head for figures. After the Duke of Windsor died, the Duchess felt insecure and frightened. She couldn't grasp what money she had, and she acquired the rich woman's paranoid horror of taxation. Maître Blum had a realistic picture of the Duchess's assets and was well qualified to advise her on her tax situation. When Maître Blum made the Duchess feel her financial situation was so dire that she was unable to buy a single new dress, she may have done it out of her protective lioness feeling for the Duchess of Windsor. Maître Blum must have sensed that the Duchess had a scatterbrained attitude towards her own finances. Maître Blum, with her tightfisted puritanical attitude towards money, would have detested this trait. When Maître Blum scared the Duchess and made her feel that ruin faced her if she ignored her advice, it was the beginning of the Duchess's prolonged dependence on her brilliant old lawyer.

As Wallis grew older, her clothes became all the more important to her. She was not a beauty. Cecil Beaton always described her as *une belle laide.* She therefore started wearing startling clothes as a way to get herself noticed. She always tried to dress "differently." She wore scarlet sashes to attract attention. She saw herself as the "siren" type. She stuck huge feathers in the back of her hair so that she looked like Pocahontas. In that period in Baltimore all the other girls from her school dressed with the utmost conformity. Wallis Warfield therefore created a scandal when she appeared wearing a monocle and spats. "Never allow a man to kiss your hand," Wallis's stuffy old Grandmother Warfield told her. "If you do, he'll never ask you to marry him."

After she left school, it never occurred to Wallis to get herself a job even though, like her mother, she was still dependent on the erratic handouts of Uncle Sol. Marriage was her only goal and to this end she tried to persuade her uncle to give her a coming-out ball. He considered doing this, viewing it as an investment. But as it was then 1914, he decided it was an improper time for such festivities when thousands were being slaughtered in Europe.

A relative of Wallis's mother who was married to a

commander of a naval air station in Florida invited her to stay. Wallis's grandmother, old Mrs. Warfield, had just died and Uncle Sol felt it would be improper for her to accept the invitation, as he felt she ought to stay in Baltimore and go into mourning for several months. Wallis became desperate. She had been asked to a few balls by school friends even though she had not been given a traditional debut. She told her uncle that if she "dropped out of sight now, she 'might as well be buried alive.' "[2] He was very angry when she defied his wishes and went off to Florida, and as her trustee he delayed payment on the sum of five thousand dollars that Wallis had been left by her grandmother.

Wallis's rebellious trip to Florida was a very important move in her life. It was there, after so many years of being prepared for nothing but marriage, that she met the first man that she was going to marry.

"I have just met the world's most fascinating aviator," Wallis wrote to her mother. Winfield Spencer was a lieutenant who worked at the naval base. The Duchess later described him:

> The eyes were surprisingly intense and bright and quick to flash in response to a quip. Above all I gained an impression of resolution and courage; I felt here was a man you could rely on in a tight place.

As a middle-aged woman, the Duchess of Windsor was asked what she thought of young girls. "Poor dears," she said. "They have all their mistakes before them."

Flying was such a novelty when Wallis met Lieutenant Spencer that there were only two naval air bases in the United States. Wallis was then nineteen and she romanticized the handsome aviator's profession. His brother fliers said that he had a "fine pair of hands," meaning that he had an instinctive feeling for airplanes.

"Undoubtedly his attraction for me was intensified by the glamour and novelty of flying," the Duchess of Windsor wrote. "He and the other officers seemed to me, at that first meeting, to belong to another race of men—godlike creatures who had descended to earth from a strange and adventurous realm."

Although Wallis saw Winfield Spencer as an infinitely glamorous figure in his aviator's uniform, her reasons for wanting to become his wife were still colored by the training she had received when she and her mother had led the scrounging and insecure life clinging to the fringes of Baltimore's patrician society. Wallis believed that only marriage could save her from the shameful feeling that she was a perpetual nuisance and a financial liability.

"Although my love for Win Spencer was real enough," the Duchess wrote, "there also lay in the back of my mind a realization that my marriage would relieve my mother of the burden of my support . . ."

Winfield Spencer was not a rich man. After Wallis married him, she had to live on his naval pay. On her honeymoon Wallis discovered that her husband was an alcoholic and when he took her to a hotel in West Virginia, he had bottles of gin secretly packed away in his suitcase.

Wallis soon learned that her husband was not a man she could "rely on in a tight place." He was moody, jealous, and savage. As fliers were forbidden to drink, Spencer would make himself "consommé," which was a soup composed almost entirely of dry martini. Wallis was naturally flirtatious and when they attended dances at the naval air base, Win accused her of infidelity and he shouted at her and insulted her in front of the wives of other aviators. Wallis, who had hoped that marriage would give her a dignified identity, started to see her marriage as a trap and a hellish prison. Once her husband began drinking, she was frightened to be alone with him. He was a wife beater and he would tie her to the bedpost and leave her there all day. He liked to put her in what he called "solitary." If Wallis was locked up, it relieved his terror that she might deceive him.

As a child she had developed a terror of being alone. When her husband locked her up and left her for hours while he went off round the local bars on an alcoholic rampage, Wallis went into a state of panic and the experience was torture to her.

Quite apart from Winfield Spencer's violence and sadism, Wallis soon learned that she loathed the life of the aviator's wife. She had to follow her husband to the various bases to which he happened to be transferred. She was constantly uprooted. She soon detested what she described as "gypsy pilgrimages to new stations for brief sojourns in rented bungalows or tasteless Government housing."

All her life she had been made to save and budget; she had never been able to live out her dreams of Southern lavishness and comfort. She therefore resented the smallness of Winfield Spencer's naval pay.

One day Winfield Spencer, as usual, locked her up in the bathroom and went out, leaving her there for hours. Wallis became frantic. She tried to pick the lock with her nail file. But she failed to get the door open. Wallis cried and she raged. But no one heard her screams. Her husband finally came back and let her out. It was then she decided she was going to leave him.

When Wallis informed her family that she wanted a divorce, her announcement caused them almost as much consternation as the Duke of Windsor created much later when he told his royal parents that he wished to marry a divorced woman. Queen Mary lost a vast amount of weight after she was told about her son's decision, and when Wallis's mother and her aunt, Bessie Merryman, heard about her intentions, they also went into a state of shock. They told Wallis that divorce was "unthinkable." No woman in her family had ever done something so wicked. They implored her to reconsider her decision. If Wallis were to divorce Winfield Spencer, she would be giving up something for nothing. They told her that "something" was much better than "nothing" even if it was sometimes difficult to live with. While she was married, Wallis at least had her husband's naval pay. If Wallis were to get a divorce, she would have no means of supporting herself. She would have to rely once again on the charity of Uncle Sol. They warned her that Uncle Sol would be appalled when he heard about his niece's immoral decision.

Wallis reminded her aunt and her mother that they were both widows. She described the horror of her life with Winfield Spencer and told them she felt they had been very lucky in their widowhood.

Wallis had to go to her uncle's bank in order to break the news to him. Uncle Sol was as angry and disgusted as her mother had guessed. He told Wallis that he refused to allow her to bring such disgrace on her family. The Warfields had been respected and distinguished leaders of society since 1662. They had never had one divorce. They had always seen marriage as indissoluble. He asked Wallis this outraged question: If she were to leave her husband, "What will the people of Baltimore think?"

Uncle Sol was so angry that Wallis weakened. She agreed to rejoin her husband, who was stationed in Washington. She made one more attempt to patch up her disastrous marriage. The reconciliation was a failure. Winfield Spencer started drinking even more heavily and his behavior was as obnoxious as it had been in the past. Wallis and her husband quarreled incessantly.

One evening Wallis prepared dinner for him and Winfield went out on a drinking spree, leaving her to eat alone. Her husband returned around two in the morning, bleary-eyed and aggressive. Wallis then told him she had made her decision. She was not going to be dominated by the conventions of her family. She wanted to get a divorce. Her announcement sobered him. "I've had it coming to me," he said. "If you ever change your mind, I'll still be around."

Wallis's stepfather, "the Seedless Raisin," had died leaving Wallis's mother in her habitual state of penury. She was living in Washington where she had got herself a job as a housekeeper. When Wallis left her drunken, brutish husband, she moved in with her mother. Marriage had not been rewarding for either of them. Mother and daughter once again had very little to live on except their wits and the generosity of their relatives.

After Wallis informed Uncle Sol that she was determined to get a divorce, he wrote her a very stern letter in which he warned her to "expect no help of any kind from me."[3]

When Wallis was a small child and unable to swim, her mother had thrown her into a swimming pool and forced her to learn. There had always been a ruthlessness in the way her mother had taught her to be a survivor. This capacity for surviving was one of Wallis's strengths in the periods when she was unmarried. It only became her misfortune when she ended up under the care of Maître Blum, once again in solitary, endlessly surviving in her prisonlike palace in the Bois de Boulogne.

After her first marriage broke up, Wallis lived on $225 a month which she received from Win Spencer. She did not have the money to get a divorce. But she had charm and vivacity and she managed to get herself invited to parties. She had many admirers who asked her out to dine. Most of her meals were therefore free. She learned to become very good at poker and her winnings helped her to supplement her income.

Her life when she was unmarried was aimless and it was also very restless. As a child she had a desperate longing to "stay put," but as an adult she was always compulsively moving. She disliked taking exercise but she never stayed still in a room. Laura, the Duchess of Marlborough once told me she felt this was the reason why she always kept her perfect figure.

"Wallis never stopped moving."

"Moving to where?" I asked her.

"Moving . . . Moving . . . It didn't matter where Wallis was moving to. She couldn't bear to be off her feet. She kept jumping up to pouf a cushion on the sofa. She centered some vase of flowers on the table. She emptied an ashtray. She removed some glass. But meanwhile she was always moving. She couldn't leave her house alone. She always made them marvelous. But she was too perfectionist about them. They couldn't give her any peace . . ."

The Duchess later explained her near-fetishist's compulsion to buy hundreds of pairs of shoes at a time. "If you have enough shoes, you have the feeling you can always keep moving."

As a divorcée with a very small income, Wallis moved quite extensively in the period before she met her next husband. She went to Paris. She then returned to Washington. Winfield Spencer kept begging her to come back to him. He was at that point stationed in China and Wallis went off to see him in Hong Kong, hoping that she could still repair her marriage. She was starting to feel lonely and she began to think, like her mother, that "something" was better than "nothing."

Her reconciliation with her husband only lasted two weeks. Win was drinking as usual. He liked to frequent the local brothels and he tried to force her to accompany him in order to make her watch his amorous exploits with the whores. Wallis left him and moved to Shanghai. She then moved on again another thousand miles and she went to Peking. The means by which she supported herself during that period have been obscured by time but later the famous rumor was started that it was in Peking that she mastered her brilliant "Chinese Trick."

In the countless rumors that enveloped her once she became a creature of myth, it was continually whispered that she had picked up some amazing sexual trick in the years she spent in China. Some called it "the Duchess's Chinese clasp," others her "Chinese Grip." Such credence and respect were given to her oriental powers that they were even repeated in British diplomatic circles where there was once a serious belief that she was an agent employed by Hitler to use her deadly Eastern devices on the future King of England in order to weaken the British Empire.

Mrs. Mortimer, daughter of Lady Alexander Metcalfe, a very close friend of the Windsors, remembers sitting by a swimming pool with the Duchess. The Duchess was very relaxed and although I knew Maître Blum would deny it with a fury, the Duchess was apparently drinking iced vodka. Mrs. Mortimer felt this was the moment she had always waited for. The mood of Wallis Windsor was extremely good. Mrs. Mortimer didn't think that she would mind if she were the question directly: "Come on, Duchess, what's all this about your fantastic Chinese trick?" But then some unfortunate tastefulness stopped her. She lost her nerve. She felt the Duchess might find the question extremely offensive. Mrs. Mortimer never dared to pose it. An historic opportunity was therefore allowed to slip by.

After the sojourn in the East she moved back to California, and on to Washington. She then settled for a while in Virginia where she lived in a seedy commercial hotel in order to establish residence to obtain a divorce.

This was the one time in her life that Wallis decided to try and earn some money. She knew she had an eye for fashion. After she married the Duke of Windsor, it was often claimed that she did more for French and American fashion than any woman of her generation. Living alone in the rundown hotel for commercial travelers in Virginia, Wallis tried to write an article for *Vogue*. Her subject was spring hats. She polished and repolished it with all the ardor of the perfectionist. But when she finally sent it off, *Vogue* immediately turned it down.

"I still believed in marriage," the Duchess of Windsor wrote, "and that within that framework lay my true destiny and my happiness."

Alice Warfield had always believed that it was essential for her daughter's future that she go to the most fashionable boarding school in Baltimore. Within her own terms, Alice proved to be right. It was when she was visiting an old school friend, Mary Kirk Raffray, in New York that Wallis met her next husband, Ernest Simpson. He was a ship broker, half English and half American. He had an exaggeratedly English accent, and he was a very good dancer. "I had acquired a taste for cosmopolitan minds," the Duchess of Windsor wrote, "and Ernest obviously had one."

Lady Diana Cooper remembered Ernest Simpson as "such an awful, common little man." When I asked her what he'd been like she described him as "the sort of creature who was always trying to get you out into the garden. Then he would start by kissing your hand and then he'd kiss your arm right up to the elbow . . ."

Ernest Simpson soon proposed to Wallis. She did not accept immediately. She had doubts as to whether her "Southern temperament" was suited to such a "cultivated" man. But she dined out with him often, and they went out dancing. While Ernest Simpson was courting her, Wallis consulted a fortune-teller. The clairvoyant told her that she would have an "unusual death" in "an unusual place," and that in middle age she would exert considerable power through a man. Some of these predictions later turned out to have an eerie validity.

The Duchess of Windsor always had a terror of flying. She thought that her "unusual death" would take the form of a plane crash. Although the crystal-ball prophesier proved to have a certain accuracy, she was wrong to give the Duchess a fear of the skies. Her death was to be "unusual" in the fact that it was to be "unusually" and cruelly prolonged. The clairvoyant was weak when she failed to foretell that the Duchess's destiny would finally lie in the brown-speckled hands of Maître Blum.

Long after Wallis Warfield had made the Prince of Wales leave his throne for her and she'd become the notorious Duchess of Windsor she used to entertain guests at weekends in a beautiful house in the countryside outside Paris. The house was called "The Mill." On one of the walls of the house she had placed an inscription which was criticized in her heyday when many considered her to be a world arbiter of good taste. The inscription read as follows: "I'm not the miller's daughter. But I've been through the mill."

Maître Blum would have sympathized with this mural declaration. She too felt she'd been through the mill. And she was certainly no typical miller's daughter.

Her methods of trying to escape from the mill had been very different from those of the Duchess. She had rejected her family's belief that a woman must make marriage and the breeding of babies her only goal. She'd rejected their idea that a woman who refused to breed was as useless as a cow that gives no yield, a chicken that will not lay.

She'd been prepared to scandalize her family and she'd traumatized them by insisting on going off to attend the university at Poitiers, and having taken this courageous step her rise to fame had been meteoric.

The Duchess had made no such rebellion. She'd contrived all her life to see marriage as her only solution. She'd never worked in her life and she'd only been supported by men.

Maître Blum had always been self-supporting. When she had competed in a male world she had never seen herself as a siren. Maître Blum was much more aggressive than many men. When she'd married another lawyer it had been more of a convenient legal partnership rather than a romantic or domestic idyll. She'd met her first husband, Paul Weill, in the law courts. They were on opposing sides. Maître Blum was acting for the prosecution and he was acting for the defense. Predictably it was Maître Blum who won.

The late Leo Lerman remembered meeting Maître Blum in New York while she was still married to Paul Weill. He got the impression that Maître Blum was not interested in men. "She seemed to be rather frustrated at that point as if she hated being seen as an appendage of her husband because he was her senior. It was as if she longed for power. Some real power that was nothing to do with husbands . . ."

Wallis Windsor married Ernest Simpson because she saw him as a stepping-stone which could lead her to the Prince of Wales. Maître Blume's first husband was to have a similar use to her. Paul Weill represented the Duke of Windsor because he worked for the well-known law firm Allen & Overy. Although Maître Blum hated the whole concept of marriage because her family had made it so unappealing, there was an irony. Like the heroine of some sentimental novel, it was through marriage that Maître Blum was to find fulfillment—it was through her marriage that Maître Blum was to "get" her Duchess.

CHAPTER FOURTEEN

$\mathcal{W}$hen I wrote a profile of Maître Blum for the *Sunday Times*, it was the last time that I had any personal dealings with the Duchess of Windsor's controversial old lawyer. I wrote a piece that was bland and praising to the point of sycophancy. I said that Maître Blum was a marvelous old figure noted for her loyalty and devotion to the Duchess of Windsor, and as I wrote this, I realized that Maître Blum always managed to get her way.

Maître Blum lived in a bubble fantasy with her Duchess. But her fantasies were violent. In her novels she killed off her characters with a sublime disregard for plot and plausibility. Maître Blum was very frightening because there was no way of knowing to what extent she was prepared to enact her pipe dreams of vengeance. She saw herself as beleaguered in an impious world that refused to recognize the divinity of the Duchess of Windsor.

Her cause was a very strange one. But there was no doubt Maître Blum was a fanatic, and like all fanatics, she seemed very dangerous.

Out of cowardice that masqueraded as courtesy, I sent Maître Blum a copy of her profile before it was published. Her response was immediate. She sent a telegram to the editor of the *Sunday Times*. She didn't find the article at all satisfactory. She warned him that if it was ever published, serious lawsuits would follow.

I then received a letter from Michael Bloch. He said that Maître Blum was very distressed by the article and she was thinking of taking legal action. As Michael Bloch's letter had a London address, I telephoned him to ask what objections Maître Blum was making. He sounded very shaky. He said that a few evenings ago, Maître Blum had telephoned him from Paris and she'd been screaming and ranting and she'd kept him up all night. He'd never experienced anything like it. He'd always been aware that she had a fearful temper but this was the first time he'd really known her to go out of control.

"But what does Maître Blum object to in the article?" I asked him. "Surely I've written rather a flattering portrait."

"That's what I thought," Michael Bloch said. "I don't know why it's made her so furious. I thought your article was very flattering indeed."

"How can Maître Blum sue?" I asked. "I've only written how accomplished she is."

"I've tried to tell her that," Michael Bloch said. "I don't know why it's made her so enraged."

Michael Bloch secretly wished that Maître Blum hadn't sent such an aggressive telegram to the *Sunday Times*. He couldn't see how she could possibly sue my article. He didn't know what had come over her. She was certainly a curious character. Her belligerent and impetuous behavior had put him in a very awkward position because he was hoping the *Sunday Times* might eventually serialize his book on the Duke in the Bahamas. As he was acting as Maître Blum's spokesperson, the more trouble she made for the *Sunday Times* the less they would be anxious to publish any of his extracts. He still wanted us to meet so that he could show me the changes that Maître Blum wanted made on her profile.

I met Michael Bloch for lunch in a restaurant. Francis Wyndham joined us because Maître Blum had threatened to sue the *Sunday Times*. Michael Bloch had a copy of my article. Maître Blum had scrawled it with her "amendments." They were written in red ink in her spidery handwriting.

Michael Bloch had grown a tiny mustache which sprouted as a scruffy patch of black fur on his upper lip. He didn't appear to be very keen to show us Maître Blum's amendments.

In my article I had written that the Duchess of Windsor now lives in a prisonlike house in the Bois de Boulogne. Maître Blum had changed this. She had scratched out my sentence and she had rewritten it. Her amendment was interesting because it was a perfect little example of the way Maître Blum was prepared to scratch out facts and replace them with her own idealized version of the history of the Duchess. "The Duchess of Windsor," Maître Blum had written, "now lives in a house that resembles Buckingham Palace."

Her other objections seemed to spring from personal vanity. Maître Blum was distressed that I had called her one of the oldest lawyers practicing at the French bar.

"But surely that is true," I said to Michael Bloch. "I can't see why Maître Blum shouldn't be proud of it."

He admitted it was true. But Maître Blum was funny on the subject of her age. He felt it would be much wiser if I took it out.

I'd also written that Maître Blum now devoted most of her energies to representing the Duchess of Windsor. I'd foolishly imagined Maître Blum might relish this picture of the way she spent her life. On the contrary, she hated it and this was one of the reasons she was planning to sue.

Michael Bloch explained that Maître Blum had many Parisian ladies in their eighties. They still came to Maître Blum asking for her to arrange their divorces. If they were to read that she devoted most of her time to the Duchess of Windsor, she might lose them as clients. Francis Wyndham tried to make Michael Bloch more specific. He wanted to know just how many Parisian ladies in their eighties came to Maître Blum seeking divorces. Michael Bloch looked embarrassed but he would not tell us the exact number.

He then told us that Maître Blum had invited him to stay with her in her "propriété" in the French countryside in August. She had given the Duchess's love letters to a French historian. As this man couldn't understand English, Michael Bloch had translated them for him. He couldn't disclose the name of the historian. Maître Blum had sworn him to secrecy.

Francis Wyndham interrupted Michael Bloch. He wanted to know why Maître Blum insisted the French historian be nameless. Presumably he was a reputable figure. If Maître Blum had given him the Duchess's love letters, his name would be disclosed eventually. What was the point of Maître Blum concealing his identity?

"It was all very complicated," he stuttered. "Maître Blum can be rather strange." He claimed she would kill him if he explained why the French historian's name had to be concealed. But he could tell us the reason why Maître Blum had invited him to her country house. She wanted to have a session in which the French version of the Duchess's love letters would be read aloud. But thinking of the Duchess lying in such poor condition in the Bois de Boulogne, there was something tasteless about Maître Blum's sickly plan to hold this sentimental reading.

When Michael Bloch finally went wriggling off holding Maître Blum's profile, the menacing telegram she had sent threatening lawsuits seemed infantile. Maître Blum had created a storm in a teacup. My profile had obviously been insufficiently effusive to soothe her immense vanity. But she could hardly sue in a negative fashion because things she would have liked to have seen written about herself, in her special fusion with the Duchess of Windsor, had not appeared in my article.

Maître Blum had once used litigation as a scourge. Now that she had total control over the Duchess, she seemed to be mindlessly waving her threats of lawsuits as if they had become a reflex action.

The Duchess of Windsor overexcited Maître Blum and released everything that was uncontrollable and extravagant in her nature, but although the Maître loved to identify with the Duchess, she was a very different character.

"No one who succeeded in getting into as much trouble as I have managed to do at one time or other could be credited with having a clear-cut objective,"[1] wrote the Duchess in her autobiography.

Maître Blum could never have given such a description of her own career. Maître Blum had always set herself very clear objectives. She had never drifted around penniless, picking up "tricks" in China. She had never bobbed her way to fame by getting herself invited to dances and relying on the chancy introductions that take place at cocktail parties.

After Wallis Warfield met Ernest Simpson and he proposed to her, she had grave doubts about accepting his offer. She moved again and went all round Europe with her aunt. There she received the news that Uncle Sol had died. She returned to New York and found he had not forgiven her for her divorce. He had left her a very small legacy. She then went back to France and stayed in the Côte d'Azur with some old friends, the Herman Rogerses. There she heard that Ernest Simpson had left New York and gone to London where he was working in his father's firm. Later the Duchess claimed that she admired his "high qualities of mind and stability of character." But on the subject of Ernest Simpson, she never sounded very sincere. She liked the idea of going to England. It would be yet another move. She wrote to him, "telling him that I was now sure in my heart—I was ready to marry him."

Wallis went off to England and there she married Ernest in the Chelsea registry office. Simpson described their marriage as "a cold little job." Once she started to live in London with Ernest Simpson, it was the first time that

Wallis had ever had her own home. Ernest bought her a flat in Bryanston Court. Wallis finally had a staff, a cook, a chauffeur, a housemaid, a parlor maid, and a part-time maid. Her circumstances were much better than they had ever been before.

But for someone as overcharged and restless as Wallis, her married life was very boring. Ernest worked all day in his ship brokerage firm and he disliked going out at night. He always felt tired at the end of the day. As a divorcée, Wallis had always stayed out extremely late. If she went to a ball, she'd always tried to make everyone go on to a nightclub and once she'd got there, she immediately wanted to move on to some more exciting nightclub. Often she had stayed out so late in New York that when dawn was breaking, she had come out of drinking clubs to find the streets empty and as she could get no other transport, she had bribed some passing milkman to let her ride home on his horse.

Ernest earned a small but steady salary and Wallis was forced to budget. Ernest was meticulous and he made her spend one evening every week going over all the household bills and examining what she had spent on clothes. If they went to the theater, Ernest noted the price of the tickets and insisted that some economy should be made on various expenditures on food in order to meet this financial outlay. Wallis's Southern dream of a lavish, carefree lifestyle had still found no expression. "We lived frugally but well," the Duchess of Windsor described her life with Simpson; "to be able to splurge at Fortnum & Mason on a jar of caviar, brandied peaches, or avocados was a special treat."

Wallis had nothing to do all day while Ernest was in his office. She had always been notorious for her "pep" and now it had little outlet. She spent her mornings shopping, although her staff could have done it for her. She annoyed her local butcher and fishmonger because she had an obsession that every fish, steak, and game bird she bought had to be precisely the same size. She had a horror that the last guest who was served at her table could find himself offered a smaller portion than the guests who had been served before him. This little running battle that the Duchess carried on with the shopkeepers in Paddington was typical of the perfectionism that later made her famous for serving some of the most delicious food in Europe. But in that period it maddened the English butchers and fishmongers. They complained she was being "American"— that she expected everything to be turned out to an identical mold in the way the Morris cars were manufactured.

Wallis herself never became an excellent cook, nor did she choose to become a good seamstress. She had watched her unlucky mother spend an entire lifetime cooking and sewing, but although she had been given an aversion to these pursuits of "gentle rearing," she had acquired an instinctive appreciation of good food and she knew how good clothes should be made. Despite the restrictions that were imposed upon her by Ernest's meticulous budget, she still dressed herself with flair and distinction.

Ernest Simpson had an English sister living in London, a Mrs. Maud Kerr-Smiley, who considered that Ernest had married beneath him. She treated Wallis with much the same condescension that Wallis's mother had been treated by the Warfields. Mrs. Maud Kerr-Smiley tried to give

Wallis lessons on being "English" as if she were teaching her a foreign language. Wallis loved to go into her kitchen. Although she always disliked getting the "smell of bacon" in her hair, she still had a compulsion to praise or criticize the cook. She was always suggesting culinary innovations and producing inventive recipes. Ernest's sister tried to discourage Wallis from going into her own kitchen to teach her that in England such behavior was considered "common."

Wallis did her best to learn various little tricks that would make her seem more "English." She stopped saying "O.K.," for her sister-in-law considered this to be as bad as dropping an *h*. When she went to dinner parties, she no longer waited for all the other guests to be served before she herself started eating as she had been taught to do by her mother. She got the impression that to be "English" you had to talk all day long about the British royal family. Every morning she therefore read and reread the Court Circular. This column in the London *Times* informed her of every function attended by the British royal family and acquainted her with all their activities.

As Wallis had very little to do, all her energies went into decorating her flat. When she wasn't shopping for food, she went "antiquing." She picked up clever bargains in sale rooms. She endlessly moved her furniture into different positions, but the effect never really pleased her.

She made one mistake which she had to live with because Ernest's budget was strict. She wanted to make her dining room seem larger than it was. She therefore covered its walls with a paper that depicted spreading meadows peopled by rust-colored shepherds and flocks of grazing sheep. The effect was not what she had wanted, for all these animals and figures seemed to enter her dining room and clutter it rather than give the impression of an airy expansion. But she made the room glow with ivory-colored candles and when Ernest allowed her the money, she decorated her table with orchids.

Sibyl Colefax, at that time the most fashionable English interior decorator, described her flat as "slightly second-rate." But when the Prince of Wales started to visit Bryanston Court, he liked the way she had done it up and told her he hoped she would give him some ideas for decorating his own house, Fort Belvedere.

Once Wallis had done up her flat, she started giving many little dinner parties. She invited various diplomats, American expatriates, and the business associates of her husband. She mixed her own cocktails in a shaker and she created an informal, pleasant atmosphere. She was starting to form a little court. Ernest called it the "Bryanston courterie."

In this period when she was married to Ernest Simpson, she once traveled back to the United States because her mother was seriously ill. When Wallis went to see her on her deathbed, her mother asked her if she was wearing a brown dress.

"Yes, mother," Wallis said.

"Thought so," the old woman snapped. "Whatever made you choose such an unbecoming color?"

Wallis could never really please her mother, just as in a much later, sadder phase of her life, she could never totally please Maître Blum. Her straitlaced old lawyer could only really love and approve of the Duchess of Windsor if she reformed her and made her exactly like herself and Queen Mary.

But Wallis's last meeting with her mother was not a total disaster. It made the old woman happy to know that at least Wallis was married. She could never be shaken from her belief that when it came to matrimony anything was better than nothing. Fate was cruel to Wallis's mother for she was never to know that one day her daughter was to make what was sometimes called the "match of the century." Nor was she to know that Ernest Simpson was to be as awed and excited by his wife's relationship with the English King as she would have been. He did so much to promote the love affair and facilitate its progress that he became a European laughingstock. He was to be the in-spiration of the quip "the unimportance of being Ernest."

After making her trip to say good-bye to her mother, Wallis went back to Bryanston Court and went on with the dull routine of her days of endless shopping for food and fur-niture. Once again she studied the Court Circular and got some pleasure from following all the engagements and move-ments and appearances of the Royal Family. "The stately language delighted me," she said. She loved sentences like "His Majesty graciously replied."

Ernest was also spellbound by the British royal family. In hushed and reverential tones he would tell Wallis some-thing that Queen Mary had done at a charity bazaar, some-thing that the King, George V, had said to a disabled veteran. But although he fed Wallis with this kind of information, her description of her marriage is still a bleak one. "I spent many a miserable hour wondering what would become of me, and whether, like a bottle of champagne kept too long in an icebox, I would find that the bubbles had been chilled out of my spirit."

In order to relieve her feeling of restless depression, Wallis took a trip round France with her aunt, Bessie Merryman. There she recklessly decided to invest the remains of Uncle Sol's tiny legacy and buy some very good French clothes. Ernest Simpson desperately tried to discourage her. But Wallis refused to listen to him. It was to be a good investment, in her own terms, for when she was invited to a house party in Melton Mowbray, where she was to have her fateful meeting with the Prince of Wales, it was one of these French dresses that gave her confidence. It was a dress made of blue gray with a cape of nutria.

Later describing her dress, the Duchess said: "This, I felt confident, would meet the most exacting requirements of both a horsey and princely setting, and would give me the added assurance that came from the knowledge that in the dress was a little white satin label bearing the word 'Molyneux'."

Wallis had the most frightful cold when she first met the Prince of Wales. Her head was stuffed up and every bone in her body was aching. She was terrified she wouldn't do the right curtsy and Ernest was as terrified about this as she was. She had to keep clinging to the comfort of her little white satin label. Driving down to the country house where she was to meet the Prince, she later admitted that she only wished she were dead.

The Prince of Wales was wearing a tweed suit with loud checks when she first met him. She found him attractive with his boyish snub nose, his tousled blond hair, and his sad expression. She was puzzled why he seemed to be such an unhappy man. This was not all that surprising for he'd had a peculiar childhood.

The first five years of his life, he was brought up by an insane nanny. The Palace only noticed there was something very wrong with the woman who had total charge of the heir to the Empire when she finally suffered a severe nervous breakdown and had to be dismissed. It was then discovered she had never taken any time off since the Prince had been born.

This unbalanced nanny adored the little golden-haired baby, but as a result she was pathologically jealous of his mother, Queen Mary. Every day the royal children had to be brought in to see their parents for a few minutes. The Prince's nanny resented this. When she carried him into some state room to see his mother, she would dig her nails into him with such viciousness he would start to scream. As it was considered unthinkable that the royal couple should have to put up with the bawling of an infant, the nanny then had the excuse to rush the little Prince out of their presence and take him back to the nursery where she could reign. When the Duke of Windsor was two years old, Queen Mary remarked that she found her son "jumpy." As his only contacts with his parents had been accompanied by sensations of severe physical agony, this was not too surprising.

At the house party in Melton Mowbray the Prince tried to make conversation with Mrs. Simpson. He noticed that she had a fearful cold. He therefore asked her if as an

American, she missed the comforts of central heating. Wallis was immediately sharp with him. She was always going to treat him in a dismissive fashion and from the start he relished the way she was prepared to put him down.

"I am sorry, Sir," she said. "But you have disappointed me."

"In what way?"

"Every American woman who comes to your country is always asked the same question. I had hoped for something more original from the Prince of Wales."

"I moved away to talk to the other guests," the Duke of Windsor wrote much later in his autobiography, "but the echoes of the passage lingered . . ."[2]

When Wallis first embarked on what was then known as "the romance of the century," she could never have guessed that one day Maître Blum and Michael Bloch would meet in the French countryside in order to hold a sentimental reading of her translated love letters.

The more I thought about the reading that Maître Blum had arranged, the more it disturbed me. The Duchess had led a much more rackety life than Maître Blum; she had got herself into much more trouble. When the Duchess started having an affair with the Prince of Wales, she was so hated she couldn't walk safely in the London streets. People would come up and stick pins into her. No one had ever stuck pins into Maître Blum.

It therefore seemed unfair that at the end of the Duchess's life, Maître Blum should zoom in and appropriate all the Duchess's gains without having lived through any of the vicissitudes by which they had been acquired.

Maître Blum, as a woman in her eighties, could display

her own very valid tokens of distinction. She was an "Officer du Légion d'Honneur." She was a "Commandeur de L'ordre National du Mérite."

At her age, Maître Blum could be resting on her laurels. Her beloved country, France, had awarded her its very highest honors. It therefore seemed outrageous that she should now be taking all the sad remaining trophies of a much less fortunate old lady.

She had seized the Duchess's body which she loved because it had once been so close to royalty. But she was also doing something much worse than that. Maître Blum was taking much more than any human being should be allowed to take from another. She had seized the Duchess's "royal insignia," her "emblems and tokens indicative of anything." She had seized all her royal drums and swords, her jewels and her furniture. Not content with that, Maître Blum had now appropriated the poor Duchess's love letters. In her insatiable lust for power, her behavior was becoming unspeakable. She was trying to take unto herself all that was left of the very soul of the Duchess.

Very soon after this lunch with Michael Bloch, I heard a new depressing rumor about the Duchess of Windsor. A certain Austrian baron apparently had once been a great friend of Wallis. He now lived in Buenos Aires and two years ago, he had suddenly received a telephone call from Paris. To the Baron's astonishment it was the Duchess of Windsor, and she was crying. She asked her friend why he never telephoned her any more. Had he dropped her like everyone else now the Duke was dead? The Baron had tried repeatedly to telephone the Duchess. But he had never got through because Georges, the butler, always answered and said she was too ill to speak, and he'd been given orders by Maître Blum that the Duchess could not be disturbed.

The Baron had become worried, the Duchess sounded so odd and distressed. He got on a plane that very day and flew to Paris. He went to the Duchess's house and Georges refused to let him in. He had returned enraged and frustrated to Buenos Aires.

Apparently the Baron had been the only one of the Duchess's friends who had been able to get through to see her. On a subsequent trip to Paris, he had refused to bow down to Maître Blum and he'd kept insisting he wanted to see the Duchess, and after a long time Maître Blum had relented because the Baron had threatened that if she persisted in keeping the Duchess hidden from her old friends, he would inform the press and Maître Blum would get some very bad publicity.

When the Baron had finally managed to get into the Duchess's house, he had been appalled by what he had found. The Duchess had shrunk to half her original size and she seemed to be unconscious. She was lying in bed looking like a tiny prune. She had turned completely black.

I tried to track down this Baron in order to verify this grisly rumor. I was unable to trace him, but this image of a black Duchess still haunted me.

The Duchess seemed such a lonely and deserted figure, condemned by Maître Blum to this life without death, a blackened victim of the modern miracles of science. If the Duchess was really now the color of a prune, it gave a pathos to the description that the Duke had once given her: "To me Wallis has always been a blithe spirit—gay, quick, unconquerable. She has an article of faith that enables her to face the future with untroubled heart—'Don't worry. It never happens.' "[3]

CHAPTER FIFTEEN

*M*any of the Duchess's old friends were dead, but it appeared that Lady Monckton was still alive. She was the widow of Walter Monckton, the brilliant barrister who had represented the Duke of Windsor at the time of the abdication. It was with Walter Monckton that the Duke took a stroll through the cedars of Fort Belvedere and first confided his desire to give up the throne in order to marry Wallis. "Listen, Walter. One doesn't know how things are going to turn out. I am beginning to wonder whether I really am the kind of King they want. Am I not a bit too independent? As you know, my make-up is very different from that of my father. I believe they would prefer someone more like him. Well, there is my brother Bertie."[1]

When the clash between the heir to the throne and his government broke in the British press, Wallis was unable to bear all the adverse publicity. Photographs of her face were blown up and they appeared grossly magnified on the front page of all the British newspapers. These photographs were accompanied by viciously hostile captions and censorious denunciations. The Duke of Windsor described her ordeal in *A King's Story*. He wrote "the world can hold few worse shocks for a sensitive woman . . ."[2]

Wallis received a flood of hate mail and she was terrified by threats to blow up her house. She decided to get out of England and she fled to France where she stayed with her old friends the Herman Rogerses in Cannes. This became the subject for a popular joke. "Question: Why does the future King of England need a can opener? Answer: Because the woman he loves is in Cannes."

Walter Monckton had helped the Duke of Windsor write the abdication speech once he left his throne for Wallis. Walter Monckton had been one of the few who remained loyal to him and he had accompanied the deposed monarch when he finally left his country on the destroyer *Fury* in order to rejoin Wallis across the Channel.

Walter Monckton had been such a key figure in all the dramas of the Windsors that I hoped his widow might know what state the Duchess was in.

I discovered from Lady Mosley that Lady Monckton was now living in an old persons' "home" near Newbury. I was warned that I might find her mind had gone. There were rumors that she spent most of her time in her "asylum" wearing coronation robes and saying she was off to the House of Lords.

When I arrived at her "home," Lady Monckton was not wearing an ermine tippet and scarlet robes. She was dressed very quietly in a tweed suit and a beige blouse.

She came tottering out of a television room, held up by two nurses. She seemed extremely pleased to see me. "How lovely you've come," she said. "I understand you've just come in from Hyderabad." I wondered who she thought I was. Could it possibly be Lady Mountbatten?

Lady Monckton was now eighty-four and it soon became clear that like many old people, Lady Monckton only seemed to be senile when she was speaking about her un-promising present. When she spoke about her past, she became perfectly lucid. Whether she went off rambling or whether she spoke realistically, Lady Monckton was ex-tremely sympathetic.

Her "home" was very comfortable and pleasant. It had once been a grand country house and it had beautiful, well-kept grounds and the leaves of its copper beeches glowed reddish purple in the sunlight, and golden pheas-ants were meandering in a stately fashion across impeccably well-mown lawns. Inside there had been some attempt to make the "home" seem like a cheerful and idyllic grand English country house. Fires had been lit in the fireplaces and above them were ancient portraits of somebody's an-cestors to give a feeling of continuity. Only a faint smell of antiseptic and the terrible state of the inmates ruined the imposing atmosphere. Having lost all their faculties, they sat motionless in their various chairs. Some of them looked at television with their eyes closed. Kindly nurses helped them dress and undress. Tea and biscuits were brought to them at suitable intervals. Often they took naps to while away the long, pointless hours, so their trays were left un-touched. There was little evidence that the golden pheas-ants and the splendor of the trees in the beautiful grounds by which they were surrounded could bring them much pleasure. Their biggest moment of struggle and drama was the time when two nurses carried them limping painfully to the lavatory and then brought them back to a bed or a chair.

Lady Monckton told me she didn't live in the old persons' home. She had just taken a flat there and she only planned to stay one week. She enjoyed being in the country for a few days. But she didn't intend to stay. She insisted that she traveled incessantly. She adored travel and she was always on a jet. If I wanted to write to her, there was no point in writing to her present address. She waved her hand disparagingly at another white-haired woman who was passing by us bent over double as she was half carried to the lavatory by a brisk and encouraging nurse.

As a young girl, Lady Monckton had been a great beauty and she was still a very handsome woman. Like the Duchess, she had caused a scandal in her youth. She had fallen in love with Walter Monckton and left her husband, Lord Carlisle, to live with him. To many of her contemporaries "living in open sin" was seen as a crime. The criticisms that had once been leveled against her were very typical of the attitudes of the period. "It's so awful of Biddy to have an open affair like this—it's really too awful of her, when Britain is at war."

Lord Monckton had been dead for many years. Sitting round the fire in her "home," Lady Monckton said she was meeting her husband next week. They both planned to fly over to Paris. They were going to see the Duchess of Windsor.

"How is the Duchess?" I asked.

Lady Monckton hadn't heard from her lately. She'd been told the Duchess was not very well. I asked if she knew that the Duchess was being cared for by her lawyer? This question seemed to scare her. It made her mind more confused. Her eyes glazed. Her voice started to sound much older and more quavery.

"Maître Blum? Maître Blum?" she repeated vaguely. "Oh yes, I've heard about the Duchess's lawyer."

Maître Blum was obviously not a figure whom she wished to discuss. Maître Blum represented the undesirable present.

I told Lady Monckton I had brought her something that I thought might interest her. Lady Mosley's book on the Windsors had just come out. When I gave a copy to Lady Monckton, she was thrilled like a child. "Oh, what a really lovely present! How clever of you to know how to bring me exactly what I wanted. I can show it to all the others who are living here. They will all be fascinated. But could you please write my name on it? It's much safer."

I wondered if the doddery, broken-down inmates of her "home" sometimes stole each other's belongings and that was the reason she wanted her book to be labeled in the way that the clothes of children are marked in boarding schools. Her "home" was only chilling because it reminded one of a boarding school. Everyone there seemed to be spending their days like prisoners longing for the end of term. The beauty of the well-mown lawns outside couldn't compensate for the misery that the inmates of this institution exuded in their fear and hopelessness.

I asked the nurse for a pen and as I started to write Lady Monckton's name in the flyleaf of the book, she seemed to sense I was just about to write the wrong one and she ordered me to write "Bridget de Maury." She spelled it out for me. When I checked on this name later,

I discovered it was a name she had never held at any moment of her life. Presumably she used this invented identity to prevent her from feeling she inhabited her "home" near Newbury.

Once Lady Mosley's book on the Windsors was placed on Lady Monckton's knee, her whole manner changed. Her eyes focused properly. They no longer looked lost and glazed once she started staring at all the old photographs of the Duchess. When she spoke, her voice no longer sounded quavery and uncertain as it had done when she had wandered into fantasy. The book had taken her back into the past and while she was there, Lady Monckton was not at all senile. She recognized with amusement all the dresses that she'd seen the Duchess wear. She knew which photographs of the Windsors were the good ones and she was irritated by the ones she saw as bad. She claimed that the camera had always been very unfair to the Duchess. Wallis had always been much more attractive in real life than photographs had ever made her appear. Cecil Beaton had always said exactly the same.

"It's enthralling. This is really enthralling," Lady Monckton kept repeating as she turned the pages. When she came across a picture of the Duchess wearing a white dress in an old interview she'd done for television, Lady Monckton became very annoyed. "How could they have made her wear that dress, when they must know white is so bad for television."

I asked Lady Monckton which of her surviving friends was now closest to the Duchess.

"Well, I suppose I am," she said. "Lots of people

didn't like the Duchess," she added. "They found her a cold woman."

"Did you find her cold?"

"No, I didn't. I don't think the Duchess was cold. I liked her very much. But people were always being nasty about Wallis. You must remember how jealous people felt when the Prince of Wales fell in love with her."

"Was the Duchess in love with the Duke?" I asked.

"Oh no, the Duchess was certainly never in love with the Duke."

Lady Monckton spoke with a certain impatience as if she found the question irritating and mindless.

"How do you know?" I asked. "Did the Duchess tell you that?"

I felt guilty to be asking this infirm and kindly old lady such delicate questions. My curiosity seemed morbid. But it appeared to please her and she seemed anxious that I continue. She had once been the best friend of the Duchess. She therefore was glad of a chance to talk about her. She appeared to be desperately lonely, but she felt less so when someone was interested in her past.

"The Duchess never told me she wasn't in love with the Duke. The Duchess didn't need to. I could tell. You can always tell when people are in love. You only have to be in the same room."

"Did the Duchess simply want to be Queen?"

"Yes, I suppose she did. But she was too American to realize that could never have been possible. As an American she couldn't understand the way the English regard their King."

"If the Duchess was never in love with the Duke, when he abdicated and she had to marry him, it must have been some kind of tragedy for her."

Lady Monckton nodded. "The Windsors may have had the 'romance of the century.' They certainly never had the 'love story of the century.' "

"Was their marriage a nightmare?"

"No, it really wasn't a nightmare. You see he was always so madly in love with her. I remember that once I was staying with them both in Paris. Wallis had gone to the hairdresser. The Duke got himself into the most frantic state. He was pacing round and he couldn't stop looking at his watch. 'Why isn't Wallis back?' 'Why isn't she back?' he kept asking me. I tried to explain that it takes quite a lot of time to have your hair set. One always had to explain that things took time to the Duke. He always got so upset when Wallis was late coming back from fittings and things like that . . ."

"Was it terrible for the Duke when the Duchess fell in love with Jimmy Donahue?"

"Yes, it was. But Wallis would never tell me anything about Jimmy Donahue. She felt I wouldn't approve. She was right not to tell me. You see, I was extremely fond of the Duke. I knew about Jimmy Donahue of course. Everyone told me. What a very unfortunate liaison . . ."

A nurse came up and said that Lady Monckton ought to take her nap. Lady Monckton looked desperate. She obviously didn't want to be interrupted. I felt she would have liked me to have brought her a bottle of champagne and while we drank it, she would have liked to go on talking about the Windsors. The nurse said that Lady Monckton must not be allowed to be overtired. Lady Monckton looked even more unhappy and cornered. "This is the nicest visit I've had for a very long time," she said to me. She kept thanking me for Lady Mosley's book. "Do you really mean that I can keep it?"

She ignored the nurse who was gently trying to get her out of her chair. She started looking once again at the photographs of the young Duke and Duchess. The nurse then became firm with her. Lady Monckton had really got to take a rest.

I couldn't see any real reason why Lady Monckton shouldn't be allowed to become overtired if she was enjoying herself for one moment. Emotionally she had returned to a happier previous existence. For a brief space in time she had escaped from her gracious, but grisly asylum. She'd escaped from the soulless prison of medical regulations and routines. Even if my visit were to exhaust her, I couldn't see that it mattered. She didn't have many taxing duties which she had to fulfill in the morning.

But the nurse was merciless. She said that visiting time for Lady Monckton was over. And the bossy nurse in her starchy uniform introduced such a sour dose of the present that she made her old patient cease to be lucid.

"Don't let the Duchess have this book," she said. "It wouldn't be good for her. She won't really want to look at these pictures. They'll remind her of the past, and after that she'll want the book. But you must never let her get hold of it. If the Duchess wants something, she always gets it. We have seen that."

I said good-bye and thanked her. She tried to follow me out through the door although the nurse gently dissuaded her. I wished I could take her with me, she looked so desolate and deserted. She seemed to be on the verge of tears. I wished I could drive her to the airport where she could get on a jet and fly to Paris to join the young Duchess and her dead husband. I wished she could have a glamorous dinner with the Duchess, that all the flowers on the table could be sprayed with Diorissimo.

But none of these wishes were realistic. Lady Monckton was never going to see her best friend again. Even if she were to find the strength to get to Paris, Maître Blum would never allow her to visit the Duchess. It was much too late for that.

As Lady Monckton was obviously much too old and ill to help me, I decided to go and see Lady Diana Cooper. She was lying in bed in her house in Little Venice. She had the carefully shaded lights of the actress and she was looking very beautiful. "I suppose you want me to do something about the Duchess," she said the moment I entered. "I know she's been locked up by her awful old lawyer. But there's nothing anyone can do about the Duchess. You've got to understand that."

"Couldn't the royal family do something about the Duchess?"

"I adore the Queen Mother," Lady Diana said. "I see the Queen Mother as almost perfect. How could she be bettered? The Queen Mother is really nearly perfect. But her one weakness is the Duchess. She still feels very unforgiving towards her. It's funny when the Queen Mother is so loving in other respects. But she still feels it's the Duchess's fault that her husband, George VI, died."

"But didn't he die of cancer?"

"Yes. He did. But the Queen Mother feels he only got it because he couldn't bear the strain of being King. She called it the 'intolerable honor.' That's exactly how she described it to Duff [Cooper]."

Lady Diana said that the Duke of Windsor had never wanted to be King either. "When he was Prince of Wales he always told me that. He said he would make a very bad King. He was meant to marry the Queen Mother. She was the girl that the Palace saw as perfect for him. She was very attractive. Everyone in those days was in love with her. But the Duke would have never dreamt of marrying someone so suitable. He wanted something more unconventional. He wanted someone like Wallis."

"Were you a close friend of Wallis?" I asked her.

"I knew her quite well. I used to go down to Fort Belvedere and stay with them both. The Fort was marvelous. I adored it. It was like a wonderful, absurd toy castle with all its turrets. Even the sentries outside seemed unreal. One felt they were little toy soldiers. The Duke made the atmosphere very informal and therefore it was always fun to stay there. He hated anything stuffy. The Fort was the only home he loved. He had a horror of pompous Buckingham Palace."

"What was the Duchess like?" I asked.

"The Duchess was much less nice, and also much more

interesting than they made her appear in the television series. They made her seem rather insipid in that television thing. And the Duchess was not in the least insipid."

Lady Diana said that she had gone with the Windsors on the famous Mediterranean cruise they had taken on the yacht *Nahlin*. It was the first time the Duke had taken Wallis anywhere quite so openly. Ernest Simpson had been left behind. She remembered that one evening on the yacht Mrs. Simpson had been wearing the most incredible dress. It was made of some marvelous filigree material embroidered with dragonflies. At dinner the Duke was clumsy. He moved his chair and managed to put its leg on Wallis's dress so that the hem got torn. Mrs. Simpson got in a rage with him. Everyone on the yacht had been astonished that she dared to get so angry. No one had ever heard anyone be so violently rude to the future King of England. When Wallis spoke so furiously to the Prince, it was the first time that it became clear that they were lovers. No one had really known what their relationship was before until she raged at him. There had been all sorts of rumors, but the Prince and Mrs. Simpson still could have been only friends. The Duke became desperately upset. He kept apologizing. Finally they both went off to their cabin. And presumably their quarrel was made up in bed. They both seemed perfectly happy in the morning.

Lady Diana also remembered a much later occasion with the Windsors. The Duchess gave a huge and luxurious dinner party in their house in Paris. Jimmy Donahue appeared after dinner. Someone knocked over a glass of champagne. The Duchess of Windsor was carrying an os-

trich fan that represented the Prince of Wales feathers. Seeing the spilled champagne, the Duchess immediately bent
down and mopped it up using the Prince of Wales feathers
as if it were a dishrag.

"She shocked us," Lady Diana told me. "It had to
mean something. We all found her behavior very odd. The
whole atmosphere became incredibly tense."

Later the whole party went on to a fancy dress party
given by the most notorious gossip columnist of her period, Elsa Maxwell. The Duchess was wearing a blue wig
and a red dress. She was still holding her soaking and be-
draggled Prince of Wales feather fan. "That was pretty odd
too," Lady Diana said. "Particularly as the Duchess was
usually so violently fastidious."

Elsa Maxwell had hired the band from the Duke's favorite nightclub, the Monseigneur. The Duke was apparently delighted and he seemed to enjoy himself. But
around four in the morning the Duchess as usual wanted
to move. She wanted to go to the Monseigneur nightclub.
She seemed to have forgotten that she wouldn't find the
band she loved there. She was already dancing to it with
Jimmy Donahue in Elsa Maxwell's house. Someone reminded her of this. The Duchess then insisted the entire
band be moved back to the original nightclub from which
it came. The Duchess got her way. The entire party, plus
the band, moved back to the Windsors' favorite nightclub.

"In those days," Lady Diana said, "they sold flowers
and bottles of scent outside nightclubs. Once we got to
the nightclub, Jimmy Donahue really showed off and he
went to town. He bought all the ladies flowers and ex-

pensive bottles of scent. But we all got very tiny bottles and rather measly little bunches of roses. But I can't tell you the size of the bunch of roses that Donahue bought for the Duchess. She also got a huge flagon, a sort of jeroboam of scent."

According to the account given to me by Lady Diana, once the Duchess returned to the Monseigneur she proceeded to dance endless dances with Donahue. She kept asking the band to play the favorite tunes of Jimmy and herself. She demanded they play "C'est Si Bon" and "La Vie en Rose."

The Duke started looking more and more distraught. The Duchess finally stopped dancing with Donahue and she came back to the "Windsors' special table." She asked the waiters for a vase. When it arrived, she took Jimmy Donahue's roses and her soggy ostrich fan and she shoved them into the vase together. "Look, everybody!" she said. "The Prince of Wales plumes and Jimmy Donahue's roses!" The Duke immediately started to cry, he felt so humiliated.

"It was ghastly," Lady Diana told me. "The whole evening was ghastly. And once it was over, I ended up alone with Donahue. I had to drop him home in a car. I couldn't bear him. He was so pleased with himself. He lolled around on the car cushions looking as puffed as a toad because he had proved he had the power to cause distress. I thought he was seriously cruel and common. I really loathed the way he talked about the Duchess. The car had no glass partition and he embarrassed me because the chauffeur could hear everything we said. 'Don't you love "Our Duchess?" ' Donahue said to me. 'Don't you think "Our Duchess" is fantastic?' "

Lady Diana had tried to snub him. "I happen to be the daughter of a Duchess," she said that she'd hissed at Donahue. "So Wallis can't ever be 'Our Duchess' to me."

I asked her if it was true that Jimmy Donahue had boasted that he had "abdicated" when his romance with Wallis ended.

"Oh, I'm sure that Donahue said that. It's exactly the sort of ghastly thing that a swinelike man such as Donahue was bound to say."

I told Lady Diana that I'd just seen Lady Monckton in her "home" near Newbury. "I hear she makes no sense," Lady Diana said. "She's much luckier than me. I make perfect sense and I am absolutely miserable. I loathe being old. I hate every second of my life. My eyes, my ears, are going. Everything is going. All I enjoy now is driving my car. And I suppose I won't be able to do that much longer. I can't walk a step without it hurting. But let's have a drink," she said. She started to get out of bed.

"Let me get the drinks," I said. "Don't you walk if it hurts."

"I don't care if it hurts. I am determined to be able to get a drink. If one can't even move to get a drink—what's the point of anything?" She got the drinks and then returned to bed. "I'm not meant to drink," she announced, "that's why I am going to have a very large drink—naturally."

She said that she felt that old people like the Duchess and Lady Monckton were the lucky ones.

"Surely the Duchess isn't luckier than you," I said.

"I'm certain that the Duchess is much luckier than me," Lady Diana said firmly. "She probably doesn't know the appalling things that are happening to her. Maybe the Duchess has really turned black. Maybe she is being kept alive by artificial means. Maybe her frightful old greedy lawyer has seized all her possessions. It doesn't really matter to the Duchess—not if she doesn't know."

"But maybe the Duchess does still know," I said. "Maybe the Duchess is not unconscious all the time. Maître Blum says she never stops talking. Have you realized that Maître Blum wants the Duchess to live to be a hundred?"

Lady Diana admitted that if the Duchess occasionally regained consciousness, even for a moment, her plight was not in the least enviable. She was very glad that she herself had no valuable possessions. She saw this as a safeguard. No lawyer, male or female, would think it worth their while to keep her alive. She would certainly loathe to be kept alive until she was a hundred.

"I still don't believe that the Duchess minds about the horror of her existence. I really detest mine," Lady Diana insisted. She seemed determined to see the Duchess of Windsor as fortunate. She told me she had another old friend, Enid Bagnold the playwright.

"Enid is now ninety-two and she is as mad as a coot. She's become totally gaga. She hardly makes a grain of sense when I go to see her. But Enid claims that old age has been the happiest time of her life. I wish I could feel that too . . ."

Lady Diana poured herself another drink. "You see it doesn't matter if you become incontinent and have to bear all those kinds of humiliations, not if your mind has gone."

Later I talked to a close friend of Enid Bagnold and I

told him Lady Diana claimed she was enjoying a very happy old age. He said that it was nonsense. Enid Bagnold was not at all happy. She was in a desperate state of ill health and she minded it just as much as anyone else. She liked to pretend to Lady Diana Cooper that she was ecstatically happy. Old ladies had their own form of one-upmanship. Through the years, all the women of Lady Diana's generation had always been very jealous of her beauty, charm, and fame. Enid Bagnold had therefore devised this effective little pretense to make Lady Diana envy her. By making claims that she enjoyed an insensate happiness in her old age, she had finally turned the tables and made her indomitable and beautiful old friend regard her with jealousy and awe.

After more drinks, Lady Diana complained that everyone saw her as one of the lucky ones. She adored her family. She had not yet had to be put in a "home." She had lots of marvelous friends. She still had many visitors. She had not been captured by Maître Blum.

"People say it's so wonderful that Lady Diana Cooper can still go out to parties and the opera. But what's the point of her still going to all these wonderful things?" she asked me. "What is the point if she feels absolutely ghastly every moment she's there?"

I couldn't think of any good answer to give her. I hoped Lady Diana wasn't being as honest as she sounded, that in certain moods she didn't find her old age quite as unremittingly hellish as she claimed. I would have liked to think she was putting on a little act for my benefit—the reverse act of her friend Enid Bagnold. But Lady Diana's huge, blue, famous beauty's eyes had an expression of desperation while she was talking about her present life.

"Age is the bilge we cannot shake from the mop," wrote Robert Lowell. And wondering if it were correct that the deserted, blackened Duchess of Windsor should be seen as more fortunate than Lady Diana who had retained her liveliness, her popularity, and her charm, I had the feeling that Maître Blum had found a brilliant device by which she could shake off more bilge than many women of her years. Maître Blum didn't seem very troubled by the problems and humiliations which beset the elderly.

At an age when many women start to feel useless, defeated, depressed, and unwanted, Maître Blum had found love, and possibly even more difficult, she had found a brand-new sense of purpose. By forming her eccentric passion for the Duchess of Windsor she had found something she passionately wanted to live for. While she loved and controlled the Duchess, while on occasion she could feel she was the Duchess, there was no reason for Maître Blum to sag and lose her wits and become despondent and go into a state of physical decay.

With the "step of a young girl," Maître Blum was still buzzing around Paris. She was still permanently "en voiture." The Duchess had once wanted to keep endlessly moving. The Duchess was now inert but that did not matter to Maître Blum. She felt that she was carrying the Duchess just as St. Christopher carried Christ, that nothing need stop their double lives from moving.

The Duchess seemed to be so many things to Maître

Blum. Having traumatized her family by her refusal to see marriage as her only goal, now late in life the Maître could feel her parents were placated. Now that emotionally she'd become the Duchess of Windsor, she'd fulfilled every dream they had ever had for her. Maître Blum had far exceeded all their wildest expectations. She'd become the little girl that got the Prince.

Maître Blum had been childless most of her long life but now towards the end of her days she had ceased to be barren. While she devoted herself to mothering the helpless Duchess once again her life had been given new and extra meaning.

According to Michael Bloch, Maître Blum still had a flood of ancient Parisian ladies who poured into her office seeking her help with their matrimonial difficulties. She also continued to derive great joy and stimulation from her various international libel suits.

Just when many women of her age felt annihilated by their failing faculties and only wanted to live in the past, Maître Blum saw the years that lay ahead of her as glorious. Whether the Duchess of Windsor had turned black or not, Maître Blum believed that she would only get more and more beautiful. Maître Blum was unique in her generation. She saw a future in which she would keep covering the Duchess of Windsor with flowers, she could therefore face it with anticipation rather than terror.

When I went to see Laura, the Duchess of Marlborough in her flat in Montaqu Square, she was in a dressing gown but

round her neck were three rows of huge and perfectly match-
ing pearls. She was still very fit and active and I hoped she
might do something about the Duchess. She had heard the
Duchess of Windsor had been taken over by her lawyer.
It made her angry.

"Wallis was a very nice woman and she doesn't de-
serve this awful end. Poor little thing, locked up by her
servants."

She didn't believe that Maître Blum had any romantic
attachment to the Duchess of Windsor. "Wallis's possessions must be worth a fortune nowadays." It was then that
she confirmed that Wallis had definitely owned Queen
Alexandra's jewels, and she remembered the time that
burglars had broken into her house and stolen a lot of
them. "All those jewels were replaced by the Duke. The
replacements may not be royal but they are still madly
valuable jewels. I would love to know what has happened
to them . . ."

The Duchess of Marlborough said that she was one of
the few people that had been willing to have the Windsors
to stay, once the Prince abdicated. "People didn't want to
meet them. It was difficult to find anyone who would
come to dinner with them."

Talking about the Duchess's current situation, she suddenly said she felt it was really the Duchess's fault. "Only
a woman would get herself into such a ludicrous predicament. This sort of thing would never happen to a man.
Men knew how to fend for themselves. If the Duke had
survived the Duchess, he would never be locked up now
by his lawyer. He wouldn't have had all his possessions
seized. It just never could have happened to him. Women

are so hopeless. They have to have a husband. They can't manage alone. Women can do what they like while they still have a husband.

"No one could have behaved worse than the Duchess when she got her infatuation with Jimmy Donahue. She really flaunted her awful affair in a way that was quite unnecessary. She tormented the Duke . . . But she could only get away with such behavior because she still had a husband . . . The Duke was like her umbrella. Once the Duchess lost her husband she ceased to function. She took to drink and she collapsed entirely and she allowed herself to get into this absurd situation . . . The Duchess was perfectly intelligent . . . I find her situation really irritating . . . How could she allow this stupid thing to happen to her? It makes me feel impatient with women in general."

"Do you understand why the Duchess became so infatuated with Jimmy Donahue?" I asked.

"None of us could understand it . . . Jimmy Donahue was the most dreadful creature . . . But I can only tell you that Wallis was just as besotted by Jimmy as the Duke was besotted by her. At one point she would have given up a throne for Donahue."

"Did Jimmy Donahue kill a waiter?" I asked. I remembered that Lady Tomkins had mentioned what she called an "inadvertent" killing.

"He may have done." Laura Marlborough gave a sniff of disgust. "Nothing that Jimmy did would surprise me . . . He was an alcoholic, he was a drug taker. He was sadistic and depraved and seriously vicious . . . I do know that he castrated a young soldier."

"Castrated a young soldier!" Every piece of information I received about Jimmy Donahue was always shocking.

"Oh yes . . . It was a huge scandal at the time . . . Jimmy went off to some queer bar in Manhattan with a bunch of queer friends. Jimmy picked up a group of servicemen and he took them back to his mother's New York apartment. Then he plied the soldiers with champagne and probably drugs. Jimmy was always plying everyone with everything. He loved plying. He loved the power he got from his money."

"And then what happened?" I dreaded hearing her answer.

"One of the young soldiers got so drunk that he passed out . . . Jimmy thought it was funny to undo his fly buttons and pull out his penis . . . I understand that Jimmy was stoned at the time and so were all his friends . . . Then Jimmy thought it was hilarious to get a sharp razor in order to shave off the fellow's pubic hair . . . Of course the soldier woke up and he started thrashing around, terrified, and somehow his prick was cut off. I was always told that it was Jimmy who did the actual cutting . . ."

"Did the young soldier die?"

"No, he didn't . . . But that was only luck. It wasn't anything to do with the kindly behavior of Jimmy Donahue . . . Jimmy wouldn't allow his friends to take the soldier to hospital. They wrapped him in a blanket and they shoved him into Jimmy's car and Donahue drove him to one of the New York bridges and then he dumped him out on the side of the road and he left him there like refuse."

"How was the soldier saved?"

"I think that a police car came by and the police heard him screaming. Anyway he was rushed to hospital and the surgeons managed to save him."

"Was Donahue prosecuted?"

"No, he wasn't. The soldier never sued. Jimmy's mother, Jessie Donahue, was able to hush up the horror of the whole thing by using the Woolworth millions. She gave the soldier 200,000 dollars to keep him quiet and I think she paid the press. Jimmy had to go to Mexico for a while until the whole nightmare was forgotten . . . But then he was back and bobbing round New York buying champagne with the Duchess of Windsor in love with him . . ."

Laura Marlborough said that she didn't blame the Duchess for her weird infatuation. Most people had unsuitable infatuations at some point in their lives. At the time she had blamed her for making no attempt to be discreet about the incomprehensible affair she was having. She had gone to every fashionable restaurant and nightclub in New York alone with Donahue and there she was to be seen giggling and openly flirting with Jimmy. At that point the Windsors had been one of the most famous couples in the world so the scandal she had created had been enormous.

"I remember taking the Duke home one night from a Paris nightclub and he was in floods of tears because the Duchess had vanished somewhere with Donahue. It was bad enough for the Duke that the wife he adored was in love with another man . . . But Wallis made the Duke look particularly ridiculous because he had given up the throne for her . . ."

Laura Marlborough went on to say that the Duke of Windsor had told her that he hoped that the Duchess would die before he did.

"He knew something awful would happen to Wallis if she survived him. He loved her so much that he was always worried as to what would become of her once he was gone."

The Duchess of Marlborough was the only English friend of the Duchess who nearly tried to find out what was happening to her. She told me she was determined to fly over to Paris. She was going to march up to the Duchess's house and ring the bell. If Georges tried to stop her from coming in, she was going to make a stink. She was not going to be stopped by any butler.

Then she wavered. She told me that it was rumored that Georges had been armed by Maître Blum, that he'd been given orders to shoot any person who tried to see the Duchess. On hearing this I understood why the Duchess was always placed in the American Hospital every time her butler went on vacation. It had made no sense before.

"I don't particularly wish to be shot in the leg by Georges," Laura Marlborough said to me. I found this very understandable. It was a strange and terrible image—this tall, stately, and elegant old Duchess being shot like a rabbit by Georges.

Laura, Duchess of Marlborough actually booked herself on a plane to Paris. She seemed to have every intention of investigating the situation. Then at the very last moment she canceled her flight. She told me that she had a cold and she had to restring her pearls.

The Marchesa Casa Maury, previously Freda Dudley Ward, was the last old lady that I went to see in my search for news of the Duchess of Windsor. She had been the Duke's mistress for fifteen years while he was still Prince of Wales. The Prince had abandoned her once he met Wallis.

When I telephoned her, she said that she couldn't tell me anything about the Duchess of Windsor. She would only waste my time. She could hardly remember the Duke. It was all so long ago. She hardly remembered anything about the whole thing. But if I still wanted to come round and see her, she would be delighted to see me.

I heard the Marchesa Casa Maury had broken her hip and had recently been in the hospital. I imagined she would be in bed. But she was sitting in a chair in the living room of her little Chelsea house. She apologized for not getting up as I came in. She pointed at her steel medical stick with disgust. "I've asked my doctor when I can get rid of this horrible thing. Do you know what he had the cheek to say? You are never going to get rid of that. At your age you must accept you are always going to need a stick. Oh, I thought it was so incredibly rude! Goodness it made me angry! But I'm going to show him. Once of these days I am going to walk into his office. And I'm not going to be leaning on any stupid stick."

She had taken some trouble with her appearance. She had put on lipstick and on her cheeks there were bright patches of rouge. They were slightly misplaced—just a little too low. But on the Marchesa they neither looked sad nor whorish. She made them seem both appropriate and festive. She was wearing a bow tie which appeared pleasantly saucy.

A Spanish maid brought me a vodka and Freda Casa Maury had a very large Dubonnet.

"I'm afraid that I am going to waste your time. You know that I never even met the Duchess. And I don't remember much about the whole thing. It's all so long ago . . . So much life has happened to me since all that . . . I really don't remember it."

The Marchesa paused, and then she spoke with both anguish and defiance. "Quite honestly, I don't want to remember it. At the time it was all really painful."

I felt I ought to leave. It seemed tactless to stay on. The Marchesa had never even met the Duchess of Windsor. She didn't want to talk about the Duke. The whole subject seemed to upset her. I decided to ask the Marchesa an innocuous question. After that I would thank her for seeing me and go.

"Do you remember any of the tunes that you and the Duke used to dance to?"

She seemed to like being asked this. She suddenly laughed. "Of course I remember the tunes. One always remembers the tunes . . ."

The Marchesa smoked incessantly. She had all the equipment of the chain-smoker on a table conveniently close to her chair. She had three packets of cigarettes, three boxes of matches, three lighters. She was like an advertisement for smoking, this gallant, old, humorous lady of eighty-six. She kept coughing and then inhaling smoke back into her cough.

"We never stopped dancing," she said. "The Duke was mad about dancing. In a way that was all we did—well, not quite." She gave another little laugh.

"I doted on the Duke," she said. "He was so handsome and glamorous and amusing. I was so flattered that he liked me. I don't think I was in love with him. I didn't dare let myself fall in love with him. I always knew it would have to end. I was married and I had two children. From the first time I met him, I could never forget that it would soon have to end . . ."

"And your husband?" I asked. "Did your husband mind?"

"Oh, no. My husband knew all about my relationship with the Prince. But he didn't mind. If it's the Prince of Wales—no husbands ever mind."

The Marchesa had once been the acknowledged mistress of the Prince of Wales. I asked her if this had made people jealous of her? Had her relationship aroused a lot of rancor and spite?

"Oh, no. It made everyone be especially nice to me. They were very nice to me because they thought that would bring them closer to him. He was going to be the King—well, you know . . . You can imagine how close everyone wanted to be to him. When he first started with the Duchess, everyone was extremely nice to her. No one said a malicious word about the Duchess in the beginning. Later, once he had abdicated, they said the most frightful things about her."

The Marchesa said she used to get a lot of abusive and

anonymous hate mail. She still remembered being shocked and distressed by a particular letter she had received from a clergyman. "The old brute had signed his obscene letter. I really didn't expect such a letter from a clergyman . . ."

I asked if she and the Duke had been able to meet openly.

"Oh, we didn't have to meet in secrecy like you would now. We weren't tormented by the press like those poor girls who go out with Prince Charles. I never had crowds of newspapermen waiting outside my door with flashing lightbulbs. I don't know when all that sort of horrible thing started . . ."

I asked her how she had first met the Prince of Wales. "I suppose it was rather romantic. I met him through a zeppelin raid. It was wartime, you see. Not the second war—the first war. I had gone out to dinner with some bloke, I can't even remember his name. We were walking back home when the sirens went. We saw a house. There was some kind of party going on there. We rang the bell and asked if we could take shelter until the raid was over. You could do that in wartime."

The Marchesa helped herself to more Dubonnet. She seemed to want to talk about the past. I no longer felt I ought to go.

"We took shelter in the cellar of the house," she said. "After the raid was over, the hostess who was giving the party asked if we would like to come up and join the dance. At the beginning I didn't want to. I felt embarrassed. I didn't want the poor woman to think she had to invite me just because there had been a raid. The hostess pointed to a blond young man. She said that he was very keen that I join the party. Anyway—eventually I did join it. At that point I had no idea who the blond young man was. It was only later I found out that he was the Prince of Wales."

"Was the Duke very sexy?" I asked. It was a heavy, silly question. But we were both getting quite drunk and I didn't feel she would mind.

"Yes, the Duke was very sexy." She hesitated and then qualified her statement, "Well, the Duke was quite sexy —he was like most men . . . well, you know . . ."

"And the Duke was never homosexual? People like to say that he was."

"Oh, no. The Duke was never homosexual. I know people like to say that he was. They like to say that about all men who are royal. If the Duke had been homosexual, I'd have known. We knew all about homosexuality even in those days. But he was a pretty miserable fellow, the Duke."

"Miserable?" I didn't know what she meant by this.

"He was always crying. He was always in floods of tears. It was usually because he'd had some row with his father. The Duke hated his father. The King was horrible to him. His mother was horrible to him, too . . ." The Marchesa suddenly spoke with anger. "You can't imagine how horrible they both were to him. If his life was a bit of a mess, his parents were to blame. They made him what he was."

"Did the Duke hate his mother?"

"No. The Duke loved his mother. But his mother

wouldn't let him love her. She always took the King's side against him. His mother would only do what the King wanted. And that didn't leave the Duke very much."

The Marchesa said that I could never imagine how terrifying George V and Queen Mary seemed to their children. The King and Queen were very frightening just as a couple, they were both so cold. And then they were made to seem even more petrifying because their royal position was regarded by the entire country with such respect, sanctity, and awe.

The Marchesa remembered that the royal children had to appear at breakfast before the King arrived. One morning the Duke's brother, Prince George, was five minutes late. He came into the dining room and he was so frightened of his father that he fell down on the floor in a dead faint.

"Can you imagine the terror that he felt?" the Marchesa asked me. "Can you imagine the sort of terror that would make a huge teenage boy collapse on the floor?"

The Marchesa said that while she was having her romance with the Prince of Wales, the Palace sent spies on them. "Everything we did, the King knew all about it the next morning. That was very unpleasant. You see, we knew our own friends were spying on us and sending reports to the Palace. It was not very nice to know that your close friends were prepared to spy on you—that they were quite prepared to be that disloyal, just in order to please 'The King.' "

The Marchesa said she thought all this blind worship of royalty was stupid and destructive, that it was bad for those who worshiped, bad for those who received that kind of adoration. She knew that it had been very bad for the Duke. He was always aware that people only adored him because of his position. He would have liked to have been loved for what he was. But of course he enjoyed all the fuss that was made of him as well.

"Did the Duke find all his royal duties very boring?"

"Yes, he did find them boring. Many of the royal family's duties are very boring, of course. But then, remember, all of us have quite boring things we have to do in our lives. And we don't get all the adulation and the good bits that the Duke also got. You've got to take the rough with the smooth," the Marchesa said. "That's what the Duke could never accept. He refused to take the rough with the smooth. And as Prince of Wales, you can believe me, that he got an awful lot of smooth . . ."

When the Marchesa was young, she had thought that the hysterical passion that everyone in her time felt for the monarchy would soon die out.

"One just thought it couldn't last. It seemed too silly to last. Don't you think it's all rather silly? But I was wrong because I think it's got worse. It's really amazing to me, but now I really think it's got worse . . ."

She still felt the present royal family behaved very differently from George V and Queen Mary. She didn't believe the present Queen ever bullied her children. The present British royal family seemed much nicer and happier and more human.

"The Duke was made wretched by the strictness of his father. He couldn't do right in the eyes of his parents. Everything he did made them furious."

The Marchesa said the Duke had always been in violent rebellion against his father. He only liked dancing so much because dancing was disapproved of by the King. "The Duke was always in rebellion. In a way that was his trouble. His life was one long rebellion . . . It hasn't turned out too well for him . . . And I'm afraid that awful woman, the Duchess, has made him become very nasty. He never used to be nasty. But now I hear all these stories that he has become so mean with money—that he never tips his servants. He didn't used to be like that. She must have made him like that."

I wondered if she had taken in that the Duke was dead. She seemed so lucid and articulate it was startling when she suddenly referred to him in the present tense.

"Was the Duke abject?" I asked. "In all the anecdotes I've read about him, he comes out as rather abject."

"No, he wasn't abject. At least he was never at all abject with me. But I have to admit he was rather abject in regard to his parents. And perhaps he is rather abject with the Duchess . . ."

"Was the Duke frightened of the Duchess in much the same way he was frightened of his parents?"

"I suppose he was. I think he may have been a masochist. Is that what you call it nowadays? Maybe he was always a masochist. I just didn't realize it when we both were young. It didn't really show then. Maybe the Duke was always going to be rather nasty. Maybe it had nothing to do with the Duchess. It's so hard to know what people are going to turn into. You can't really tell—not when you are young."

The Marchesa said she still blamed herself for having

been so conventional. "I would never have dreamt of doing anything to upset the monarchy. That's why I knew our romance would never last. In that way I was never fair to him. My attitudes were just as bad as those of the Palace. If I'm honest—I took exactly the same position as his parents. When I heard he had abdicated to marry the Duchess—I really admired him. It was very brave of him. It couldn't have been easy for him to throw all that up . . ."

"You never once met the Duchess of Windsor?"

"No. Thank God. I never once met the Duchess of Windsor."

The Marchesa Casa Maury pronounced the Duchess's name with great animosity. Obviously time had not healed the resentment she felt for her rival. When she constantly spoke about the Duke in the present tense, it was as if he had not completely died for her.

"I didn't know anything about the Duchess for quite a long time," she said. "I remember that one of my children was desperately ill. I was in the most awful state about her. I was dashing in and out of the hospital. I was in such a frantic state that I hardly noticed that the Prince hadn't telephoned lately. Usually he telephoned me all the time." The Marchesa suddenly looked very upset. She smoked feverishly.

"I decided to telephone the Prince at Buckingham Palace. I got through to one of the telephone operators on the Palace exchange. He knew me very well. He had always put through my calls to the Prince. The telephone operator sounded very funny when I spoke to him. I heard this odd sort of gulping noise. He didn't seem able to speak. I suddenly realized to my horror that he was crying. 'Everyone seems to have gone mad round here,' he said."

The Marchesa herself looked very distressed and close to tears. "The Prince had given orders that none of my calls be put through. I never heard from him again. He never even wrote to me, not even a postcard. After all our years together, I felt he ought to come round and see me and tell me about the Duchess. I wouldn't have made a scene. You see, I knew it always had to end. From the very start I knew it always had to end."

"The Duke seems to have been very callous and cowardly," I said.

"I'm afraid he was. I wonder if the Duchess made him behave like that. I minded the way he treated my children more than I minded the way he treated me. You see, he had been like a father to them. They adored him. But once he met the Duchess, they never heard from him again . . ."

She suddenly seemed to be getting upset. She started gulping her Dubonnet rather than drinking it.

"The Duke did something that really shocked me. It was so petty and cruel and it really hurt me . . . He had arranged for one of my daughters who was quite small at the time to receive a pearl from a jeweler every time she had a birthday . . . The idea was that she would have a necklace by the time that she was grown-up . . . The idea was rather charming . . . But then you won't believe it . . . The moment he met the Duchess he canceled the order with the jeweler! I thought it was really shocking that the Duke, who had more jewelry than anyone in the world, would take away a tiny pearl necklace from a child."

"Do you know what is happening to the Duchess at this moment?" I wanted to change this subject which she still found a very painful one.

"No, I don't know what's happening to the Duchess. What is happening to her?"

I told her about the Duchess's peculiar situation. I described Maître Blum and I explained that she had locked the Duchess up.

The Marchesa started to laugh hilariously.

"I thought the Duchess had been quiet lately. It's never been like the Duchess to be so quiet."

I told her that it appeared the Duchess of Windsor was in a pitiable condition, that it was rumored that she had turned black.

The Marchesa started shaking with laughter. "I really shouldn't laugh," she said. "But I just can't help it. Poor Duchess. It's awful for her. But somehow I can't help finding it terribly funny."

She then said that she was certain I had made the whole thing up. I'd invented it all because I wanted to please her.

This made her laugh even more. Tears were rolling down her cheeks.

When she stopped laughing, she said that none of it really mattered in the end. I wasn't certain what she meant.

"Love affairs . . . They don't really matter in the end. They seem so important at the time. But in the end they don't matter." The Marchesa looked down at the steel medical stick she hated. "I wonder what does matter in the end." She seemed bewildered. "Family, I suppose . . . I had all my grandchildren around here the other day." Her face lit up. "It was amazing to find oneself head of such a large, lovely clan."

As I was leaving, she apologized for having laughed so much about the Duchess. She then started laughing again. "I really shouldn't find it so funny. It's awful of me to laugh about it. Do you promise you didn't invent it all? There's something so comic about the situation. It's the idea of that horrible old lady being locked up by another horrible old lady . . ."

CHAPTER SIXTEEN

*T*wo years after I interviewed Maître Blum, the Duchess of Windsor was still alive. I received only unrelated little snippets of information about her, but anything that threw light on her "special" hot relationship with her lawyer continued to intrigue me. Debrett's Peerage had written to Maître Blum and sent her a copy of the formal entry they'd made for the Duchess's biography. Maître Blum had approved it except she insisted with threats of possible lawsuits that they add that the Duchess was the author of a cookbook. This culinary enterprise has curiously never reached a publisher, although the fame of its author might well have made it a best-seller. It appears to exist only in the vibrant imagination of Maître Blum, very like the lost shoulder of General Spillmann. But then the able old lawyer was always resolutely determined that her client go down to posterity as hardworking.

Maître Blum then suddenly gave out an announcement to the press in which she claimed that the Duchess of Windsor had made a miraculous recovery and it was now a problem as to how to amuse her. Maître Blum said that the Duchess was sitting up and was listening to Cole Porter.

During a visit to Paris I met the owner of a chain of French hamburger joints. During the course of the conversation, he mentioned that an antiques dealer had recently offered him a collection of the Duke of Windsor's Sèvres snuffboxes. He had turned them down. He had no interest at all in acquiring them. He asked me about the Duchess. I explained that Maître Blum had made it impossible to know. The French hamburger king found this ridiculous. It must be possible to ascertain her condition. He had a friend who was a detective. The detective was Sicilian. He had contacts with the French police. He suggested I go to see the detective. Out of curiosity I made an appointment with this man. The detective was very bronzed and handsome. He was cynical and cool and could have played James Bond in a spy movie. I wondered if he sometimes used his good looks in order to seduce and thereby elicit information. I still felt it was doubtful his charms would be very effective if he attempted any seduction of Maître Blum. I explained that I wanted to know what was happening to the Duchess of Windsor. He said he would make inquiries in Paris.

When I got back to London I decided to tell Lord Mountbatten's daughter, Countess Mountbatten, that Maître Blum was selling off the royal Sèvres snuffboxes. She sounded immensely upset on the telephone. I asked if Lord Mountbatten had always known Maître Blum would do this kind of thing. "I'm afraid Daddy always knew," she said. "Yes, I'm afraid Daddy always knew. Yet there is so little the royal family can do." She said she would still arrange for the Queen to be told about the sale of the royal snuffboxes. Apparently the Queen was staying at Sandringham. Countess Mountbatten promised to see that the news was broken to her immediately. Later she telephoned to

say that the Queen had been informed. When I next saw
the Queen performing her royal duties on television, she
looked rather cross, but that could have been my imagination. She certainly had a look of frowning preoccupation
and I wondered if it could have been produced by the
unwelcome news that Maître Blum was taking liberties
with the royal snuffboxes.

When he finally telephoned me, the Sicilian detective
gave me a discouraging report on the results of his inquiries. The Duchess of Windsor had been sequestered by
Maître Blum and no one seemed to have any news of her.
He had found a doctor friend who had questioned a physician at a cocktail party. He claimed he was only one of
her many doctors. The physician maintained that the
Duchess was very well. She was not at all senile. She was
not on any life supports. She had only one problem. As
she was an old lady, the Duchess sometimes felt rather
tired.

The detective had also got hold of an ex-bodyguard
of the Duke of Windsor. He had arranged for him to call
round to have tea with Georges, as these men had known
each other in the old days. The ex-bodyguard had gone
round to have tea with the Duchess's butler but he had
not been allowed to see the Duchess of Windsor. Georges
had kept him in the kitchen. Georges said the Duchess
wished to see no one. Nobody could visit her any more.
The Duchess had fewer nurses than in the old days. The
only person who never stopped coming to the house was
her lawyer, Maître Blum.

The detective said that the Duchess of Windsor was

so well-protected that it would need some kind of helicopter raid to get into her house and find out what was happening. He warned me that would be against the law and therefore very expensive.

"How do you know the Duchess of Windsor is still alive?" the detective asked me. I insisted she must, surely, still be alive. It would be illegal to suppress the news of her death. Maître Blum would surely never dare to do that.

The detective gave a cynical laugh. He agreed that the suppression of a death was considered a highly serious crime in France. It was an imprisonable offense. Many deaths were suppressed all the same. Usually it was because there were trusts involved. But there were sometimes various other motivations. If there were valuable possessions to be disposed of, less attention was attracted if their disposal took place over an extended period.

His assessment of the Duchess's situation was a sinister one, but later it seemed it was mere fanciful surmise. Hugo Vickers, the biographer, met the head of the American Hospital in Paris. When he asked this doctor about the health of the Duchess of Windsor, he said she had been admitted to the American Hospital eight months ago. Her condition had been so pitiable it had upset the nurses. In his opinion, the Duchess of Windsor was being "too well looked after."

I then met a woman who was a patient of Maître Blum's niece, who was a Parisian doctor. Maître Blum had apparently told her niece that the Duchess was "all wired up." Maître Blum's niece claimed her aunt was devoted to the Duchess. Maître Blum had announced that she herself never wanted to have a frightful end like the Duchess. If she ever got into such a desperate condition, she wanted her niece to give her an injection.

Maître Blum's position sounded very callous. This hypocritical old lawyer wanted an injection for herself and yet maintained a pious respect for life when it was the life of the Duchess.

Soon after hearing about Maître Blum's private wish for an injection, I learned that she herself was writing a book about the Duchess of Windsor. She had sent an outline of her intended project to the British publisher Andre Deutsch. If the Maître was planning to write the final word on the Duchess, all the fury and the lawsuits she had brought to bear on the other authors who had written about the Windsors became more explicable. Yet Maître Blum was violating her legal oath by writing this book. She was making use of a famous client for her own financial gain. But Maître Blum always knew how to justify her actions.

$\mathcal{T}$he last time I was in Paris, out of a driven curiosity I went to look at the Duchess's house in the Bois de Boulogne. It was raining when I reached 4 route du Champ d'Entrainment. It looked as bleak and deserted as before. One single window was still unshuttered. It was very silent. I could hear no strains of Cole Porter.

On an impulse I rang the bell of the huge steel gate that guarded the Duchess's driveway. Georges, the butler, answered, speaking on an intercom system.

I said that I was the niece of Mrs. Brinsley Plunket. *"Oui, oui."* Georges remembered her very well. She used to come to the Duchess's dinner parties. I said that Mrs. Brinsley Plunket wanted to know how the Duchess was.

"Toujours le même, Madame. Toujours le même."

I told Georges that Mrs. Brinsley Plunket would soon be coming over to Paris and she was planning to come and see the Duchess.

"Non! Non!" Georges sounded terrified and unnecessarily hysterical. *"Elle ne peut pas voir la Duchesse! Personne ne peut voir la Duchesse!* No one can ever see the Duchess . . ."

I asked Georges to tell the Duchess that her old friend sent her love. He assured me he would tell the Duchess that evening.

Her butler suddenly made Wallis Windsor sound surprisingly healthy, normal, and aware, a figure who was perfectly capable of receiving an affectionate message from one of the old friends she entertained so lavishly in her heyday.

The rain was pouring down. I felt the Duchess's butler should have opened the steel gate and spoken to me personally rather than talking only on the intercom. Why was he so frightened to open the gate? I thanked him for taking my message to the Duchess.

I decided I would return to the Duchess's house and bring her some flowers. Surely if I brought flowers, Georges, as the Duchess's butler, would have to receive them personally. Would he be rude enough to thank me on the intercom and tell me to put them down in the street outside the great gate that cut her off from her friends? If Maître Blum had given orders the gate must never be opened, Georges would obey her. It seemed so unlikely the Duchess would ever get my flowers, that I only bought her a cheap little bunch of anemones from a Paris stall. If I bought her some tremendous bunch of orchids, I assumed it would only be appropriated by Maître Blum.

When I got back to the Duchess's house, I once again rung the bell of the forbidding gate. Georges answered on the intercom and I told him I had brought flowers from Mrs. Brinsley Plunket.

Rather to my horror, there was a buzzing sound. Georges had opened the huge steel gate. I had a feeling of panic as I became aware of the wretchedness of my little bunch of wilting flowers. To make it worse they were wrapped in a very unpleasant plastic. I realized I should have brought the Duchess a vast and memorable tribute from some leading Paris florist. The Duchess of Windsor had once taken more pains with her floral decorations than any other great hostess in Europe. My flowers were totally inadequate. Her butler would rightly feel outraged when he saw them. He could not possibly consider them a tribute. He had to see them as a downright insult to the Duchess.

As I walked up the drive, I noticed how ill-kept the Duchess of Windsor's grounds had become. No one had swept her lawns and they were littered with dead brown leaves. There was an ornamental tree growing in front of her house. It had become so neglected that it was encircled by rings of repulsive yellow ocher fungi, which rose for several feet in great flopping layers. The fungus that was killing this delicate tree presented a very melancholy and memorable image.

Georges was standing in the doorway of the Duchess's house. His wife was standing there too. Georges looked like a distinguished and silvery diplomat. He was formally dressed in his butler's black. His teeth looked beautifully capped. He had very good French manners. He introduced his wife and said she was called Ophelia.

Georges repeated that he remembered Mrs. Brinsley Plunket very well. She was *charmante*. She used to be a great friend of the Duchess. In fact he thought she had been the last person to dine with the Duchess. Maître Blum claimed she herself was the last person to have dined with the Duchess. Either the Duchess's butler or her lawyer had made an error. Georges said that he had been with the Duchess for longer than he cared to remember. He'd been with her thirty-four years. It was very sad what had happened to her. His eyes filled with tears when he mentioned her name.

The house was in darkness because the shutters were drawn. From the doorway one could see a shadowy hall with some furniture and a staircase leading up to a balcony. From the ceiling there hung the Duke's sad-looking Garter banner from St. George's Chapel. The chill of the interior of the Duchess's house was indescribable. It no longer seemed like a house. It had the creepy and oppressive atmosphere of a morgue.

"How is the Duchess?" I asked her butler the answerable question.

He shrugged and his eyes became moist. The Duchess was completely paralyzed. She couldn't even move her little finger. She had been like that for three years.

"Has she become very small?" Georges looked taken aback. He was obviously astonished by this question.

"Yes, the Duchess is very small." Her butler made an expressive signal with his hands that indicated that the Duchess of Windsor was the size of a baby. It seemed much too crude and tasteless to ask Georges if the Duchess had turned completely black.

"Is she in any pain?" I asked.

The Duchess was apparently not in pain. She had three nurses, Georges insisted.

The silence in the Duchess's house was unearthly. Her bedroom was up on the passage that ran to the left of the balcony. There was no sound of a nurse. No one moved around in the Duchess's passage. No one ever went to the lavatory. There was certainly not one note of Cole Porter.

"I imagine that it is impossible to see the Duchess," I said to her butler.

He made an imaginary line with his finger and drew it across the front door. "No one passes beyond here," he smiled and he showed his capped teeth.

If I were to push past him and run up the stairs to see whether the Duchess was there, I wondered if Georges would shoot me. I couldn't see the bulge of a gun underneath his impeccable butler's uniform. But the risk didn't seem worth taking.

"Is there anything anyone can do for the Duchess?" I asked him.

Georges shook his silvery head.

"Rien, Madame, rien."

I kept Georges talking. I was unwilling to leave this house where I was so close to uncovering the fate of the Duchess and yet deprived as usual by Maître Blum from having access to the truth.

Standing outside the front door, I encouraged Georges to reminisce. He seemed quite glad to take a sentimental stroll down memory lane and he tearfully described the splendor of the Duchess's establishment in the good old days. He reeled off the names of the guests who had attended her magnificent banquets and choked as he recalled their social importance.

It struck me that whatever future dreams of "golden

carrots" he lived on, the present life Georges led was a dismal one. With his worship of glamor he must find it deadly to be shut up all day in this dilapidated dark tomb of a house with only his furious spouse Ophelia for company. He had nothing to do except prevent the world from discovering what state the Duchess was in and as even her closest friends had tired of trying to ascertain her condition his task was hardly very challenging.

All the time he was speaking to me his wife stood and glared at us both. I wondered if she detested all this talk of the past. George was in raptures as he reconstructed the good old days when he had fawned over the Duchess.

Michael Bloch had told me that the Maître had an enlightened, modern, and lenient attitude towards homosexuality so it was conceivable that she allowed the butler to invite young men to the Duchess's house and the tedium of his vigil was occasionally alleviated.

During my long conversation with the butler I never stopped listening for some sound to come from the upstairs landing where I knew the Duchess's bedroom to be located. The staircase which led up to it was a short one and standing under the portals of the front door of the Duchess's house it would have been very easy to hear any movement of the three nurses who were allegedly attending her. But nothing stirred. The unearthly stillness persisted. I went on talking to Georges until I had convinced myself that the butler and Ophelia were the only occupants of the Duchess's run-down house. But what did this mean? Had Maître Blum elected to take on the onerous burden of the Duchess's medical care herself? Always passionately parsimonious, had she volunteered to sacrifice herself in the interest of sparing the Duchess from unnecessary expenses?

If this were the case Maître Blum was clearly neglecting her patient. It was obvious from the butler's behavior that Maître Blum was not in the house at this given moment. She would have been outraged to discover that he was prepared to open the front door to a stranger. So the Duchess was either upstairs unattended, or . . . The Sicilian detective's theory no longer seemed so farfetched.

If I was to try and take the butler by surprise and make a sudden run to the Duchess's bedroom and there discover it was empty I realized that Georges would really have no choice but to shoot me. He would be unmasked as an accomplice to Maître Blum's crime and he could face imprisonment. It didn't seem a good way to die.

He apologized that there were no flowers in the Duchess's hallway. There used to be so many glorious flowers in her house in the old days. It had all been so different then. The memory made his eyes fill with tears.

I awkwardly handed him my insignificant bouquet of flowers and I thanked him. He hardly looked at them. There was therefore no need for me to feel embarrassed. He took them as if he were receiving a solitary flower that had been tossed onto the Duchess's grave.

I left Georges and Ophelia standing in the doorway of the Duchess's house. I went down the derelict drive and once again passed the decorative tree with its horrible fungi. The Duchess of Windsor, who had lived through so many eras, had entered a new epoch and she was now living, or allegedly living, in a France under Mitterrand. Her huge house now belonged to a socialist government. I wondered if as a committed left-winger Mitterrand approved of her tenancy, if he knew that Maître Blum was neglecting the upkeep of French government property.

I took one last look at her window that had no shutters. Like the Great Gatsby, the Duchess had come a long, long way to this "blue," if leaf-strewn lawn. If she had given the British monarchy the "greatest jolt in its history," she had also been its greatest booster. The British went into raptures when the Queen Mother attained her eightieth birthday. The Archbishop of Canterbury in St. Paul's gave thanks to God for the Queen Mother and for his son, Jesus Christ, and it was most important that he thanked God in that order. And yet no one gave any thanks to the Duchess who was lying miserably alive in Neuilly under Maître Blum's despotic surveillance. The nation seemed to forget that without the American Duchess of Windsor, the British would never have had their adored Queen Mother. The Duchess had also been overlooked when Prince Charles married Lady Diana. The press created a minor uproar and they started asking the whereabouts of Queen Alexandra's jewels. According to royal tradition, Lady Diana should have worn them on her wedding day. Lady Diana was never able to wear these jewels, but the royal marriage went off perfectly well without them. If the Duchess of Windsor deprived the Princess of Wales of one of her royal rights, she had already paid the British back far more than they seemed prepared to estimate. Without the Duchess, they would have been deprived of one of the most popular princesses in their history.

The Duchess of Windsor had once been the very symbol of jet set frivolity. Through the long agony of her death, she had finally acquired a greater stature. Looking at her unshuttered window, I felt that in the loneliness and pain of her end, the Duchess had become a figure of tragedy.

Mrs. Simpson had burst into tears when she heard the news that the King of England had abdicated. Staying with her friends the Herman Rogerses in their villa in Cannes, she ran into the lavatory and she hid herself. When she cried on realizing the full and irreversible impact of the Duke's historic decision, she could never have prophesied that while she lay dying, the microphone on which Edward VIII broadcast his famous speech would be displayed on British television. Mrs. Simpson could never have foreseen that the microphone itself would one day be able to make her late husband's speech from a tape that has been cunningly inserted inside it, so that the public is now able to hear the microphone renouncing the throne "for the woman I love," just as many times as they are interested to hear it.

As I took a last look at her beautiful and desolate house, I wondered when the Duchess would ever be released so that her coffin could be escorted to England by the current British ambassador. When would she ever be taken in state and allowed to lie beside her royal husband in the burial ground of Frogmore?

The Duke was not in the important mausoleum in the royal cemetery. He was not with Queen Victoria, George V, and Queen Mary. His grave was tucked away at the side near various minor royalties. Maître Blum must know about this and it was unlikely that it pleased her.

If the Duchess was one day to get to Frogmore, presumably Maître Blum would be her chief mourner. She would arrive in the royal graveyard swathed in the same black weeds she'd worn for General Spillmann. Yet Lady Mosley had said that the Duchess hardly knew Maître Blum until her mind became enfeebled, and it was unlikely her old lawyer would mourn the loss of the "pep," the jokes, and the vitality that the late Duke and the friends of Wallis Windsor had once found lovable.

Staring at the spikes of barbed wire fencing that encircled her house, I felt the Duchess of Windsor had always been locked up. As a child she had been imprisoned by the snobbish conventions of Baltimore. She had been shut in the bathroom by Win Spencer, her drunken, jealous first husband. Ernest Simpson had restricted her in a different way. The boredom of her life with him had made her feel like a bottle of champagne that had been kept too long in the icebox. When the future King of England abdicated for her sake, she had no alternative but to marry him. Once he had renounced so much, it was very difficult for her ever to leave him, although he was so dependent on her, so unflaggingly besotted, that the obsessional nature of his need for her must have often seemed like a prison.

The Duke's attitude that found expression in his favorite song, "I want to be—a bee in your boudoir   And 'bee' in your boudoir all day" had to have been very burdensome for the Duchess. For thirty-five years the Duke of Windsor had been a bee in the Duchess's boudoir and when she tried to escape with the exhibitionistic and *louche* and sadistic Jimmy Donahue, her flight had been doomed; for in her attempt to flee from the gold cage of the Duke's doting and uncritical love, she sought approbation from a man who by the very essence of his nature could only see her as a "fantastic Duchess" and never really like her at all.

Then the Duke died and the Duchess fell into the hands of Maître Blum. The Duchess had always been a figure of myth, and it was this myth that had captivated her old lawyer. The Duke had seen the Duchess's character as "elusive" and now the Duchess's actual physical condition had been made totally elusive by Maître Blum, adding to myth. Was she black? Or was she radiant? Was she pipe-fed or was she talkative and witty and listening to Cole Porter? Was she a long time dead as the Sicilian detective had surmised? Had her lawyer decided to retain her beloved bones so that they would be kept where she wanted them—forever on French soil? Would a substitute body eventually go off to the royal burial grounds of Frogmore, escorted by the British ambassador? Would the Duke end up in death lying beside a bogus Duchess?

All these questions might never be answered. All that

was certain was that for Maître Blum, with her eccentric, octogenarian passion for the Duchess, Wallis Windsor could only get more and more beautiful. In life or in death, for her lawyer she would always be the golden girl who got the Prince. For Maître Blum that was all that mattered.

After ten years under the supervision of her lawyer, the Duchess of Windsor died after a long illness in her house in Paris on 24 April 1986 in her ninetieth year.

———

On 29 April 1986 her funeral took place at St. George's Chapel, Windsor, in the presence of the Queen and the Duke of Edinburgh, The Queen Mother, the Prince and Princess of Wales, other members of the Royal Family, and Michael Bloch. Maître Blum did not attend. The Duchess was buried privately beside the Duke of Windsor in the royal family's burial ground at Frogmore. The Queen broke down momentarily and cried at the internment.

———

Within days of the Duchess's death, the *Daily Mail* was serializing intimate letters between the Duke and Duchess, given them on the authority of Maître Blum and edited by Michael Bloch.

———

Altogether, Michael Bloch produced five books based on his research into the Windsor papers, access to which was given him by the estate of the Duchess of Windsor. Two of these books appeared before the Duchess's death.

———

In April 1986, Mohamed Al Fayed, the proprietor of the Ritz Hotel in Paris and chairman of Harrod's in London, was asked by the mayor of Paris, Jacques Chirac, to take responsibility for the Windsors' residence in Paris on the same terms under which they had leased the house from the French state. He quickly changed the locks and then had the house thoroughly restored.

———

In April 1987, the Duchess's jewels were sold at Sotheby's in Geneva, for prices vastly exceeding the estimates. The total of the sale was $50,281,887.

———

George Sanegre died in August 1989, aged 71.

———

Maître Blum died in Paris on 23 January 1994 at the age of 95.

NOTES

CHAPTER ONE

1. Quotations in this chapter are from J. Bryan III and Charles J. V. Murphy, *The Windsor Story* (New York: Morrow, 1979), pp. 559–60, 569.

CHAPTER FIVE

1. Bryan and Murphy, *The Windsor Story*, p. 516.

CHAPTER SIX

1. The Duchess of Windsor, *The Heart Has Its Reasons* (New York: David McKay, 1956; London: Michael Joseph, 1965), p. viii.

CHAPTER SEVEN

1. Peter Coats, *Of Generals and Gardens* (London: Weidenfeld and Nicolson, 1976).
2. Laura, Duchess of Marlborough, *Laughter from a Cloud* (London: Weidenfeld and Nicolson, 1980), pp. 94–95.
3. Ibid., pp. 97–98.

CHAPTER NINE

1. *American Mercury*, June 1944.
2. Cleveland Amory, *Who Killed Society?* (New York: Harper, 1960).

CHAPTER TEN

1. Virgil Thomson, *Virgil Thomson* (New York: Alfred A. Knopf, 1966), p. 320.
2. Ibid., p. 388.

CHAPTER THIRTEEN

1. Quotations in this chapter are from the Duchess of Windsor, *The Heart Has Its Reasons*, chaps. 1–7, unless otherwise noted.

2. Bryan and Murphy, *The Windsor Story*, p. 12.

3. Ibid., p. 17.

CHAPTER FOURTEEN

1. Quotations in this chapter are from the Duchess of Windsor, *The Heart Has Its Reasons*, chaps. 12–15, unless otherwise noted.

2. The Duke of Windsor, *A King's Story* (New York: G. P. Putnam, 1947), p. 257.

3. Ibid., p. 359.

CHAPTER FIFTEEN

1. The Duke of Windsor, *A King's Story*, p. 320.

2. Ibid., p. 329.

About the Author

Daughter of the Marquis and Marchioness of Dufferin and Ava, LADY CAROLINE BLACKWOOD was born in 1931 and grew up in Northern Ireland. Her first husband, Lucian Freud, whom she married in 1953, has immortalized her youthful beauty in several of his finest portraits; she was later married to the American poet Robert Lowell; she had four children. Her first novel, *The Stepdaughter*, was published in 1967 and won the David Higham Fiction Prize; her last book, *The Last of the Duchess*, was published in 1995. In all, she published five novels, four nonfiction works, and, with Anna Haycraft, an idiosyncratic cookbook entitled *Darling, You Shouldn't Have Gone to So Much Trouble*. Resident in her later years in Sag Harbor, New York, she died in New York City in 1996.